The
QUANTUM
LEADER

The

QUANTUM LEADER

A REVOLUTION IN BUSINESS THINKING AND PRACTICE

DANAH ZOHAR

Prometheus Books

59 John Glenn Drive
Amherst, New York 14228

Inquiries should be addressed to
Prometheus Books
59 John Glenn Drive
Amherst, New York 14228
VOICE: 716–691–0133
FAX: 716–691–0137
WWW.PROMETHEUSBOOKS.COM

20 19 18 17 16   5 4 3 2 1

Library of Congress Cataloging-in-Publication Data

Names: Zohar, Danah, 1945- author.
Title: The quantum leader : a revolution in business thinking and practice / by Danah Zohar.
Description: Amherst, New York : Prometheus Books, 2016. |
     Includes bibliographical references and index.
Identifiers: LCCN 2016019736 (print) | LCCN 2016031006 (ebook) |
     ISBN 9781633882416 (hardcover) | ISBN 9781633882423 (ebook)
Subjects: LCSH: Leadership. | Organizational change. | Quantum theory. |
     Physics—Philosophy.
Classification: LCC HD57.7 .Z65 2016 (print) | LCC HD57.7 (ebook) |
     DDC 658.4/092—dc23
LC record available at https://lccn.loc.gov/2016019736

Printed in the United States of America

For Stephen ChingChun Meng.
Much-loved friend and colleague and a true servant leader.

"Most transformation programs satisfy themselves with shifting the same old furniture about in the same old room. Some seek to throw some of the furniture away. But real transformation requires that we redesign the room itself. Perhaps even blow up the old room. It requires that we change the thinking behind our thinking—literally that we learn to rewire our corporate brains."

—Danah Zohar

"The answer is to overturn all that was once believed reasonable and rational."

—Zhang Ruimin, CEO, Haier Group, China

CONTENTS

ACKNOWLEDGMENTS

My greatest thanks for help with this book go to my colleague Chris Wray, with whom I have engaged in creative dialogue throughout. Chris and I continue to work together as we evolve our thinking about Quantum Systems Dynamics, and Chris travels globally with me to deliver workshops on quantum management. I would also like to thank Stephen Meng and Professor Kai Sung for their help in getting me to know China and for introducing me to Chinese companies and business schools. I am grateful to the strategy department of the Haier Group in Qingdao for arranging my valuable visit to their company, and to the Center for Confucian Entrepreneurs and East Asian Civilizations at Zhejiang University in Hangzhou for the interest staff there (especially Professor Zhou) have taken in my work. I would also like to thank Chen Feng of the Tian Jian Water Company in Hangzhou for his hospitality and for making his company available to me for research purposes.

INTRODUCTION

WHY BUSINESS
NEEDS A REVOLUTION

Our capitalist culture and the business practices that operate within it are in a crisis. Capitalism as we know it today—an amoral culture of short-term self-interest, profit maximization, emphasis on executive bonuses and/or shareholder value, isolationist thinking, and profligate disregard of long-term consequences—is an unsustainable system. In *Spiritual Capital*, I described it as a monster consuming itself.[1] The financial collapse that rocked the global economy in 2008, and from which we have yet to recover, brought this home to some business leaders, but most have continued with "business-as-usual." It's the only game they know.

This book offers a radically different model for business structure and practice and a new kind of leadership thinking that can make it a reality. It offers a different model for leadership itself and for the inner and outer dynamics that drive a different kind of leader. I call this "the quantum leader."

Corporate leadership faces the greatest technological upheaval and the greatest need for creative restructuring since the Industrial Revolution. Without clearly recognizing it, corporate leaders are challenged by external forces to build a radically new leadership culture from the ground up. These same challenges face leaders at all levels and in all sectors of society.

This new culture must define a new leadership paradigm that can deal creatively with rapid change, complexity, uncertainty, risk, global-interconnectivity, decentralization, and greater demands for ethics and meaning from employees, customers, and citizens. This requires not just new thinking, but new metaphors, new assumptions, and new values. There is no more powerful model for such a paradigm shift than the revolution in scientific thinking that gave us quantum physics and chaos and complexity science.

It is not new to turn to science as a powerful metaphor for new thinking in the social sciences, including management theory. The mechanistic physics of the sixteenth and seventeenth centuries, particularly the beauty and simplicity of Isaac Newton's three laws of motion, inspired nearly every creative thinker whose ideas were to shape Western culture for the next 300 years. The psychology of Freud, the political thought of Locke and John Stuart Mill, the capitalist philosophy of Mill and Adam Smith, the sociology of August Compte, the scientific management thinking of Frederick Taylor, and logical positivism—all were consciously modeled on Newton's thinking. Even today's neuroscience and the computer models of mind favored by cognitive science bear this influence. All are passionately materialist and reductionist, choosing to reduce all complex systems to simple, atomistic, law-abiding working parts.

The existing, business-as-usual paradigm owes a great deal to the thinking, assumptions, and values of Newtonian science that gave rise to the Industrial Revolution. If we don't understand this history of how we got to where we are today, we won't understand the source of a kind of thinking that still holds business minds prisoners. Newtonian business thinking assumes that corporations and markets are like machines, capable of operating with simple, law-abiding certainty and predictability, that they are stable and controllable and best managed in a way that eliminates risk and assures equilibrium.

By contrast, the thinking associated with quantum physics and chaos and complexity science stresses the creative potential of uncertainty. It tells us that creative systems are complex, powerfully interlinked, and best left to self-organize in dialogue with each other and with their environments. They are at their best at "the edge of chaos," the point of maximum instability in a system that allows freedom to innovate and to reinvent the rules.

I have been fascinated by quantum physics since my early teens. I first "discovered" the atom when I was thirteen years old and knew I wanted to become an atomic scientist. When fifteen, I read David Bohm's classic textbook on quantum physics, and that changed everything I thought about most everything. I framed answers for myself in terms of quantum physics to all those big questions adolescents ask about life and meaning, and I spent my teenage years smashing atoms in a cloud chamber with an electron accelerator I had built in my bedroom. I won lots of science contests and, eventually, a physics scholarship to MIT. During my time at MIT I realized I was more interested in the philosophy and worldview implicit within quantum physics than the physics itself, and I took my degree in physics and philosophy. It is that new quantum worldview that provides the philosophical framework of this book.

Our worldview is our understanding of the way the things and people we experience "hang together." It embraces everything from the cosmic level of our understanding to the everyday. In the Middle Ages, Western cultures lived within a Judeo/Christian worldview that told how God created and ordered the world, lay down standards and a moral code for human behavior, and even the hierarchical structuring of the family and society at large. In the seventeenth century, this was replaced by the mechanistic "Newtonian" worldview that described the universe and all things within it as a giant clockwork machine consisting of atomistic, fragmented parts ruled by deterministic laws. Materialism became the dominant value, and human life lost its larger meaning.

This book focuses on the implications for leadership and management of a new, emerging quantum worldview. The quantum worldview portrays a universe that is constantly evolving, consisting of holistic, deeply interconnected self-organizing systems that explore the future by trial and error. In the human dimension of the quantum worldview, meaning, purpose, and motivation replace mechanistic laws as the dynamic organizing principles of our lives and organizations.

I have spent my life writing books about the new perspective the quantum worldview brings to all aspects of daily life and everyday problems—a shift from fragmentation to holism, from certainty to uncertainty, a greater understanding of the role relationships play in our lives, a more meaningful role for human beings, our values and motivations and interventions, an emphasis on potentiality and "what might be" rather than just on "what is," a shift away from materialism, a whole new framework for thinking itself. Though two later of these books were actually written for a business audience, it was the first, *The Quantum Self*, that led quite unexpectedly to a now twenty-five-years' long career as a business thought leader and management consultant. A professor at a London business school asked me to speak to his MBA students about *The Quantum Self*. That, in turn, led to further invitations and engagements in the business world ever since.

That London business school professor, Ronnie Lessem, was prescient and way ahead of his time, perhaps the first to realize that ideas drawn from quantum physics had something new and important to say to business. Today, increasing numbers of business leaders share his view, and I no longer meet blank expressions when I tell them about my own quantum work with companies. But they want to know more. They want to know whether these new ideas from physics can help them understand why most business systems are broken and whether they can help them find new ways of leading, structuring, and transforming their organizations in the face of challenges they don't know how to meet. This book is for them, and for the many more business leaders who have yet to realize they have a problem.

Imagine you are a business leader and your company isn't doing as well as you would like. You feel your business practices and your approach to or style of leadership could be more effective, so you call in the consultants with their coaching and promised transformation programs. But none of these transformation exercises seem to make any real difference. They move the furniture about in the room, and for a while it *looks* different, but before long you realize it is the same old furniture in the same old room. You've got rid of some of your staff, reengineered your working practices, trimmed your middle management, and made an effort to "communicate more." You've defined your "company values" and printed them on little cards for employees to carry in their wallets. But nothing significant has changed. This book suggests how to redesign the room itself, perhaps even how to blow up the old room and start afresh. It invites leaders to "rewire" their brains and reinvent themselves, to *think* in a new way and thus to *be* in a new way. It invites them to become "quantum leaders."

Quantum leadership emphasizes the importance of trusting people and the system, building relationships and teams, remaining flexible and in dialogue with changing circumstances, being open to and ready for many possible futures. It also means an emphasis on meaning, vision, and values, particularly the value of *service*. As we shall see, the quantum leader is a "servant leader." Where "Newtonian" organizations are run like machines, quantum organizations are respected as living systems, what biologists call "complex adaptive systems." Living systems are in a constant creative dialogue with their environment; they are sensitive to and readily adapt to change. They thrive on risk and creative mistakes (mutations), they are "bottom-up" and self-organizing, and they are at their best in unstable circumstances. Understanding that their organizations are living systems, living *organisms* with brains, gives quantum leaders new power to understand themselves and their needs and new power to work *with* rather than *against* the inner dynamics of the organizations and people whom they lead.

Critical to the needs of both leaders and those whom they lead is a sense of meaning, an understanding of *why* they are doing what they are doing, a sense of the wider context and consequences of their actions, a lived sense of the values that underpin and guide those actions. The emphasis in quantum thinking on the importance of asking good questions (Heisenberg's Uncertainty Principle) on the values that drive our questions, and of the contextual nature of problems and problem-solving, addresses these needs.

The Newtonian thinking that drives the business-as-usual leader is all about efficiency, about *how* to get the job done. It is value-neutral. The Newtonian leader's emphasis on "management by objectives" breaks down the essential holism and complexity of problems into a linear stream of single, separate goals, each to be achieved in turn. The achievement of the final objective is seen as a sum of its (isolated) partial objectives. Quantum leaders respect efficiency and profit, but they see a focus on meaning, service, relationships, and values as the best way to generate these. They realize that short-term goals are shortsighted and often self-destructive, and that placing problems and ambitions within the wider context of a long-term perspective generates better overall success. They see all objectives as contextual, thus looking for the big picture, that greater, systemic whole that is larger than the sum of its parts, and that will enable them better to understand and use the parts (whether these be capital, plant, or people).

Quantum leaders learn how to work with and thus thrive on uncertainty and instability. They know that creativity and innovation are best nurtured at "the edge of chaos." They see the lack of certainty and clear boundaries as an opportunity for experiment and creative exploration. Where Newtonian leaders prefer to play a "finite game," quantum leaders are at their best with the "infinite game." Finite players play *within* the rules, *within* the boundaries. Infinite players play *with* the boundaries. They make up new rules, invent new games.[2] We will see that many of the new tech start-ups, in both the West and China, play by quantum rules.

Newton stressed there is only one path from "A" to "B," one God's eye view on the universe. Newtonian leaders too often buy into the idea that there is one best solution, one best strategy, one best answer. This tunnel vision can lead to one big failure. Quantum systems simultaneously try out *many* possible paths from "A" and usually end up creating a new "B." Quantum leaders envision many possible outcomes of a situation or problem and explore, with the greatest possible range of input from others, many possible ways of addressing them. This leaves them better prepared for rapid change and unpredictability and with a better understanding of the complexities at play.

Newtonian leaders are "top-down." "I am the boss. I make the decisions. I know best. I am in control." To make this work, they manage hierarchical organizations. Quantum leaders rely far less on hierarchy. Yes, a quantum CEO must still make the final decision, but he/she sees employees as co-creative partners and draws widely on their thinking and expertise. He/she makes use of inter-connected networks, dialogue groups, teams-within-teams. Teams are given more room for taking initiative and self-organizing their work structures and practices. The quantum organization has many inter-acting centers of power.

Newtonian leaders stress answers and guaranteed outcome. They are risk-averse and punish people for mistakes. Quantum leaders encourage questions and experiment. There are no "stupid" ideas, no "mistakes" that don't present learning opportunities. This encourages the risk necessary for innovation.

To become a quantum leader requires nothing less than a different perspective on reality (a new worldview), both the leader's own inner reality, and the outer reality within which that leadership will be practiced. The two are not separate. Thinking is a way of being, and I argue that *being* a leader is what leadership is about. New being needs new thinking. It requires the balanced employment of physical, mental, emotional, and spiritual intelligence, an ability to use the *whole* brain. I argue that quantum thinking, thinking modeled on the nature and processes of quantum systems, can meet these needs.

We know today that the brain is "plastic," that it constantly "rewires" itself in dialogue with experience, the environment, and with the process of thinking itself.[3] The way we think is influenced by the brain's neural wiring, but that wiring itself is in turn influenced by the way we think. The way we think plays an active role in structuring the way we use our brains, in the way we cocreate reality, and in the kind of social structures and organizations that we design. This book adopts David Bohm's view that all the problems of the world are problems of thought. If we are Newtonian thinkers, we use our brains in a partial, left-brain dominated, Newtonian way and create Newtonian organizations. If we are quantum thinkers, we use our whole brains, combining the skills of its left and right hemispheres. And we create quantum organizations. Quantum thinking is the key to becoming a quantum leader.

This book will outline the basic principles and skills of quantum thinking, derived from the properties and processes that allow complex adaptive systems ("living quantum systems") to thrive on uncertainty and instability and to be in co-creative dialogue with each other and with their environments. (I point out that many highly respected, contemporary physicists and neuroscientists argue that the brain actually works as a complex adaptive system, using a blend of quantum processes and neural complexity to generate consciousness, or "mind.")

The book will offer readers things they can do and practice to nurture their quantum thinking. It will illustrate all conceptual points with concrete examples drawn from the good and bad business practices of real leaders and real companies. And it will offer practical suggestions for how to employ quantum thinking in real-life business situations. The whole of Part III is devoted to methods of practical implementation, to practicing the methodology of QSD, *Quantum* Systems Dynamics.

Business organizations are essentially dynamic energy systems. A powerful force in shaping these is the motivations that drive our decisions and actions. These motivations act like chaotic "attractors" and direct our behavior. Linking the nature of a leader's motivations with the extent to which he/she employs Newtonian or quantum thinking, the book will also explore how quantum leaders can raise their own and their employees' motivations from the all too familiar fear, greed, anger, and self-assertion that dominate current corporate culture to the more positive motivations of exploration, cooperation, creativity, and service. And it will make the case that acting from higher motivations, having a deep sense of purpose based on strong values and a broad-based vision of what your company is *about*, will lead to a far more healthy "bottom-line" than mere obsession with efficiency and short-term material profit.

The systems dynamics view of organizations that, working in dialogue with my colleague Chris Wray, I adopt in this book is the most radical and original thing about the book. Systems dynamics itself has been around for decades, successfully pointing out that working parts are best understood as systems that have feedback loops that can reinforce some patterns or behaviors and give rise to new patterns or behaviors. Traditional systems thinking suggests methods to detect best ways to employ interventions that produce desired effects. Its methodology relies heavily on the mathematical modeling systems. But it has failed to consider what is uniquely different about working with *human* systems. And business organizations are, of course, human systems.

When presenting Quantum Systems Dynamics (QSD), I am offering a new business philosophy/vision applying to all human groups and organizations. This vision is inspired by ideas drawn from the new thinking found in quantum physics. In its more practical sense, QSD is a methodology for transforming business and social thinking, being, and practice inspired by the dynamics of quantum physical systems as mirrored in human consciousness.

QSD applies the dynamics that make complex adaptive systems (all living systems) creative and adaptive to the dynamics of specifically human systems. Human beings have brains, each with its right and left hemispheres and their differing thinking skills. Human beings have biases, motives, values, purposes, and a need for meaning. All these are at play in the dynamics of the organizations within which they work. Indeed, I go further. I argue that organizations themselves have brains, biases, motives, values, purposes, and meanings.

The practical methodology of Quantum Strategy Dynamics involves teaching leaders to use the central ideas derived from quantum physics ("quantum thinking"), to understand and work with the Scale of Motivations first presented in *Spiritual Capital*,[4] and to work with my twelve principles of transformation (Chapter Twelve). In addition, they are taught to use meditation, reflective thinking (a method original to myself), and Bohmian dialogue techniques[5] (already used by some companies) to surface the assumptions, values, motivations, etc. at work within their present business model. They are then invited to consider *many alternative* models and, hopefully, to arrive at the "quantum" position of being able to think and work at the edge of all models. This turns the traditional model-dependent systems dynamics on its head.

Astute readers of the book will realize that many of the problems facing business today are actually problems of our wider culture and can thus feel discouraged. They might say, "The problems are so big, what can *I* do?" This is in accordance with the quantum insight that everything is connected to everything else. But I see this as a creative challenge, hopefully even a source of inspiration. True, many business problems are cultural and global problems. But I believe that, in our world today, business is the only institution that has the money and the power and the global reach to bring about the cultural and global transformation that we need. Quantum business leaders are pioneers who have the power to take us into the future.

PART I

A QUANTUM APPROACH TO BUSINESS THINKING

CHAPTER 1

ENTERING THE QUANTUM AGE

In late 2014, *China Daily* published a profile of Haier's CEO Zhang Ruimin titled "A Chinese Business Model For the Internet Age."[1] The profile highlighted Haier's radical management approach, company culture, and corporate structure. It stressed Haier's flatted, entrepreneurial platform structure, its borderless management methodology, its culture of constant self-questioning and co-creation, and its consumer-driven design and manufacturing practice. In November of that same year, in a letter inviting me to meet Zhang, a member of Haier's Strategy Department wrote,

> What Haier has embarked on early this year is an effort to transform itself into an efficient platform for "makers." It is an overarching strategy adopted by its CEO Mr. Zhang Ruimin. We have been following your Quantum Management thinking and believe it is the one that can guide our path in the implementation of the strategy.[2]

Haier is China's global domestic appliances and "white goods" manufacturer, a semiprivately owned company that has seized 14 percent of the global market. It is one of many Chinese companies embarking on a new quantum management revolution, taking Chinese business thinking into the Quantum Age. There are others in the West's Silicon Valley, companies experimenting with radically new structural and leadership practices, companies taking their lead from thinking in the "new" sciences born in the twentieth century and now really shaping the world in the twenty-first.

It is not new for management thinking and practice to take its lead from science. For the past three hundred years, science has been the dominant influence behind nearly all human thinking and activity. Through applied science, first the Industrial Revolution and then subsequent revolutions in medicine, public health, the nature of war, transportation, and now the still unfolding computer revolution, technology has transformed beyond all recognition the way we live and relate on this planet. In terms of technology alone, there has been more change in the past fifty years than all previous change since the Stone Age.[3]

But the scientific *thinking* of the past three hundred years, the research, the discoveries, the theories about how life and the universe have evolved, of what they are made, of how they function, has also transformed beyond all recognition our thinking about ourselves. They have changed our assumptions about how we function, of who and what we are, of our place in the general scheme of things and thus the meaning of our lives. The scientific thinking of the seventeenth-century physicist and mathematician Isaac Newton has pervaded every corner of the human mind, and thus all the creations and products of our minds.

Newtonian science gave rise to a general Newtonian worldview. Still today, Newton's model of a machinelike, clockwork universe in which all things are determined by three simple iron laws, and thus all things are certain and predictable, underpins the Newtonian psychology we assume about our own behavior and relationships; it underpins the Newtonian medicine still practiced in our hospitals, and the Newtonian management taught by our best business schools. Newton's ideas about atoms underpins our Western taste for individualism, our fear of the collective, and even our preference for Western-style democracy. Though you are most likely wholly unaware of it, if you live in or are influenced by the Western world, you live with a Newtonian mind-set and believe in a Newtonian you.

But a radically new way of thinking runs through the scientific work that first began with the discovery of quantum physics at the start of the twentieth century, and we have yet to catch up with it. New concepts, new categories, a wholly new vision of physical and biological reality mark a sharp break with nearly everything that science held dear or certain in earlier centuries. The transition to this new thinking has been so profound and so abrupt that it constitutes a Second Scientific Revolution. This new scientific revolution, I believe, promises a revolution of comparable magnitude in our understanding of ourselves, a new way of living in society and a new way of doing business. At the deepest level, it would be a spiritual revolution. Just as Newtonian science gave rise to an all-embracing Newtonian worldview, quantum science lays the foundation for a new Quantum Age.

The old science was framed by Absolutes—absolute space and absolute time, absolute certainty. The new science stresses the relative and the indeterminate, the uncertainty that lies at the heart of all reality. The old science told us that mind and conscious observers play no role in the making or running of the way things are in the physical universe. Material reality is just "out there" and I a passive witness, someone who just finds myself in a world of forces beyond my control. The new science says we live in a "participative universe" where conscious observers/agents make reality happen, where we are responsible for not just our own actions but for the world itself. Where the old science stressed continuity and continuous, linear change, the new science is full of quantum leaps, complexity, catastrophes, and sudden surges into chaos.

The old science portrayed a physical universe of separate parts (atoms) bound to each other by rigid laws of cause and effect, a universe of things connected by force or influence. Quantum science gives us the vision of an entangled universe where everything is subtly connected to everything else, indeed where everything is a part of everything else. Influences are felt in the absence of force or signal; correlations develop spontaneously ("synchronicity"); patterns emerge from some order within. Where the Newtonian scientist reduced everything to its component parts and a few simple forces acting on them, the quantum or complexity scientist focuses on the new properties or patterns that emerge when parts *relate* to form wholes. A universe where nothing new or surprising ever happens is replaced by a self-organizing universe of constant creation. The quantum scientist learns that things cannot be described in isolation from their environment or context, and that wholes are greater than the sum of their parts. In the new science, organized simplicity gives way to self-organized complexity. We are in charge, and nothing is simple.

Most people have heard of quantum physics, but they imagine it hasn't anything to do with them. It's something about how atoms, and even smaller particles inside atoms, behave. It's obscure, mathematical, and some people say rather weird. Most people are not alone. The founding fathers of quantum physics did not understand it either, and some felt they never would. Einstein called it "Alice in Wonderland physics" and compared it to "the system of delusions of an intelligent paranoiac, concocted of incoherent elements of thought."[4] He had helped to invent quantum physics, but he never came to like it.

Yes, quantum physics is very different. That's what makes it interesting. It has the capacity to change everything. It is all around us. It's inside us, inside our bodies and our minds, and inside nearly every technological gadget on which we've come to depend. We actually live today in a quantum world, and once we fully grasp that, nothing will ever be the same again.

Look up into the evening sky on any early autumn afternoon and marvel at the mysterious flocking activity of hundreds of birds. It is quantum signaling between electrons in the birds' eyes that enables their coordinated flight. Large-scale quantum phenomena play a key role in plant photosynthesis, the functioning of cells in the human body, the synchronized firing of neurons in the brain, and perhaps even in the mystery of human consciousness. All the technology that defines the twenty-first century is quantum technology. Superfluids, superconductors, laser eye surgery and all laser technology, PET scans, silicon chips and thus all our laptop computers, smartphones, tablets, even Nintendo, X-Box, and Wii are quantum technology. The whole digital communications revolution is a quantum revolution. The Age of the Internet is the Quantum Age.

"Few modern physicists think that Newtonian physics has equal status with quantum physics, even in the 'real world' of everyday life," says Vlatko Vedral, Oxford University's professor of quantum information. "It is but a useful approximation of a world that is quantum on all scales."[5] A world that is quantum on all scales! And yet, most of us are still trapped in an outdated Newtonian worldview that dominates our best thinking about ourselves, our societies, and our organizations. It's time to catch up!

THE QUANTUM WORLDVIEW

The new quantum worldview means many things—an emphasis on wholes rather than parts, an emphasis on relationship rather than separation, both/and and many ways rather than either/or and just one best way, an emphasis on questions rather than answers, on potentiality rather than just the here and now, humility in the face of one's own thinking, integration rather than fragmentation, complexity rather than simplicity. We shall be looking at all these in depth in the chapters that follow. But the quantum worldview also promises to restore meaning and a sense of purpose to our lives and leadership. Finding a deeper meaning for these troubles many leaders.

A business leader who survived the 2011 Japanese tsunami said afterward, "Every day now I think about the meaning of my life and what I am here to do."[6] A senior executive from Sweden wrote to me, "I'm still young, I have a beautiful family, plenty of money, and I'm at the top of my profession, but I'm not happy. I'm making money, but I'm not serving any of the things that I care about."[7] Lord Andrew Stone, former managing director of Marks & Spencer PLC, told me, "I often wake at four in the morning, asking myself what it's all about, what it all means. I feel if I can't find answers to these questions, I might as well chop myself."[8]

The search for meaning is the primary motivation in all our lives. It is this search that defines our humanity, that possibly makes us unique among earth's creatures. And it is when this deep need for meaning goes unmet that our lives come to feel shallow or empty. We "lose the plot." To function as full (and fulfilled) human beings, we need meaningful answers to questions like: What is my life all about? What does my job mean? What is the meaning of this company I have founded or worked for? Why am I in this relationship? What does it mean that I will die someday? Why commit myself to one thing or another, to one person or another—or to anything?

When we can't find the answers, we find ourselves in a state of crisis, a crisis of meaning. We may experience this in different ways, as feeling lost, being rudderless, listless, depressed, or bored. For a business leader, the lack or loss of meaning can result in occasional cynicism and a short-term pursuit of profit at any cost.

We are by definition a questioning species, but of all the questions that we ask, four stand out as the essential questions that frame any meaningful worldview. In various forms, they occur in all the world's great spiritual traditions, and they set the agenda for finding deep meaning and a sense of existential security in our lives. These questions are: Where do I come from? Who am I? Why am I here? and What should I do? In my own way, I've been asking these questions since I was five years old, and simply asking them anew as the years go by has been my essential spiritual practice. I would like to share with you the "answers" I have found in my own evolving quantum worldview, in hope they can offer a quantum perspective on the spiritual foundations of leadership itself. As Christopher Giercke, CEO of Altai Himalaya, an Asian company that provides fashion goods exclusively to Hermès, says, "A leader has to see himself in a cosmic context, to get a perspective on where we fit in, just how small we are and thus how important it is that we cooperate with and serve one another."[9]

WHERE DO I COME FROM?

If I were to ask you how old you are, you would almost certainly tell me your chronological age, measured by your date of birth—twenty-five, forty-five, sixty-five, etc. If I then said to you, "But remember that you are a child of your culture," you might say that in that case you are perhaps one hundred years old, or three hundred years old, or even, taking the longer view of the Western or Eastern traditions, two thousand or five thousand years old. If I said, "But, oh, you are a child of life on earth," you then would say that you are one and a half billion years old. But in fact, each of us is thirteen and a half billion years old.

Each of us was here at that moment of the big bang, when the massive expansion of a singularity gave rise to all that was to come. We were here when, a split second later, the big bang gave rise to the quantum vacuum, space, time, and the Higgs field. We were here when that first fluctuation of the Vacuum, the "wrinkle in time," gave rise to mass and energy and gravity, and when these then gave rise to a fiery plasma and cosmic radiation. We were here with the creation of particles and forces, stars and planets, and none of these is truly inanimate, none wholly without some primitive form of agency, volition, and sense of direction, even a sense of purpose. As quantum physicist David Bohm says, "Even the electron is informed with a certain level of mind."[10]

We carry the whole history, purpose, and intent of the universe in our bodies and in our minds. Our bodies are made of stardust; our minds obey the same quantum laws and forces that bind the universe together. And I believe that each of us is destined to retell this story of our origins in whatever the language and culture of our times. This could be why all the world's great creation myths, from the ancient Babylonian to the contemporary quantum, tell much the same story, each in its own way.

We also carry within us the whole history of the evolution of life on this planet. In the simplest layer of our bodily organization we find structures like those of single-celled animals such as the amoeba. They have no nervous system, all their sensory coordination and motor reflexes existing within one cell. Our own white blood cells, as they scavenge for rubbish and eat up bacteria, behave in the blood stream much like amoeba in ponds.

Simple many-celled animals like jellyfish still have no central nervous system, but they do have a network of nerve fibers that allow communication between cells so that the animal can react in a coordinated way. In our own bodies, the nerve cells in the gut form a similar network that coordinates peristalsis, the muscular contractions that push food along. More evolved animals develop increasingly complex nervous systems, and eventually primitive brains. The most primitive part of our own brain, the brain stem, is inherited from reptiles, and is often called "the reptilian brain."

With the evolution of mammals a forebrain developed—first the primitive forebrain of lower mammals ruled primarily by instinct and emotion (and containing our emotional center, the limbic system), then the cerebral hemispheres, with all their sophisticated computing ability, the "little gray cells" that most of us identify with the human mind. Just as we carry the whole history of cosmic evolution within our consciousness, so we think and function with the whole history of life's evolution on earth.

Then there is the whole history of our great and ancient cultures, with their myths and superstitions, their moral laws and values, their art, music, and stories. How many of us are still afraid to step on a crack, to travel without a talisman, or to feel uneasy about Friday the thirteenth? How many educated people think, in times of defeat, of Sisyphus, who pushed a boulder to the top of a hill only to have it roll back down again, or of Icarus, who flew too close to the fire of the sun?

The logic and reason taught by the Greek philosophers and the rational intelligence measured by our IQ tests are only the tip of our mental iceberg. Many of these beliefs from the evolution of our culture are contradictory or mutually exclusive, but we think, and make our decisions and commitments, drawing from them all. Hence the mess we make of things! Jungian psychology, with its eye on the many layers of the unconscious, has always stressed that we are only about one percent civilized.

From our genetic history we inherit physical features, talents, diseases, and behavioral traits once belonging to distant ancestors. In the East, and increasingly in the West, many people believe that we inherit, and/or accumulate, a karmic history, a destiny and a set of life challenges that passes from one generation to the next, from one act or decision of ours to the next. And then there's the influence of our parents, from whom we inherit values and habits, aspirations and our starting point in life, problems and challenges, neuroses, and sometimes even psychosis.

When we ask where we come from, we must know that we come from all these things. They are part of who we are, the story of how we came to be here, the meanings that we have inherited and that provide a large part of our lives' context.

WHO AM I?

Here am I, my body made of elements that once were stardust, drawn from the far corners of the universe to flesh out, however briefly, the pattern that is uniquely me, my soul a thing that can breathe in, and in some meaningful sense remember, the enormity of such awe-inspiring origins. But who, or what, is this "I" that I think I am? Where do I begin, and where do I end?

According to the most advanced form of quantum physics, quantum field theory, the very first thing that was created after the big bang was what physicists call "the quantum vacuum." And in the language of physics, everything else that exists is an excitation of, or vibration of, this vacuum—metaphorically, a wave upon the sea of existence. The vacuum is badly named, in that it is not "empty." Exactly the opposite. The quantum vacuum contains the potentiality for everything that has existed, everything that does exist, and everything that ever will exist. It permeates the universe; it is everywhere and "inside" everything.

The quantum vacuum is also known as the "zero point field," and this helps us better to picture it at least metaphorically. It is the field of background energy on which the universe is "written," on which you and I are written, and the writing takes the form of dynamic energy patterns each of which stands out as an existing thing with defining qualities. I, at my most primary, am an evolving pattern of dynamic energy written on the quantum vacuum. Again, "a wave on the sea" of existence. And just as the waves on the sea form and reform and are never still, the dynamic energy pattern that is me is never still and never exactly the same from moment to moment of a whirlpool. And the "whirlpool" itself will have an altered shape. *I am a process of constantly shifting and changing flow playing out its drama against the background of the quantum vacuum.*

The quantum vacuum is the ground and source of everything and everyone that exists, conscious and unconscious, the driving force that causes the universe to evolve as it does, the prime substance that gives rise to all substance, the "prime mover" behind all movement, the reason for things being as they are, the sense of direction, the purpose behind things, the essential purpose coursing through our lives. Many contemporary physicists have presented good arguments for saying the quantum vacuum is conscious, even that it is Prime Consciousness. It is without question the *source* of consciousness, because it is the source of everything, and consciousness is "something."

If the vacuum *is* conscious, it could be said to have a mind, and existing things, with their distinctive excitations/vibrations, would be like the brain waves that make up the patterns of every mind's thoughts—those alpha, beta, theta, and gamma waves that neuroscientists measure with EEG machines. We could think of the vacuum as "the God within physics," and thus ourselves as *thoughts in the mind of God*. This is the underlying truth of Eckhart Tolle's words in *The Power of Now*: "You are here to enable the Divine Purpose of the universe to enfold. That's how important you are."[11]

This is a very far cry from the reductionist myth that tells us we are but accidental and random collocations of atoms in a universe without purpose or direction, or nerve pulses and chemical reactions in brains that are not conscious. Rather, as excitations of the quantum vacuum, we are co-creative agents of the field of existence, the agents through whom the God of physics acts in the world—agents through whom this God within physics feels its own way forward into an uncertain future.

WHY AM I HERE?

In the Jewish Kabbalah, we are told the origins of creation and the purpose of those of us who are its consequence. It is said that there was a world before our world, a perfect world filled with the essence of the light of Godhead. But this world became so filled with light that it could no longer contain itself. It burst, and the fragments of its light (the "divine sparks") were scattered throughout our world. This story tells us that the purpose of humankind is to gather up these fragments and reconstitute the original holy vessel. We do this, it tells us, by building relationships that can bind the fragments into a loving and meaningful whole.

Quantum physics tells a very similar story. In this story, there was a Vacuum before our Vacuum. This first Vacuum became a singularity that could no longer contain itself. It burst with the big bang, giving rise to our Vacuum and to all of creation that followed. This creation, too, contains fragments of that original light, fragments that physicists tell us are evolving toward ever greater complexity, toward ever greater wholeness, and thus toward ever greater meaning. Physicist David Bohm argues that this innate sense of cosmic direction is written into the teleological laws of physics, into the dynamics of the universe itself.[12]

In the quantum laboratory, the way a physicist sets up an experimental apparatus determines whether he/she will get a series of waves or a stream of particles. The Heisenberg Uncertainty Principle tells us that the questions we ask determine the answers we get. This is true in life as in the laboratory. The way that the infinite potentiality latent within any person, relationship, or situation unfolds into a given actuality depends upon us. Through our thoughts, our decisions, our "experiments," and our actions, we create meaning, and thereby we create existence. This makes us partners in the evolution of the universe. We are here to make reality happen. With our lives and work and leadership, we make the world. We are here to take responsibility. In the words of *The Bhagavad Gita*:

> What the outstanding person does, others will
> try to do. The standards such people create will be
> followed by the whole world. . . . If I ever refrained
> from continuous work, everyone would immediately
> follow my example. If I stopped working I would
> be the cause of cosmic chaos, and finally of the
> destruction of this world and these people.[13]

WHAT CAN I DO?

Howard Lutnick is the CEO and chairman of Cantor-Fitzgerald, a global financial services firm specializing in bond trading. Before 9/11, Cantor-Fitzgerald had 688 employees based in the USA. All worked in the Twin Towers, and all died when those towers collapsed. Lutnick himself, covered in dust, walked away from the scene of the devastation but could not walk away from the nightmare itself. "I felt everything was lost, everything was finished," he told Piers Morgan on CNN on the tenth anniversary of 9/11. "I thought I would just move to Colorado with my family and live a life of quiet retirement. Making money just didn't matter anymore. Money no longer had any meaning. I couldn't live for it."[14] Just one thing changed Lutnick's mind.

"I thought," he said, "of those 688 families left behind. I thought, 'What will become of them? Who will take care of them?'" Financially, Cantor-Fitzgerald was ruined by the disaster. There was not even money to meet the payroll demands of European employees. But Lutnick got on the phone to his London headquarters. He asked his staff there to work twenty-four seven, without pay, for a month to rebuild the company. If they would do that, he promised, he would commit 25 percent of all future company profits to supporting the families of the lost American colleagues. "That *meant* something to me," he said. "I would be rebuilding the company *for* something, for something that wasn't just money."[15]

Cantor-Fitzgerald was rebuilt and prospered, and Howard Lutnick conceived a new paradigm for business itself. He called it "philanthropic capitalism"—capitalism that takes as its aim the making of money for a higher purpose, the making of money for what that money can achieve in the wider world. In talking to Piers Morgan about the financial crisis still threatening the global economy in 2011, Lutnick suggested that wealthy businessmen should take their money out from under the mattress and invest it in creating jobs. "That's the real meaning of business," he said. "It's not about making money. It's about creating jobs."[16] Lutnick had found his own personal meaning, and the meaning of business in general, in *service*. I doubt he has ever read *The Bhagavad Gita*, but he might well have spoken Krishna's words himself:

> True sustenance is in service; those who do not
> seek to serve are without a home in this world. . . .
> Strive constantly to serve the welfare of the
> world; by devotion to selfless work one attains
> the supreme goal of life. Do your work with
> the welfare of others always in mind.[17]

Like an elementary subatomic particle arising suddenly from within the vapors of a Wilson cloud chamber, leaving its track, and then disappearing back into the vapor, each of us arises as an excitation of the Quantum Vacuum, leaves a trail in this world, and then returns once again to the Vacuum. This is our journey in bold outline. In living it, as James Joyce wrote in *Portrait of the Artist as a Young Man*, each of us must, away from home and early friends, learn "what the heart is and what it feels." Each of us must "go to encounter for the millionth time the reality of experience and to forge in the smithy of [our souls] the uncreated consciousness of [our] race."[18]

Along the way in our journey, we must acquire wisdom. We must learn of life's complexities and nuances and unavoidable contradictions, its tragedies and losses, and learn to feel compassion for it all, most especially for ourselves. We must learn not to expect more of others, or of ourselves, than they can do, and to have the capacity to forgive them (and ourselves) for what they can't. We must learn to live life's questions, to acquire patience, fortitude, and resilience, and learn both generosity and humility. Above all, we must find our purpose and what Don Juan calls our "place"[19]—the center of our power.

Poet and playwright Archibald MacLeish defines this place for the potential quantum leader, "the hero in the play."[20]

> Who shall be the hero in the play?
> And where, upon what stone or throne or will or
> Word or plinth or power shall he stand
> To still the world to peace again; to poise
> Eternity upon a turning pole
> Again: to make us men:
> To make us whole?[21]

The thinking and practice of the quantum leader is outlined in the following chapters.

CHAPTER 2

THREE LEVELS OF
REAL TRANSFORMATION

We know a great deal today from science and psychology about transformations in both physical and living systems. Many of these are universal, some specific to living systems, and a few are specific to human beings because of our intelligence, complexity, and particular psychology. The human self has three levels: the mental, the emotional, and the spiritual—that deep layer of the self from which we are in touch with questions of meaning and value. It is crucial to emphasize again, and to remember when I use the term throughout this book, that *spiritual* need not have any religions associations. Human beings can be members of any religion or no religion, they can even be atheists, and still have spiritual needs, values, and visions.

In human beings, the mental aspect has to do with things we normally associate with explicit thinking, our ability to solve problems, to follow rules, to achieve goals. But *which* problems we choose to solve, what goals we think it *worth* attaining, and our *willingness* to follow rules all spring from our emotional and spiritual dimensions—from our aspirations, our ambitions, our associations, and from our visions and deepest values. Aspirations, ambitions, and associations have obvious cultural and emotional origins—social values, peer pressure, personal relationships, childhood experiences, and so on. But the latest depth psychology provides evidence that all are underpinned by our quest for meaning, by our visions and deepest values, that is, by our spiritual side.

Because organizations organize human beings, they, too, have mental, emotional, and spiritual dimensions. The mental side of an organization is its overt thinking processes, its organizational model, its explicit rules, the reasoning used to set priorities and achieve goals. In Newtonian organizations, with their emphasis on rules and efficiency, this mental aspect has been split off. Such organizations ask, "What is the best (the cheapest, the most efficient) way to do x?" They seldom ask, "Is x worth doing?" or "What does it *mean* that we are doing x? What does it mean for our employees or our customers or the wider community? Would it be better if we did y instead?" These are not purely mental questions. In organizations, as in human beings, the questions of what priorities to set or which goals to pursue are emotional and spiritual questions. They spring from the organization's basic vision.

In any human being or in any human organization, real change requires a fundamental shift at each of the three levels of the self—and this change must be reflected at the personal, the cultural, and the structural levels of the organization. Change at any one level on its own is ineffective, yet most change processes do focus on just one level. Some appeal to our minds, some to our emotions, and a few to our spiritual level. Some concentrate on transforming individual attitudes and practices, some on changing the company culture, some on reinventing the organizational structure. The result is that people or organizations get out of balance, precocious in some ways, backward in others. For the whole system to thrive and change, progress must be balanced. Transformation must be achieved at all levels.

The human self does not consist of a series of little boxes separately labeled "Mind," "Heart," "Spirit." No more does an organization just consist of a series of smaller divisions separately labeled "Product Development," "Marketing," "Finance," and so on. Both are Newtonian models based on the premise that the world consists of separate little atomistic bits. Freud took these models into psychology; Frederick Taylor introduced them into management. In both cases they have led to notions that change or transformation can happen piecemeal, working on different parts of the system independently.

Today we should know better. All the new sciences of the twenty-first century, both physical and biological, are holistic. The whole is greater than the sum of the parts. They show that the world does not consist of separate, isolated parts but rather of intricately entangled systems. A change in any one apparently separate part affects the whole. Quantum physics tells us that the universe actually consists of patterns of dynamic energy, self-organizing wave patterns like so many whirlpools, the boundaries of each interwoven with those of all others. If we could look through a quantum microscope, the whole effect would look like the interlocking patterns of waves on the sea. From chaos theory we learn about the famous "butterfly effect"—the world's physical systems are so interrelated that sometimes the mere flapping of a butterfly's wings in Beijing is enough to cause a tornado over Kansas City. At our own level of daily reality, such holism has been brought home to us most forcefully in our understanding of the complex and interrelated factors that have contributed to the world's environmental crisis. Both the latest thinking in human psychology and the systems approach in management thinking have taken such insights onboard. Some of the newer economists realize it. There are no high, impenetrable walls around the world's apparently separate systems. There are no hard boundaries dividing regions of the self. Our mental, emotional, and spiritual dimensions are interwoven, each feeding—and feeding on—the others. The same is true of the supposedly separate divisions of our organizations.

Western culture has always had a propensity to split things up into little boxes. It goes back to the atomism of the ancient Greeks. But there has been an accompanying and equally distorting Western tendency to split the mind or soul off from the body, or the spiritual from the physical. Both the early Greeks and the Christian Church taught such dualism. In the seventeenth century, the French philosopher Rene Descartes gave this a very modern twist by saying, "I know that I have a mind, and I know that I have a body. And I know that the two are completely separate. I *am* my mind. I *have* a body."[1] Isaac Newton took this split as the basis of his new physics, excluding everything mental or psychological from his new physical laws of the universe. The mechanistic culture to which this physics gave rise, the culture that still dominates the thinking of most of us today, applies the Newtonian categories of the machine to human beings and to human organizations.

Freud looked for the "laws and dynamics" that governed the psyche and insisted that human behavior was fully determined by such laws and their interaction with childhood experience. Adam Smith looked for the laws and principles that guide the market economy and insisted we could use them to predict and control market behavior. In management theory, the British engineer Frederick Taylor insisted that every organization is bound by underlying laws and principles and that human beings within the organization act accordingly. Discover your company's underlying laws and you can work with them to predict and control the behavior of your markets, your employees, and your production. In the language of today's computer-speak, the whole thing is *programmed*.

Iron laws, prediction, control, programs. These are the bywords of Newtonian physics and mechanistic culture. They are keywords in Newtonian management thinking. But how accurately do they reflect today's world or meet the needs of today's companies? How do we predict and control complexity? How do we program chaos? Where are the iron laws that guarantee the behavior (and therefore the creativity and the productivity) of what managers call "intellectual capital"? How do we quantify and measure the more human characteristics and motivations and uniquely human potential in those people that companies describe as their "greatest assets" or their "competitive advantage"?

Human beings do have some mechanical characteristics. Our muscles work very much like machines, and indeed it was human muscles that the technology of the Industrial Revolution began to replace. There are also mechanical aspects of our minds, aspects that are indeed programmed. Our rational, rule-bound, problem-solving, goal-oriented thinking operates very much like the program of a common personal computer (PC). And it is those mechanical aspects of the mind that computers are replacing in large numbers. The corporate world does not need more human "thinking machines." Silicon chips are cheaper, faster, and more reliable. Rather, the "intellectual capital" that companies need to nurture today involves those characteristics of human beings that *no* machine can duplicate, those special qualities of people that can't be programmed.

Computers don't have emotions. They don't feel pain or frustration;

they don't laugh at jokes; they don't write poems; they certainly don't have spiritual needs and insight. A company's IT system can't question itself; it can't think outside the box; it can't reflect on failures or conceive new approaches to problems. These are the things that link the human self with its world and the human employee with his/her creativity. Computers don't *have* selves. In human beings, thinking is not split off from emotion and spirit—our creativity and uniqueness depends upon these more complex sides of the self. So does our capacity to have vision, to dream, to assign meaning to our projects.

Equally, just as vision is inseparable from our spiritual intelligence, our capacity to handle ambiguity, uncertainty, and complexity is bound up with a combination of emotional and spiritual intelligence. Our striving, our drive toward perfection, our dedication, and our need to serve are all bound up with our spiritual intelligence. And these are the human qualities for which organizations must make room—indeed must nurture—if they want to unleash the full potential of human creativity and productivity.

Ironically, it is these very qualities of emotional and spiritual intelligence that many corporate transformation programs strive to develop. At least they try to tap the *net result* of their employees having such qualities. Most corporate leaders would like to have a workforce, or at least a managerial team, that can think on its feet, be creative, thrive on complexity, take responsibility, and give its all to the firm. This is why they spend millions on "change agents," consultants who specialize in managing transformation. But most change agents are themselves mechanistic and haven't a clue what deep transformation means, never mind what it requires. Most don't know where to begin, so they satisfy themselves with schemes for downsizing or "restructuring," with introducing a "change vocabulary," including charts that say "vision" and "values" and "leadership." They give two-day workshops on "creativity" and "embracing diversity." But they don't "change the room"—they work within the *existing* culture or structures. And Newtonian organizations have no existing structures that foster emotional intelligence, let alone structures that foster the creative abilities of spiritual intelligence. Newtonian organizations have no inner capacity for fundamental transformation.

THE NEED FOR A NEW LEADERSHIP PSYCHOLOGY

Most people who think about the challenges facing management and leadership know that something is stuck. The consultants and the gurus introduce one gimmick after another, and unwittingly maintain mechanistic assumptions about human behavior derived from the old physical sciences and their methodology. Thus the unceasing attempts to analyze and measure motivation and personality as predictive tools, and the common belief that there are measurable criteria (and hence an applicable technique) for becoming a more effective leader, a better person, a good coach, and a creative individual. What CEO would pay for anything less? For instance the two-day or two-week workshops on transformation that transform nothing.

Some training managers and consultants concerned with individual or leadership development are familiar with and use American psychologist Abraham Maslow's famous "Hierarchy of Needs" (shown in Figure 1) to chart their way through the human psyche. It is one of the best and most wide-ranging models of human priorities and hence human motivations ever to be summed up in one table, and it commonly appears in the textbooks or handout booklets of change-management courses. Formed in the shape of a pyramid, human needs are divided into the "basic needs" of survival, safety, and security, and then the "growth needs" of belonging (social), self-esteem (ego), and self-actualization. By self-actualization Maslow meant the need for meaning, the deep need to feel that one's life and work are *about* something, the spiritual dimension of the self. Over the years the psychological insight of the corporate world has slowly been working its way up Maslow's pyramid.[2]

The labor unions (themselves heavily Newtonian organizations) were the first to fight for recognition of employees' basic needs for survival and security—safety measures, adequate pay, rest breaks, and so on. These are needs common in some form or other to any living organism, human or otherwise, and thus take little special account of the fully human dimension in organizations. The union reforms were necessary but not sufficient. It was for the later Human Relations Movement and its assorted transformation schemes to stress the importance of the higher, or "growth needs":

the need for work to have a personal dimension, the need for individuals to have a sense of self-esteem, the need to foster better relationships at work, the need for work-site counseling, and so on.

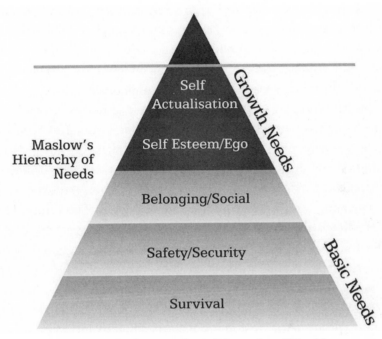

Figure 1. Abraham Maslow's "Hierarchy of Needs"

Some of this made some difference to people's tolerance or even enjoyment of work, but again it was not sufficient to deliver deep transformation. People at work could smile at each other sometimes, could leave their babies in crèches provided by the boss, could vent their frustrations to a counselor. But organizations have remained stressful places, and loneliness prevails, fear still drives the relationship between subordinates and their bosses, risk is still not adequately rewarded. From the point of view of the organization's long-term success, nothing important has changed. Thinking remains stuck, experimentation remains tentative, inflexible organizational structures still thwart human potential, and the organization as a whole resists change.

It is only very recently that Maslow's last category, the need for self-actualization, has touched business circles—among the few who begin to see the need for a more spiritual dimension in business, who see that initiative and creativity within companies, and even the ultimate survival *of* companies, is bound up with core meaning, vision, and values. These are the people who need a new, more complex psychological model that links the mental, emotional, and spiritual intelligence of employees. And they need a vision of how to use their new understanding to change the priorities, the structure, and the leadership of organizations.

The Maslow hierarchy is good. It does at least recognize that human beings have a range of needs and that the need for meaning is one of them. But the model is upside down and too hierarchical. It does not answer the need for a new corporate psychology. Maslow makes the basic need for safety and security (that is, a category of material things) the foundation of his pyramid, stressing that it is the sine qua non for sustaining life. He places self-actualization (meaning) at the apex, the ultimate goal of the fulfilled life—nice if you can get it, but really just the icing on the cake. Other needs are ranked in between. This ranking of priorities mirrors the bottom-line returns of Western corporate culture (short-term stockholder value), and that in turn mirrors the generally materialist bias of Western culture itself. It also atomizes needs into hierarchical boxes, giving the false impression that we can rank and separate physical, personal, social, and spiritual needs. Human beings are more holistic than that. So, too, would be organizations that can use full human potential to thrive on change and complexity.

In my own more recent books on spiritual intelligence and spiritual capital, I have argued that we need to invert Maslow's pyramid.[3] *The need for meaning is primary.* There are countless documented instances of people sacrificing comfort, companionship, food, even life itself, in pursuit of meaning, higher morality, or higher ideals. In the corporate world, there are countless examples of employees agreeing to longer hours and less pay if they can see that this is for the greater good of all, or in pursuit of some goal that excites them. The same is true of senior corporate executives who take vast pay cuts to move into the nonprofit sector of charities and NGOs. The people who survived prisoner of war and concentration camps in World War II were the people motivated by deeply held beliefs and values.[4] Productivity levels in automobile plants increased when people were organized into small teams that build entire cars, so that each employee had a vision of the purpose of the work and the satisfaction of seeing it completed.

It is also true that the need for meaning cannot be separated from what might be called lesser needs for security, material well-being, companionship, and self-esteem. Each level of the self suffuses every other. The self is a dynamic system, and our needs support each other in a dynamic way. The same is true in organizations. We cannot split off an organization's need for profit from its need to give employees self-esteem, nor from its need for deep vision. So many things go wrong in organizations because we don't understand this basic holistic, systemic aspect of their function. This is the message most urgently driven home by Quantum Systems Dynamics.

Throughout this book I am going to replace Maslow's pyramidal Hierarchy of Needs with the set of interlocking concentric circles shown in Figure 2. I place spiritual needs (vision, values, meaning) at the center, stressing that these needs underpin and suffuse everything else, but I also want to portray the dynamic interplay between our different needs, the different aspects or dimensions of ourselves, the different goals, pursuits, and internal structures of our organizations. I also stress throughout the book that all fundamental transformation is ultimately *spiritual* transformation, spiritual in the very broadest sense as issuing from the level of reflection, meaning, and value. This is true for individuals and for organizations. It is also crucially true that creative thinking emerges from this spiritual level, whether it is thinking about widgets, thinking about organizational structures, or thinking about long-term strategies and purposes.

In corporate language, the spiritual level is the company's basic vision and core values. Vision does not mean "our plans for the next five years" or "how we plan to achieve our goals." It is more basic than that. A company's vision is its overall—and often *unconscious*—sense of identity, its aspirations, its sense of itself in the wider world, its deeper, motivating core values and long-term strategies. In one example that I used in working with managers at Shell Oil, I asked them whether they see Shell as an oil company or as an energy company. The answer to that is key to the company's core vision. The two answers are very different, and each would lead to a different set of long-term aims and prospects, different research and development strategies, a different sense of Shell's role in the larger economy, a different sense of identity and purpose (and hence a different degree of loyalty and commitment) in Shell employees. If Shell or other companies want genuine transformation programs, they must start at that level. They must get to the core thinking (and being!) that can reach and shift that level. And they must maintain, with suitable leadership and infrastructures, their capacity to tap freshly into that level of vision whenever necessary. *A company, like an individual, must always be able to access its spiritual core.* That is the only level from which it can shift its existing assumptions, leadership patterns, and corporate structure.

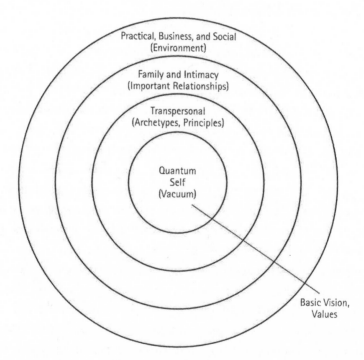

Figure 2. Layers of the Self

The rest of this book is about how leaders and their companies might do this. It is about the kinds of thinking that human beings can do and the level of thinking from which deep transformation, and therefore deep creativity, issues. We will explore together the complex organization and potentiality of the human brain (and its accompanying self) and think together how nature's best organization yet devised can be used as a model for rethinking and restructuring our own human-made organizations.

> The organization, potentiality, and thinking processes of the human brain are our most powerful model for creative thinking in organizations.

CREATIVITY AND QUANTUM THINKING

Creative thinking, the thinking that originates crucially in the spiritual level of the self, issues from a brain dynamic that functions very much like the processes and systems described by quantum physics and complexity science. Some brain scientists even argue that there is an actual quantum level in the brain, perhaps coupled with "complex" activity, that makes consciousness and creative thinking possible.[5] Whether this is true remains to be proven. But human creative thinking is so similar to the creativity of quantum processes that I find it useful to call creative thinking *quantum thinking*. For similar reasons, I often refer to the spiritual level of the self as *the quantum self*. This allows us to find a language, a set of images and metaphors, and even an organizational model for nurturing creativity and creative leadership in the existing language, imagery, and organization of quantum and complex systems and the quantum brain.

The essence of quantum physics is that it describes an unfixed, both/ and level of reality that thrives on ambiguity and uncertainty at something very similar to "the edge of chaos." The essence of the quantum self is that it describes that source of the self that precedes divisions into mind and body, into the mental, the emotional, and the spiritual, and that precedes the self's identification with existing ways to be. The quantum self is not an off-the-peg self, not a persona or a mask. The essence of quantum thinking is that it is the thinking that precedes categories, structures, and accepted patterns of thought, or mind-sets. *It is with quantum thinking that we create our categories, change our structures, and transform our patterns of thought.* Quantum thinking is vital to creative thinking and leadership in organizations. It is the key to any genuine organizational transformation. It is the key to shifting our paradigm. Quantum thinking is the link between the brain's creativity, organizational transformation and leadership, and the ideas found in the science of the twenty-first century.

Product development in business lies somewhere on the grid of criss-crossing influences that link pure science and fine art with technology (applied science) and design (applied art). Quantum thinking drives pure science and fine art; paradigm shifts in technology give rise to new products.

THE NEED TO SHIFT PARADIGMS

Many business people are familiar with the word *paradigm*, but I believe that few really understand it. Paradigm (and paradigm shifts) is another of those greatly overused, misused, and abused words that have become part of the gobbledygook of the "change vocabulary." Some people think it means a mental model or mind-set; some use it as though it is just a new idea or set of ideas, a set of habits, a style, or even a set of traditions or prejudices. A paradigm does include all these things, but it is much more.

Our paradigm, used in the proper sense first defined by American philosopher Thomas Kuhn in *The Structure of Scientific Revolutions*, is the whole perceptual, conceptual, emotional, and spiritual framework embracing our most deeply held, unconscious assumptions and values. It is the things we take for granted about any situation in life. Like a pair of glasses we wear to focus our visual world, our paradigm focuses the whole of what we take to be reality. It determines our expectations, frames the questions that we will ask, and structures our approach to what we do. Paradigms are so deep that they even determine what we *see*. When people who lived in the Middle Ages went to the seashore, for instance, they literally did not see the curvature of the horizon. To us it's obvious because we know (we have the paradigm) that the earth is round, but they *knew* the earth was flat. So a curved horizon would have made no sense to them, they had no categories to see it, and thus they *didn't* see it. Nor, it follows, did they ask questions like, "Why don't we fall off?" That kind of question is raised by our paradigm of the round earth.

Our Paradigm

Our most deeply held, unconscious set of assumptions and values

The things we take for granted

That which determines our expectations, frames the questions we ask, and structures our approach to what we do

---

We can't help having paradigms. Indeed, we need them. They are literally wired into our brains so that we have the concepts and categories necessary to digest our experience. Philosophers and neuroscientists used to think that we are *hard wired*—born with certain neural connections that frame our experience from birth and remain with us throughout our lives. This view was accompanied by the notion that we have a limited learning horizon related to aging and that beyond a certain age (about aged eighteen) our capacities start to diminish. But we know today this is not true.

Today neuroscience tells us that the brain is "plastic,"[6] ever changing and rewiring itself in dialogue with our growing experience. When we enter the world as infants, we arrive with very little of our brain wired up. We are born with sufficient neural connections to regulate our breathing, our body temperature, and the beating of our heart, but nearly everything else is pure potentiality. What diet we will be fed, what climatic conditions and germs we will encounter, what language we need to speak, what concepts we will need to form—all these are uncertain at the moment of birth. So the infant's brain is poised at the edge. Chaotic instability in its initial neural firings enables the brain to wire itself as it learns and evolves with experience.

Experiments have been done, for instance, on the language-learning abilities of human infants. The sounds that infants make in the first months after birth have been recorded, and psychologists have discovered that every human infant, everywhere on this planet, utters all eight hundred or so phonemes (sound patterns) found in the totality of *all* human languages. The infant's brain ranges across the whole spectrum of human speech. Yet within the first year of life, infants select out those phonemes relevant to the language of their own culture. They lay down neural pathways for recognizing and using those sounds—and lose the ability to recognize and use sounds not used by the surrounding culture.

Infants and children lay down new neural connections—wire their brains—of necessity at a rapid rate. They have to construct their world. Older people may be able to get by on the experience of their first eighteen years, may be able to sleepwalk through life. It is tempting to do so because growing new neural connections requires energy and can be exhausting. When we think creatively, the brain uses more energy than the whole rest of the body. But we are not condemned to be sleepwalkers. Given a motivation, given an opportunity, given a crisis, we can and do grow new neural connections at any age. Experiments have shown that people well into their nineties still have the capacity to rewire their brains. That means we have a lifelong ability to change our paradigm.

Thomas Kuhn wrote about paradigms to describe how scientists work. We usually think of science as revolutionary, "at the edge." But Kuhn pointed out that most normal science is very conservative.[7] Most scientists work *within* a paradigm, play a "finite game," and their experiments are done to validate that paradigm. It is only when the anomalies, the things that won't fit into the old paradigm, mount up that "revolutionary science" takes over. Revolutionary science plays the "infinite game," *changes* the paradigm. It has the insight and the boldness to say that the old way of looking at things won't work. But such revolutions are painful, and we resist them. The necessary casualty of a paradigm shift is nothing less than our whole way of looking at things, our sense of reality itself.

We need a paradigm to function at all, to know our way about in the world. But the danger is that we can get trapped inside our paradigm. We get used to things as they are and think that's just the way it is. New thinking becomes impossible. We become people of a single vision, a single outlook. This conflict between the need for a paradigm and the fact that it can become our prison is known as the "paradigm paradox." Science cannot be changed from within the old paradigm; neither can business. As Einstein said, "We can't solve problems by using the same kind of thinking we used when we created them."[8] To change the rules of the game, we have to step outside the game as we know it. In the same way, we can't transform the structures of organizations from within the existing structure. You have to "blow up the room." This is difficult for those who have grown up within the existing structures and have invested their whole careers in learning how to use them. Kuhn argued that a scientific paradigm couldn't shift until all the practitioners of the old paradigm had died.[9] This may be too bleak, but to change our paradigm we do have to rewire our brains. Like scientists, we are usually motivated to make the effort only when catastrophe strikes, when the old structures have failed. I think this is where we have gotten to today in business, politics, economics, and education. *Our old structures just don't work.*

Business leaders, too, like scientists, have their paradigm—their deeply held and largely unconscious set of assumptions and values, the way they see things, the questions they think it is natural to ask, the risks they think it reasonable to take. The dominant Western business paradigm is shared with the wider culture and has grown out of our whole Western tradition. It has been focused sharply by the language, concepts, and categories of Newtonian mechanistic science and includes basic assumptions like force, causality, predictability, control, and what should be taken for granted. Thus business leaders couch their analyses and future scenarios in language referring to market forces, market forecasts, chains of cause and effect ("If we don't do this, x will react like that"), and "best possible" practices and solutions. Power and control are central features of this Newtonian business paradigm. Efficiency is one of its central values.

If we want to transform the structure and leadership of our organizations, we have to address transformation at this fundamental paradigmatic level. We have to change the thinking behind our thinking. Leaders who want to initiate real change processes must in the first instance become aware that they have been acting out of a paradigm. They must see the origin and nature of this existing paradigm, its effect on their management, and its limitations. And they must get to a point where they can *feel* the reality of an alternative paradigm—or the creative excitement of standing at the edge between paradigms. They must learn to ask fundamentally new questions, bring themselves to a place where the very categories of thought and vision are different. They must come to see themselves, the world, human relations, and their companies in a fundamentally new way. If leaders can reach this point, then they will be in a position to change the room rather than shifting the same old furniture about in it. Changing the room means seeing and implementing the possibility of a fundamentally new form of organization. I call it a *quantum organization*. But building this new kind of organization means learning to think in a new way—to use *all* the brain's capacity for thought. It means becoming good at three kinds of thinking.

CHAPTER 3

THREE KINDS OF THINKING: HOW THE BRAIN REWIRES ITSELF

T he brain is the most complex organ in the body—perhaps the most complex structure in the known universe. The brain somehow produces or transmits the mystery of conscious mind, our awareness of ourselves, others, and the world. It generates and structures our thoughts, enables us to have emotions, and somehow mediates our spiritual lives— our sense of meaning and value. The brain gives us touch, sight, smell, and language. It controls the beating of our hearts, the rate at which we sweat, the pace of our breathing, and countless other bodily functions. Its outward-reaching neural fibers extend to every region of the body. It is the bridge between our inner lives and the outer world. The brain can do all these things because it is flexible, adaptive, and self-organizing. It constantly rewires itself.

The human brain is capable of three distinctive kinds of thinking. The first, rational, logical, rule-bound thinking produces concepts, categories, and mental models similar to structures described by the Newtonian particle paradigm. The second kind of thinking, associative thinking, is generated in relation to less rational experience—our emotions, our felt, bodily experience, the associations we make between elements of our experience, the patterns that we detect or recognize. Associative thinking is not rule-bound but is, instead, habit-bound. Our third kind of thinking is our creative, reflective thinking. It breaks old rules and creates new ones; it recognizes and questions assumptions and accepted mental models. Creative thinking behaves very much like the kind of systems and structures found in the quantum paradigm. These three kinds of thinking and their associated brain structures and dynamics provide a powerful model that companies can emulate when looking for infrastructures and processes that can thrive on change and uncertainty and harness meaning.

The brain is nature's most complex and multifaceted organization. All human-made organizations are in fact reflections of this natural template. Human-made organizations are approximations of the real thing based on their leaders' best ability to draw on the full resources of nature's potential. If leaders deepen their understanding of this potential—if they raise their own consciousness of brain dynamics, structure, and capacity—they will be better placed to rewire the corporate brain of the companies they lead.

THE BRAIN'S INFINITE CAPACITY TO CHANGE

As already mentioned, scientists used to think that our brains are hard-wired. We are born, they thought, with a certain number of neurons connected in particular ways, and with aging the whole network slowly deteriorates. People were thought to be in their mental prime at about the age of eighteen, after which it was to be downhill all the way! Today's neuroscientists know better. True, we are born with a certain number of neurons, and we do constantly lose some of these as we go through life. An older person has far fewer neurons than a baby. But we do constantly grow new neural *connections*, or at least we have the capacity to do so.

It is the connections between the neurons, more than their number, that create the mind and its capacities. The more complex and varied our mental challenges, the richer the array of neural connections required. The human infant is born with the basic necessities for maintaining life outside the mother's womb—neural connections to regulate breathing, heartbeat, temperature, and so on. But infants do not yet have the capacity to recognize faces and objects, to form concepts, to utter coherent sounds. These capacities evolve over time as experience enriches the infant's brain capacity. Through experience of its world, the brain lays down new neural connections. The richer and more varied the experience, the greater the maze of neural connections that forms. This is why we know that we can boost infant intelligence and even physical coordination through offering frequent and varied stimulation—brightly colored objects to look at, different sounds and voices, a range of smells and tastes, back rubs, and emotional warmth.

Infants *must* grow new neural connections in their brains if they are to have a world. Early connections provide the capacity to recognize tastes, smells, faces, voices. With increasing maturity, new neural connections allow language and concept formation; they store the facts and experiences of memory; they enable reading, writing, and general learning. There is *no limit* to how many neural connections a child's brain can grow. But in modern culture, by about the age of sixteen or eighteen (early twenties if the child continues with higher education), most of us have grown enough neural connections to coast through the rest of life. We've formed an overall picture of the world and its ways. We have formed (and wired in) assumptions on which we can act. We've formed mental models and habits, emotional patterns, patterns of response to people and situations. In short, we've wired in a basic, workable life paradigm.

Growing new neural connections for the brain's initial wiring takes a lot of energy, but the growing child is motivated by both need and curiosity. And children do have a lot of energy. As adults we are less motivated. After all, we have all those accumulated habits and assumptions to call upon when dealing with experience. As long as our initial paradigm makes sense and copes with life's basic challenges, why make the effort to change it? We have an infinite, lifelong capacity to lay down new neural connections, to change and grow our brains, but when life's events and challenges were more stable, predictable, and controllable, few people used it. *Re*wiring the brain, challenging all those initial habits and assumptions in the face of new experience, requires far more energy than the original wiring. Rewiring means the effort of deconstructing (tearing out!) all the old connections as well as laying down new ones. We resist it. So long as no great challenge rocks the boat, we resist spending energy we could save. But if things have gone badly wrong in our lives, if our original mental and emotional habits and our deeply held assumptions can no longer cope with some new challenge or experience, we *have* to rewire or go under.

Today's world is not stable, predictable, or controllable. Many of us feel that our lives, both personal and working, are spiraling out of control. The books we read at university are out of date before we graduate. The technology we used two or three years ago is reinvented before we have fully learned to get comfortable with it. Relationships, job security, what it *takes* to be qualified for work, the kinds and number of problems we have to solve, all are volatile. Rapid change and the uncertainty it generates means that most of us can no longer coast through life on what we knew when we were eighteen. Companies cannot remain sustainable on the habits and assumptions, the skills and the thinking tools that existed when they were startups. Rewiring the brain, both individual and corporate, is no longer an option; it is a *necessity*. The kind of thinking that allows us to change our thinking is now required for survival. Lifelong learning has become the rule.

MESS, WONDERFUL MESS

When he was CEO of Shell USA, Phil Carroll used to advise his colleagues, "The world is a messy place. If we want to stay on top of the corporate ladder, we must plunge into the mess. We must learn to work with the mess."[1]

The human brain is at the top of nature's intelligence ladder (so far as we know!), and it definitely got there by learning to work with mess. There is nothing planned or orderly about the brain's structure. This is just one of the things that makes it so difficult to understand. Its wiring is a bit like the twisting alleyways of a medieval city, layer upon layer of archeological history built one on top of the other and all somehow being lived in. The brain's architecture—its neural wiring—carries within it the whole history of the evolution of life on this planet, at least that belonging to the animal kingdom. And we use it all.

In the simplest layer of our nervous system, the part corresponding to the prehistory of the medieval city with its many layers of archeology, we find structures like those of one-celled animals such as the amoeba or paramecium. They have no nervous system; all the sensory coordination and motor reflexes of these animals exist within one cell. Our own white blood cells, as they scavenge up rubbish and eat bacteria, behave in the bloodstream much like amoebas in ponds. Simple many-celled animals like jellyfish still have no central nervous system, but they do have a network of nerve fibers that allow between cells so that the animal can react in a coordinated way. In our bodies, the nerve cells in the gut form a network that coordinates peristalsis, the muscular contractions that push food along the gut.

With the evolution of mammals, a forebrain developed—first the primitive forebrain of the lower mammals, ruled primarily by instinct and emotion, and then the cerebral hemispheres with all their sophisticated computing ability, the "little gray cells" that most of us identify with the human mind. Yet drunkenness, fatigue, the use of tranquillizers, or damage to the higher forebrain result in regression to primitive, more spontaneous, less calculating, less *rational* types of behavior found in the lower animals.

So despite the increasing centralization and complexity of the nervous system as it evolves, even in humans the more primitive nerve nets remain, both within the expanded brain and throughout the body. The more recent phases of our evolution have supplanted earlier phases, but they have not entirely replaced them. The experience of the amoeba, the jellyfish, the earthworm, and the ant are all embedded in our nervous tissue. So, too, are the mental and emotional processes of the rat, the wolf, the bear, and the cat embedded in our higher faculties. *We think with the whole history of evolution sleeping within each thought and in each act of the imagination.* As I argued in Chapter One, we even carry the whole history of the cosmos, the laws and forces and potentialities of cosmic evolution, within our consciousness.

Our usual business-world model of "thinking" then is inadequate to the real thing. As now made common knowledge by the new science of behavioral economics, thinking is not an entirely cerebral process. It is not something we do best or most effectively when we can be entirely cool and rational and detached. It is certainly not something we do simply and straightforwardly. We do not think only with our "heads"—we also think with our emotions and our bodies and our spirits (our visions, our hopes and longings, our sense of meaning and value). We think with all the complex and varied and messy nerve nets woven throughout our organisms. Everyday language recognizes this when we say things like, "He thinks with his guts," or "She thinks with her heart." Many leaders speak of having a "feel for the situation," described sometimes as almost "tactile."

Because the business world (like so much of the wider Western culture) has a limited picture of thinking, the structures evolved within organizations to encourage thinking, effective action, and success are also limited. Not surprisingly, the brain's thinking structures and processes are more varied, taking into account the inputs from emotion, the body, and the spirit. Today, neuroscience knows that the three kinds of thinking involved in our higher mental faculties each employs a different kind of neural structure and processing in the brain. Let's look at these in depth to see what they might say about the potentialities for business thinking.

SERIAL THINKING: THE BRAIN'S "INTELLECT"

Our simplistic model of "thinking" as something straightforward, logical, rational, deliberate, and dispassionate is not wrong. It is just a limited model of thinking that is only part of the story. It is a model derived from formal logic and arithmetic—"If x, then y," or "$2 + 2 = 4$." Human beings are very good at this kind of thinking, and, ever since Aristotle, it has been the dominant form of thinking encouraged and practiced in the Western world. This is true even more so since the seventeenth-century Newtonian Scientific Revolution and the Rationalist philosophy of Descartes that accompanied it. Our children are educated to maximize it, our leaders have been taught to value it in their strategy and decision-making, and nearly everything in Western culture has been dominated by it.

In the latest work on cognitive psychology and cognitive neuroscience, this rational, logical kind of thinking is called "System 2 Thinking" by some, "left-brain thinking" by others, and in his influential book

Thinking, Fast and Slow, Daniel Kahneman calls it our "slow thinking."[2] It is our IQ thinking. All who now refer to it distinguish it from at least one other way that we deal with, digest, and use our mental experience. I call this first kind of thinking "serial thinking" because of the very distinctive kind of working neural architecture that produces it.

The brain has three recognizable kinds of neural processing. The kind associated with serial thinking is facilitated by neurons acting as though they are *neural tracts*. With neural tracts, the neurons behave as though they are connected one-on-one in a series, like a series of telephone cables. The head of one neuron connects to the tail of the next one, and an electrochemical signal passes along the chain of linked neurons being employed for any particular thought or series of thoughts. Each neuron is switched either on or off, and if any neuron in the chain gets damaged or switched off, the whole chain ceases to function, like a chain of Christmas tree lights wired serially. PCs are wired in this serial fashion.

Neural tracks learn (are wired) according to a fixed program, the rules of which are laid down in accordance with formal logic. The learning involved is thus step-by-step and rule-bound. When we teach our children their times tables by rote, we are encouraging them to wire their brains for serial processing. This produces a kind of thinking useful for solving problems or achieving tasks. It is goal-oriented, or instrumental, how-to thinking. It is the kind of thinking with which we manage the rules of grammar or the rules of a game. It is rational, logical thinking— "If I do this, then I know that certain consequences will follow."

A great deal of thinking involved in business-as-usual is serial thinking. The analysis phase of any enterprise relies on breaking a situation down into its simplest logical parts and then predicting the causal relationships that will emerge. Traditional strategic planning assumes a game plan and a step-by-step rationale for enacting it. "Management by objectives" assumes we set clear goals and objectives and then work out a logical series of actions for achieving them. Serial computers that play chess do so by analyzing all possible outcomes of each position and then calculate the strongest, step-by-step.

Like the kind of thinking that underpins Newtonian particle science, both the structures and thinking produced by neural tracts are linear and deterministic. B always follows A in the same way. This kind of thinking does not tolerate nuance or ambiguity. Everything must be clear and logical. It is strictly on/off, either/or thinking for which only one future option is possible. Fantastically effective within its given set of rules (within its program or model), the serial thinking process breaks down if someone moves the goal posts. It is like a PC asked to do a task not covered by its program. In that case, a message flashes on the screen to tell us "system not operating." In the metaphor of James Carse, serial thinking is "finite," and it functions within boundaries, "inside the box."[3] It is of no use when we need to scan the horizon for alternative possibilities or when we have to deal with the unexpected. It is because so many business leaders are trapped in this kind of thinking that they are rendered ineffective by today's uncertainty and rapid change.

Companies have many structures in place that embody serial thinking. The eight-hour work shift itself, the time clock that signs employees in and out, the job descriptions and codes of dress, the whole bureaucratic structure describing responsibilities, codes of practice, holiday schedules, coffee breaks, and sickness benefits—all these are defined by rules applying universally to everyone and within set categories. Serial thinking underlies the factory-floor blueprint, the assembly line, or the engineer's repair manual. As I have said, it underlies the analysis process in strategic planning or managing by objectives. It underlies the structuring of organizations into separate divisions with separate functions. All serial thinking accepts the assumption that the corporate world (people, nuts and bolts, markets, customers, competitors) can be manipulated successfully through rules and strategies and five-year plans because they are themselves predictable in their behavior, just as the Newtonian universe is governed by fixed laws of nature.

The advantages of serial thinking are that it is considered, accurate, precise, and reliable so long as the system functions within the rules or the assumed model. The chief disadvantage is that it *can* operate only within a given model or paradigm, within the "rules of the game." Similarly, the advantages of serial structures within organizations are that they are accurate, reliable, manipulatable (controllable), and universal. The disadvantage is that they are inflexible and "closed-minded."

ASSOCIATIVE THINKING: THE BRAIN'S "HEART"

The second kind of thinking we can do is associative, or "parallel," thinking. Associative thinking helps us form cognitive links between things like hunger and the food that will satisfy it, between the need for comfort and the love we receive from others, between the color red and emotions of excitement or danger. Associative thinking also enables us to recognize patterns like faces or smells or similarities in our experience, and to learn bodily skills like riding a bicycle or driving a car. Our associative thinking goes on pretty much unconsciously, and this whole realm of our mental experience was either dismissed or consigned to the "dark side," the mysterious and irrational side of our being.

The neural structures within the brain with which we do associative thinking are known as *neural networks*. Each of these networks contains bundles of up to a hundred thousand neurons, and each single neuron in the bundle may be connected to as many as a thousand others. The connections between neurons are random, messy, or parallel—that is, each neuron acts upon and is acted upon by many others simultaneously. The neural networks in the brain are connected to further neural networks throughout the brain and the body. Associative thinking is thus rooted in our emotional and physical experience. *It is "thinking" with the heart and the body.*

In the latest parlance of cognitive psychology and cognitive neuroscience, the brain's associative thinking is known as "System 1 Thinking," "right-brain thinking," or, in the language of Daniel Kahneman, "fast thinking."[4] It is the source of EQ, or emotional quotient. It acts on hunches or "gut instincts." It gets "a feel" for the situation. Associative thinking is neither rational nor logical—it is too quick and too emotional for that. And yet it adds richness and depth to our mental experience. It is the poet within us, the author of metaphors and analogies. "This is like that." It is now recognized that a vast proportion of our thinking is associative, unconscious, irrational, emotional, and body-centered.[5] In the new science of Behavioral Economics, this has led to great caution about the reliability of rational models and forecasts for market behavior, indeed, for all of human behavior. Man as a "rational animal" (Aristotle) has been exposed as a myth. There is, in fact, only the thinnest top layer of rationality separating our conduct and thought from rule by the passions and the instincts.

Unlike the neural tracts of serial thinking, which become prisoners of their own mental model or paradigm, neural networks have the ability to learn and rewire themselves in dialogue with experience. Each time I see a pattern of behavior or event sequences, the neural network connections that recognize that pattern grow in strength, until recognition becomes something automatic. If the pattern alters, my ability to perceive it will slowly alter, too, until my brain has rewired itself to recognize the new pattern.

When I learn to drive a car, for instance, every move of my hands and feet is at first deliberate, and my control of the car is based upon rational calculation. With each practice run, coordination between hands, feet, and brain is more strongly wired into the brain's neural networks (their interconnections grow stronger) until, eventually, I don't "think" about driving at all unless there is some unusual or unexpected problem. Indeed, it even becomes impossible to think consciously, or at least easily, about my driving skills. When he was twelve, my son asked me, "Mum, which foot do you use to press the clutch pedal?" I couldn't answer him. I had to get behind the wheel of our car and *watch* my left foot go down on the clutch. My foot knew how to work the clutch, but my head didn't!

All associative learning is trial-and-error learning. When a rat learns to run a maze, it doesn't follow rules. It *practices*. If a trial run fails, no neural connection is wired in; if it succeeds, the brain strengthens that connection. This kind of learning is heavily experienced-based. It is also habit-bound—the more times I perform a skill successfully, the more times I use a certain strategy to solve a problem, the more inclined I will be to do it that way the next time. Associative learning is also *tacit*, or *intuitive*, learning—I learn the skill, solve the problem, but I can't articulate any rules by which I learned it, and usually I can't even describe how I did it. Neural networks are not connected with our language faculty, nor with our ability to articulate concepts. Those are "left-brain" abilities. The more "right-brain" skills of associative thinking are simply embedded in experience. We *feel* our skills, we *do* our skills, but we don't "think" or talk about them. We develop our skills because they give us a sense of satisfaction or efficacy or a feeling of reward, or because they help us avoid pain or failure.

A great deal of the knowledge possessed by an organization is tacit knowledge, knowledge that no one can frame or articulate but upon which the organization relies for its lifeblood. This tacit knowledge is in the skills and experience of its leaders and employees. An article about the Xerox Corporation in the very first issue of *Fast Company* magazine gave a powerful example of this. Xerox management wanted to cut wasted employee time, so it called in a time-and-motion expert to chart where this waste could be found and eliminated. The expert focused on the coffee machine—engineers, he concluded, spent far too much unnecessary time chatting over cups of coffee. He recommended cuts to the coffee break. Fortunately, Xerox had also hired an anthropologist to accompany the time-and-motion expert as he observed employee habits.[6]

The anthropologist asked the coffee-loving engineers to show him their repair manuals. At first, they produced their pristine, clean copies, bearing all the official procedures for installing and repairing machines. But as time passed, the engineers came to trust the anthropologist, and they showed them their "real" repair manuals, the ones they actually used when they went out on the job. These were full of dog-eared pages filled with scribbles of shortcuts and unorthodox procedures that the men had learned by trial and error when out on the job. They saved both time and money, and also gave the engineers a glee of satisfaction that they could beat the system. It was these shortcuts and unorthodox procedures that were being exchanged in conversations around the coffee machine.[7]

The upshot of the Xerox study was an attempt to capitalize on the engineers' tacit skills. The coffee breaks were not shortened, but in addition the company experimented with collating a computerized data bank of tricks learned on the job. Engineers who discovered shortcuts that saved time and money on official procedures described in the manual were given a standing invitation to add their tips to the data bank.[8] In this way, the company brain got rewired as the engineers rewired their individual brains.

In recent years, neural network computers (known as parallel-processing computers) have been perfected so that they can mimic the associative thinking skills of human beings. These computers are used to recognize handwriting, to read postal codes, to discriminate tastes and smells, to "see" and construct images of faces. And unlike serial processing PCs, neural network computers can learn and adapt their programs with experience.

The advantages of associative thinking are that it is rooted in and in dialogue with experience and can learn through trial and error as it goes along. It can feel its way in new, untried situations. It constantly rewires the brain. It is also a kind of thinking that can handle nuance and ambiguity—we can remove up to 80 percent of a given pattern, and the brain's associative processing system can still recognize what is left. A neural network computer can recognize a postal code written in millions of different samples of handwriting. The disadvantages of this kind of thinking are that it is "fast," it jumps to conclusions, and is thus often inaccurate. It is also habit-bound. We *can* relearn a skill or learn to solve a problem in a new way, but it takes time and much effort. And because associative thinking is tacit thinking, we have trouble sharing it with others. We can't just write out a formula or set of instructions and tell another to get on with the job accordingly. Each of us must learn a skill in our own way, for ourselves. No two brains on the planet are alike. No two brains have identical sets of neural connections.

QUANTUM THINKING: THE BRAIN'S "SPIRIT"

The third kind of thinking the brain can do is reflective, creative, insightful, intuitive thinking. It is the kind of thinking with which we *challenge* or *question* our assumptions, or change our mental models, our paradigms. It is the kind of thinking that rewires the brain to invent new categories of thought, that creates new patterns, new language. This third kind of thinking is rooted in and motivated by our deep sense of meaning and value. It is our spiritual thinking or our vision thinking—our SQ. I call it "quantum thinking" because its capacities and processes are very much like those used to describe the behavior of quantum systems. And it may well arise from the existence of a quantum field extending across the brain. Whether or not it *is* literally quantum, the new field of cognitive science called "quantum cognition" has established beyond doubt that human thought processes such as reflection, contextuality, the creative use of ambiguity, and decision-making do accord with the mathematical formalism of quantum mechanics.

The serial, System 2, slow thinking I described is supported mainly by the activity of the brain's left hemisphere. The associative, System 1, fast thinking is supported mainly by activity in the brain's right hemisphere, with some of it issuing from lower brain structures like the emotional center located in the limbic system. It is my view that quantum thinking is *whole brain* thinking, thinking that synthesizes and synchronizes the mental activity from all over the brain, including its bodily cues. When a quantum leader brings his/her quantum thinking to bear on solving problems and forming strategies for action, he/she is using what might be called *total intelligence*.

Computers can simulate both serial and associative thinking. PCs do something very similar to serial thinking faster and more accurately than human beings. Neural network, or parallel, computers can replicate some of our associative thinking, and these machines will certainly get better as their technology improves. But no computer so far built, or even conceived, can do anything like the creative, insightful thinking at which humans can excel. Computers work *within* assumptions, habits, or mental models. They work within the boundaries and the rules or programs. They play a finite game. Our quantum thinking moves the goal posts. It challenges assumptions, values, and mental models. It *invents* programs, makes and breaks rules. Our quantum thinking plays *with the boundaries*, constantly reinventing them. It plays an infinite game.

Serial thinking deals with the data of experience in a linear way by connecting its separate "parts," or inputs according to logical rules. In the language of quantum physics, it is "particle-like." Associative thinking deals with experience as a whole, but in a way that is blind to the parts, blind to logic and rationality. It is "wavelike." Quantum thinking is holistic, both particle-like (left brain) and wavelike (right brain) at the same time, able to integrate and analyze all the data of experience simultaneously. It integrates the thinking abilities of the brain's serial and associative systems, and unifies all the millions of sensory data and information impinging upon the brain at any moment, as well as integrates it into a unified field of experience. The best guess about the physical basis of quantum thinking is that it is enabled by a 40 Hz (forty cycles per second) oscillatory field that sweeps across the brain from the front of the head to the back, synchronizing neural activity from every part of the brain.[9] This 40 Hz field is also known as the brain's "gamma wave" activity. It is active whenever the brain is active, even in deep sleep. It is at its most coherent, most effective unifying state, when people are in deep meditation. I will discuss that later, in Chapter Fourteen, when I describe meditation as a "tool" of quantum thinking and quantum systems/strategy dynamics.

The unifying effects of the 40 Hz oscillatory field (the quantum field?) can be appreciated if we think of a simple perceptual experience. When I look at a tumbler sitting on a table, a part of my brain responds to its height, another to its shape, another part to its elliptical rim outline, yet another part to the reflections of light bouncing off it, and so on. Yet all the neurons in all these different parts of the brain responding to data about the tumbler oscillate at the same frequency, and that is what gives me my perception (and understanding) of the tumbler as a whole—and of its physical context on the table and in the room, and of its meaning to me: "This is something that can hold water that can satisfy my thirst." Similarly, when I sit at my desk, the billions of different neurons in my brain are being bombarded by countless perceptual data—visual data, tactile data, thermal and auditory data, and the internal data issuing from my thought processes and imagination. There is no central control mechanism in the brain that receives and channels all this data. There is no single "CEO neuron" that manages the lot, nor even an executive committee of neurons. Rather, my whole perceptual field and my whole sense of meaning—my sense of being in the room and knowing why I am there—*self organizes* itself out of the synchronous oscillations of the various neurons being stimulated.

Creative thinking in business at the team or corporate level—rewiring the team or corporate brain—means that we must have diffuse and flexible infrastructures that can get into a similar sort of synchronous self-organization. How to achieve this is the subject of what I call QSD, or Quantum Systems Dynamics. In the organization, we would call this kind of synchronized activity communication. IT systems can play a vital role in this if used creatively, as can the dialogue process discussed in Chapter Thirteen, or by building a strong and vital company culture that fosters shared vision and values (see Chapter Nine). The achievement of such organization synchronicity and self-organization is the rationale behind Japanese practices of beginning the working day with company songs or group calisthenics.[10] Schools often attempt it by holding morning assembly, or by beginning the school day with Mindfulness meditation practice.

Quantum thinking has the capacity to question itself and to question the environment. It is called into play when the unexpected happens, in situations of crisis or opportunity when our rule-bound serial thinking and habit-bound associative thinking can't cope. If, for instance, we are involved in a training session at a company in London and a huge Indian elephant suddenly lumbers into the room, crashing down the door as it proceeds, the following sequence of brain events will happen. In the first instance, we will be in a state of shock, not knowing what is happening or what we are seeing. We simply have no existing categories of thought (or perception) for elephants lumbering into corporate training seminars, no existing neural connections to process such events. Our brains can't handle it.

The brain's first response to the elephant is a desperate attempt to process the data with its existing categories. When this fails, the brain then puts itself on hold. It goes through a thinking process, something like, "Wait a minute. I can't make sense of this from where I am starting." The brain then begins to use its quantum thinking process to rewire itself.

It first creates some new perceptual categories that can see the elephant and place it within the context of the room. Then it sets out to create some new-meaning categories that can make sense of why the elephant is there. Perhaps it escaped from the London Zoo and made its way into the company training room. Perhaps a competing company wanted to sabotage our training session. Perhaps the instructor arranged for the elephant's arrival to wake up the participants and to illustrate the efficacy of quantum thinking.

The brain tries out all these possibilities, apparently simultaneously like quantum feelers toward the future (virtual transitions), until it arrives at a *narrative*—a mental model, a new set of neural connections—that makes sense. Having thus rewired itself, the brain is happy with the elephant's presence, even if the participants themselves are not!

All creative thinking is like learning to see the elephant. It is being able to see that our existing categories don't work or are insufficient, being able to put those categories on hold, and then being able to create new categories, some of which involve new meaning. It is our ability to do this kind of thinking that makes us truly human, and it arises from the deepest recesses of the self. But using this ability requires that we step outside our usual thinking, or usual paradigm. It requires that we gain a further perspective from which we can see the thinking behind our thinking.

QUANTUM THINKING AS HYPERTHINKING

There is a mathematical theory in modern physics known as *hyperspace*. The gist of this theory is there are not just three dimensions in space, or even just four, but N dimensions, each offering a different perspective on the last. In his excellent 1994 book *Hyperspace*, Michio Kaku uses the example of a family of carp swimming around in their pond. From their perspective, the fish have no sense that they live inside a pond, or that this pond is filled with a liquid medium called water.[11] This is just their world, and they take it for granted.

But in Kaku's example, one of the fish suddenly takes a big leap that raises him above the surface of the water in his pond. "Ah!" he says, "look where I've come from." He sees the pond and his fellow fish and the water from this further perspective, and he sees that he has come from a world of ponds and water. But now he also knows that there is a larger world outside the pond, a medium in which to move other than water. In the parlance of business and "quantum speak," he has reframed or *recontextualized* his situation. Kaku calls his new grasp of a wider perspective *hyperthinking.*

Hyperthinking is quantum thinking *par excellence*, and it is an essential skill for building Quantum Systems Dynamics. We have seen that both serial thinking and associative thinking trap us "inside the pond." The one is rule-bound, the other habit-bound, and both limit us to a single model or single perspective. This makes it impossible to stand back from a situation and question our assumptions about it. As Einstein famously said, we can never solve a problem with the thinking that created the problem in the first place.[12] The essence of quantum thinking is that it can *take us to the edge* of any particular model or perspective. It can expose the thinking that was behind our earlier thinking and thus allow us to grow beyond it. In quantum physics itself, there is no limit to the different possibilities latent within any given situation, no limit to the number of possible perspectives on the quantum world. By cultivating quantum thinking, business leaders can learn to live at the edge of all models (ways of viewing their situation, its problems and opportunities) and thus always have at hand a new perspective when adapting strategies and decision-making to ever-changing reality. This is the truly valuable lesson that business can learn from science and scientific method.

We can get a better grasp of what quantum thinking is like and what it has to offer business by looking at some dramatic contrasts between the Newtonian scientific paradigm that has dominated past business thinking and the new quantum scientific paradigm that offers business a way forward.

CHAPTER 4

EIGHT PRINCIPLES OF QUANTUM THINKING APPLIED TO LEADERSHIP

"Humanity faces a quantum leap forward. It faces the deepest social upheaval and creative restructuring of all time. Without clearly recognizing it, we are engaged in building a remarkable new civilization from the ground up. . . . This new civilization has its own distinctive outlook; its own ways of dealing with time, space, logic and causality. And, its own principles for the politics of the future."
—Alvin and Heidi Toffler, *Creating a New Civilization*

The term "quantum leap" has entered everyday speech from the language of quantum physics. It means not just a big leap, but a leap from one state of reality to another. In human terms, it is a leap from one paradigm or worldview, one framework of meaning, to another. In both business and science, it means a leap from a world we understood and could manage to one where at first nothing makes sense. It is a leap that requires us to rethink our basic categories and strategies, to alter our most cherished and deeply unconscious assumptions. A leap into the unknown—a paradigm shift. The new science of the twentieth century has made such a leap, but not without pain and confusion.

The great Danish physicist Niels Bohr was one of the founding fathers of the new science. He was among the five or six men who conceived the basics of quantum theory. Bohr was a popular public speaker, frequently asked to explain the new science to general audiences.[1] He often began his lectures with a story that he felt expressed the difficulty of such a task.

In Bohr's story, there is a young Jewish religious student who attends three lectures by a famous rabbi. Excited by his experience, the student rushes off to tell his friends about the lectures. The first lecture, he says, was very good—the student had understood every word. The second lecture, though, was even better—very subtle, very profound. The student did not understand this lecture, but the rabbi himself understood every word. The third lecture, however, was the best of all. It was so good that even the rabbi did not understand it![2]

Bohr himself, he told his audiences, was like the rabbi of the story.[3] He and his fellow scientists had described a new science that was so subtle, so deep, so profound in its implications and so new in its language and concepts that they did not understand what they had done. Nothing in their education or training had prepared them for a new physics that broke all the rules. Schooled in a framework of absolute space and time and iron laws of causality that assured certainty and predictability (and hence control), they were confronted by a quantum world that violated common sense as they knew it. Quantum space and time have little meaning. Quantum events can't be controlled. They happen with no apparent cause, and a quantum *uncertainty* principle replaces the predictable laws of nature with the slippery rules of the gaming house. Bohr called his new science "weird." Einstein said it reminded him of "the system of delusions of an exceedingly intelligent paranoiac, concocted of incoherent elements of thoughts."[4] He went to his grave trying to prove that it was wrong.

The four new sciences conceived in the last century—relativity, quantum mechanics, chaos, and complexity theory—are all different. Each best describes a different level of reality. Relativity is about very large distances and great speeds; quantum mechanics originally described the very small world within the atom. Chaos and complexity apply to physical systems on our everyday level of reality, things like the weather, the flow of streams, the beat of the human heart. Yet all these sciences share a common new paradigm. They change the rules of the game in the same way. A great deal of progress has been made this century in understanding the brain, but properly speaking, there is not yet a "new" brain science. Most neuroscientists are still trying to fit their data into the old paradigm. The exception to this is the cognitive scientists now fleshing out the new discipline of quantum cognition.

In the old science, the Newtonian paradigm, nature is seen as simple, law-abiding, and ultimately controllable. The whole science is about organized simplicity. In the new science, the quantum paradigm, nature is seen as complex, chaotic, and uncertain. This science is about learning to live with and to get the fullest potential out of complexity. Attempts at control can be counterproductive.

Newtonian Approach	Quantum Approach
Simple	Complex
Law-abiding	Chaotic
Ultimately controllable	Uncertain

Table 1. Newtonian and Quantum Approach

Of all the new sciences, quantum mechanics is generally regarded as the most fundamental. It raises the greatest challenge to our previous ways of thinking. It has also been put to great practical use in the technology that is altering our lives in this century—superfluids, superconductors, lasers, silicon chips, and now even quantum computers. Our computers, our smartphones and tablets, even my grandson's Wii, are all quantum technologies. The kind of thinking needed to understand quantum mechanics is the key to understanding the whole new paradigm that is emerging in our culture at large. In this chapter, I want to show how quantum thinking helps us to articulate the new paradigm emerging in business. I want to contrast eight key ideas from Newtonian science, and their effects on business thinking, with eight key quantum ideas and their application to new thinking about leadership.

ATOMISM VS. HOLISM

Old paradigm science, like Greek philosophy before it, is atomistic. This gives us an emphasis on separate working parts and leads to a tendency toward fragmentation. New paradigm science is holistic. Its emphasis is on relationship, and this leads to a stress on integration.

The ancient Greeks believed that matter could be reduced to its smallest bits. These were called atoms, and the whole universe was thought to consist of four kinds of atoms—earth, air, fire, and water. Newtonian physics kept the idea of atoms, though from the seventeenth century onward scientists realized there were many more kinds. Today we speak of ninety-two kinds of stable atoms, making up the naturally occurring elements.

Atoms are conceived as hard, impenetrable things. One atom cannot get inside another. Each occupies its own place in space and time and cannot be reduced to anything further. Newton suggested the atoms were linked by forces of action and reaction, giving a model of the universe that stresses impact and collision. If the atoms are to avoid collision, they must avoid each other—we call this a controlled situation, or perhaps a "compromise." The familiar desktop toy shown in Figure 3—several steel balls suspended from strings, appropriately called a "Newton's Cradle"—is a good model of the atomistic universe. When any of the steel balls strikes another, it transmits a predictable amount of force to it. The system as a whole seeks to balance these collisions by relaying the force to a ball that is at the end of the line and thus free to move.

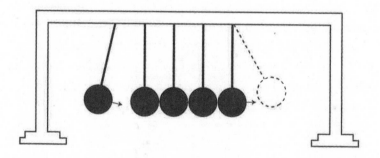

Figure 3. Newton's Cradle

FAR REACH OF THE ATOMISTIC PARADIGM

The atomistic model became the basis for the whole modern Western paradigm. Political philosophers like Thomas Hobbes and John Locke used it in their theories of social order. Individuals were conceived as the basic atoms of society, and the institutions and laws of society would be the forces that bound these individuals together, that controlled them. In Locke's liberal individualism, individual needs and individual rights became the focus of attention. The social whole was just the sum of its parts. In the words of a modern Lockian leader, Britain's Margaret Thatcher, "There's no such thing as society. There are individual men and women and there are families."[5]

Freud used Newton's atomism as the basis for his tragic view of modern psychology. In his "Theory of Object Relations," Freud said that each of us is isolated. He conceived the boundaries of the self as hard and impenetrable. You are an object to me and I just an object to you. We can never really know each other or relate in any fundamental way. I form a picture of you in my own mind, "a projection," and I relate only to that. Love and intimacy are impossible. "The commandment to 'Love thy neighbor as thyself,'" wrote Freud, "is the most impossible commandment ever written."[6]

Western medicine, Western education, and Western management have all followed the atomistic model. Doctors are taught to see the body as a collection of separate working parts, and each has its specialist physician. None is taught to see the body as an organic, living whole. Illnesses that seem to weaken the whole system like myeloencephalitis (ME) or fatigue or depression are described as "mystery illnesses." We don't really know what causes them, and treatment is at best approximate. Western education divides knowledge into separate subjects, and we become expert at some one of them. General, cross-disciplinary education beyond primary school is rare. This kind of education in itself has greatly influenced the kind of leaders we produce. Many of the most inspirational examples of leadership are men and women who dropped out of formal education early, or who followed eccentric educational paths.

Adam Smith's famous pin factory example first introduced the division of labor principle into management. If one worker concentrates on making the heads of pins and another concentrates on the shafts, more pins can be made per day than if each worker makes whole pins. Newtonian organizations are structured into separate areas of expertise, separate divisions, and each of these atomistic units is encouraged to compete with the others. The whole thing is held together by bureaucratic rules and structured hierarchically to impose maximum control from the top. "Transformation" programs are usually piecemeal, directed at improving the efficiency of some function or division. There is little emphasis on teamwork, almost none devoted to seeing the organizations as a "team of teams."

The great twentieth-century quantum physicist David Bohm described atomism as "the virus of fragmentation." "For fragmentation is now very widespread," he said, "not only throughout society, but also in each individual; and this is leading to a kind of general confusion of the mind, which creates an endless series of problems and interferes with our clarity of perception so seriously as to prevent us from being able to solve most of them. . . . The notion that all these fragments are separately existent is evidently an illusion, and this illusion cannot do other than lead to endless confusion and conflict."[7]

THE HOLISTIC VIEW OF QUANTUM PHYSICS

Quantum physics teaches that the world does not consist of any kind of separate, solid things. At the most fundamental level of reality, physical systems consist of patterns of dynamic energy represented as information. Bohm writes that the whole universe consists of interacting, overlapping patterns of dynamic energy that crisscross and "interfere" in a "pattern of unbroken wholeness."[8] Each quantum "bit" has a particle-like aspect, an aspect that can be pinned down, measured, located in space and time. But it also has a wavelike aspect, vibrations of further potentiality that, in principle, reach all the way across the universe. The future possibilities, and even the future identity, of each bit are internally bound up with the possibilities and identities of all the others. No one bit can be abstracted out and viewed on its own without loss or distortion.

The ambiguous and heavily relational boundaries of quantum entities are known as "contextualism." To be known, to be measured, to be used, a quantum entity must always be seen within the larger context of its defining relationships. Change the context, and the entity itself is different. It realizes another of its infinite potentialities. It *becomes* something different. Something more.

Old Paradigm		New Paradigm
Atomism	versus	Holism
Emphasis on separate working parts	versus	Emphasis on relationship
Fragmentation	versus	Integration

Table 2. Old vs. New Paradigm

The atomistic Newtonian organization sees itself isolated in its environment, and sees its divisions and employees isolated within its own mechanistic system. Such organizations seek to control both their employees and their environment.

The holistic "quantum organization" would be more sensitive to its context, internal and external. It would be aware, to paraphrase the famous words of the eighteenth-century poet John Donne, that no organization is an island. Quantum organizations would seek to build infrastructures that are themselves more integrated and holistic, and more in dialogue with each other and with the outside world.

At Motorola, for instance, the envisaged twenty-year transformation process was meant to embrace every employee in the company, from janitors, telephonists, and secretaries to the CEO himself. A company-wide dialogue process including every individual is integral to this program. Motorola University had a "Culture and Technology" section devoted to monitoring the impact of Motorola products, such as mobile phones, on emerging societies, like newly modernizing China.

Within Marks & Spencer (M&S) global buying trips were made by cross-departmental, cross-specialist teams. In-store merchandise displays located in specialist departments feature goods available throughout each store. Such holistic strategies are in response to customers' perceived desire to mix and match across departments. M&S has a team working in every developing country to monitor local political, social, and economic sensitivities. The company also maintains a practice with small, local suppliers to ensure that a supplier accustomed to orders of $1 million a year who suddenly does a $3 million turnover because of M&S purchases doesn't then go out of business if orders return to normal. "We don't want to be in the business of ruining other people's businesses," was how Joint Managing Director Andrew Stone put it.[9]

> We flourish when every part or partner flourishes. If those who supply us benefit in pay and conditions by making goods that please our customers, everybody wins. We even get on with our competition. They bring customers to a shopping center in which we trade, and they benefit from the "traffic" we create![10]

In China today, in Guizhou Province, big tech companies like Lenovo and Haier are pooling their research resources to create a larger collection of learning from which each can benefit.[11]

Such relational factors will certainly affect results. They should affect strategies. Competitor companies are also among an organization's customers and suppliers. Employees and junior managers are an organization's intellectual capital. As the modern playwright Arthur Miller said, "The fish is in the water, and the water is in the fish."[12] Both fish and water, both individual employees and leaders *and* their company culture, must be healthy. They are in a symbiotic balance.

The quantum organization would seek to build infrastructures that reach into and integrate the environment, infrastructures that can cooperate with the environment and cocreate a new reality for both. The ethos of cooperation and integration is very different from the ethos of control and ruthless competition.

DETERMINATE VS. INDETERMINATE

Old paradigm science is determinate. Iron laws govern all the movements of particles and larger bodies. It values certainty and predictability. New paradigm science is indeterminate. Predictability and control are impossible, even damaging. Quantum and chaotic systems thrive on uncertainty and ambiguity. Given that today's business environment is dominated by chaos, uncertainty, and rapid change, there is a need for company structures and cultures that can thrive on these.

The Western mind has always looked for the causes of events, explanations that would put experience within a workable framework. In ancient and medieval times, explanations were sought in the whims or anger of the gods, punishment for human sin, or the movements of the stars. None of these lay within human control. Newtonian science introduced a new kind of causality. Everything in the physical world happens, Newton said, because it *has* to happen. The whole universe is governed by three simple laws of motion and the law of universal gravitation. The universe is like a giant clockwork machine that God set in motion to run for the rest of time. B will always follow A in the same way if the starting position and the forces acting upon A are the same. If we know these facts about any physical situation, we can predict its outcome without fail. Knowledge means control.

In an age when human beings felt like helpless pawns in the face of unpredictable natural catastrophe, Newtonian determinism caught the general imagination. It was the new panacea, the final explanation for all mysteries. It gave rise to a faith in technique, to the great conquests of technology and to instrumental reason—the kind of reason that asks, "What is the best way to do x?"

Freud, who saw himself as the Newton of the mind, imported determinism into his new "scientific psychology."[13] In his "hydraulic model" of the self, we are divided into three compartments—the id, the ego, and the superego. The id is the basement of the self, the dark, instinctive forces of sex and aggression. The superego is the overwhelming forces of parental and societal expectations. The poor ego, the conscious self, is sandwiched between the two, pushed helplessly around from below and pressured into guilt from above. Our feelings and behavior throughout life are fully determined by these conflicting forces and the experience of our first five years.

The legal system took up Freud's determinism with its notion of the "guilty victim"—the criminal forced into crime because of an unhappy childhood, a deprived neighborhood environment, or an abusive school. Behavioral psychology described human beings as so many Pavlovian dogs, determined to act with a fixed response to any given stimulus. More recently still, artificial intelligence (AI) has told us that we are all just ambulatory computers, programmed for success or failure. Genetic scientists say that behavior patterns like addiction, criminality, and sexual orientation are programmed in our genes.

Where Newton looked for the laws of the universe and Freud the laws and dynamics of the psyche, Frederick Taylor's Scientific Management looked for the laws inherent within each organization. Find those laws, understand the machinery of the organization, and a leader can exercise control. Most senior managers in our Newtonian organizations value control above all else—control over their subordinates, control over the products, control over the market and customer desire. Advertising campaigns are designed to manipulate customer choice, not to respond to it. They plan against contingency and seek answers to questions before they arise. I saw a postcard in one executive's office that read "Control the unexpected."

There is a theorem in cybernetic theory, the science that tries to bridge the living and machine worlds, that points out the limitations of too much control. Known as Von Foerster's Theorem, it says,

> The more rigidly connected are the elements of a system, the less influence they will have on the system as a whole. The more rigid the connections, the more each element of the system will exhibit a greater degree of "alienation" from the whole.[14]

The more controlled the parts of a system, the less they contribute to the system and the less they are part of the whole. The new science helps us to understand why this is so. The new quantum organization will place more stress on self-organization.

QUANTUM INDETERMINISM

Quantum physics is radically indeterminate. Quantum events just happen as they happen, without rhyme or reason, making the prediction of any one event impossible. We can never know when any given radioactive atom will decay, nor which path an excited subatomic particle will follow in getting from A to B. Quantum bits emerge into existence out of nowhere and disappear again just as mysteriously. What is more, this indeterminism is vital to the creative holism of quantum systems.

It is precisely because the identity, the coordinates, and the possible movements of individual quantum entities are ambiguous that a whole quantum system can "fall into place," all its constituent elements integrally interrelated and working for the greater good (the eventual stability or creativity) of both themselves and the system. Because they are indeterminate, quantum entities *have no fully fixed identity* until they are in relationship. This gives the quantum system maximum flexibility to define itself as it goes along. It cocreates in dialogue with its environment. All of nature's complex systems are at their most creative when they are delicately poised between fixedness and unfixedness—poised at the edge of chaos.

Andrew Stone of Marks & Spencer said that understanding the dynamics of quantum and complex systems changed the way he managed. I saw one striking instance of this in the way he conducted a meeting of his directors. Marks & Spencer was developing a global procurement policy to supply its growing international retail sales. Stone felt such a policy needed to be written up, and he drafted a vague outline of one. When he presented this to his twelve colleagues, they said, "This is a wonderful idea, Andrew. But it's not yet practice. How do we do it?" In reply, Stone threw up his hands and said, "Don't ask me. You know I have too many ideas and never know how to put them into practice. You are great at implementing!" After moments of stunned silence followed by embarrassed guffaws, the room broke into an excited free-for-all of suggestions, plans, and schemes. Everyone had an idea.[15] The ambiguity of Stone's approach had released the creativity of those who worked with him. When a plan does emerge, it will belong to the group as a whole, rather than being a policy imposed upon them. Such an approach challenges the simplistic truth of the old dictum that "It is the business of leaders to lead." In a quantum organization, every employee is a potential leader.

IMPORTANCE OF AMBIGUITY FOR COMPANIES

Indeterminacy and ambiguity also play a significant role in the style used by many Asian managers. I worked with a group of Japanese and Korean businesspeople for over a year to set up a research institute. Time and again they gave me itineraries and stated their intentions, and then when I followed through by setting up appointments for them or clearing some red tape they telephoned at the last minute and said, "We have changed our plans." When I asked in the best Western style, "So when are you coming? What is going to happen next?" they responded, "We don't know." The vagueness continued for months while they maintained maximum flexibility. Then very suddenly, and with stunning effect, some key venture fell into place. I have found the same to be true in my recent work with Chinese companies and nongovernmental organizations. While I had been tormented by their dithering and ambiguity, they had kept large numbers of indeterminate balls in the air until just the right (best for them!) situation emerged. Such stories of protracted and frustrating contract negotiations between Eastern and Western companies are rife. The competitive advantage usually rests with the party best able to handle and use the ambiguity.

Leading chaos and maximizing creativity require learning to thrive on ambiguity. Quantum leadership implies that control give way to some more subtle, intuitive feel for the situation and the creative potential of its indeterminacy. The infrastructures and strategies of the quantum organization would themselves have to be designed to allow for ambiguity and indeterminacy. This in turn requires that the quantum leader find new reliance on trust—trust in the leader's own character and intuition, trust in the character, intuition, and leadership abilities of subordinates, and trust in the dynamics of the organization. And it requires trust in the emergent potential of "self-organization," nature's own most creative response to chaos. We can look at this next.

Old Paradigm		New Paradigm
Determinate	versus	Indeterminate
Value certainty and predictability	versus	Thrive on uncertainty and ambiguity
Control	versus	Trust

Table 3. Old vs. New Paradigm 2

REDUCTIVE VS. EMERGENT AND SELF-ORGANIZING

In Newtonian science, reduction and analysis are key. Any system or object is reduced to its parts. The parts are isolated and analyzed for ultimate properties or primary function. The whole is considered to be the sum of its parts, so we best know the whole by knowing those parts. This is hands-on science—grab the system, tear it to pieces, learn how to control the parts, gain power over the whole.

The division of labor is a reductive philosophy. Break the job down into parts and do it more efficiently. Breaking organizations into competing divisions is reductive. Each division, it is argued, can be most effective concentrating on its own region of focus, but, inevitably, it leads to Newtonian fragmentation and actual loss of overall control.

Newtonian parts are whatever they are, wherever we find them or in whatever combination. Adding A and B together just gives us A + B. A gear is the same gear and has the same function whether it is part of a lawnmower, a car, or a spaceship. Newtonian organizations tend to carry on regardless of their environments, each division going its own way, each employee following a separate job description. Such organizations are broken down and viewed in isolation from their environments with a view to maximizing control. How else could a five-year plan be inviolate except in such a vacuum? Some control is necessary, of course. But how much?

In new paradigm science, emergence and self-organization are key. Quantum wholes are *larger* than the sum of their parts. A quantum system has additional properties and potential not possessed individually by the parts. And both the parts and the whole system are contextual, context-dependent. A quantum bit is one thing in one environment or relationship, quite a different thing in another environment or relationship. Because each bit has both individual (particle-like) and system (wavelike) properties, the system properties only develop within a system, within a context. They *emerge* within the context. Thus we can never identify the nature, properties, or potential of a quantum thing without knowing its wider context. In leading quantum organizations, the leader's purposes themselves emerge in a wider, emerging context.

IMPORTANCE OF CONTEXT FOR COMPANIES

Existing systems theory talks a great deal about the need to see things in larger context. But nonetheless it remains mechanistic because it is atomistic. The parts of systems described by systems theory are not themselves contextual. They don't change *internally* through different relationships. They remain unchanging black boxes. This is one way in which quantum thinking and quantum contextualism require that, for human systems, we need to apply Quantum Systems Dynamics (see Chapter Ten).

If we try to pin down a quantum thing and isolate it from its environment, we *reduce* it. (The technical quantum term is to say that its wave function collapses. Many complex possibilities become one simple actuality.) Thus trying to control the uncertain system properties of the thing destroys those very properties. Tight control is achieved at the expense of lost potential. Fullest potential is achieved by letting the system unfold, emerge, as it will. No amount of controlled intervention can foresee and realize emergent possibilities. They just happen as they happen, in dialogue with the system's wider environment.

Similarly, the intricate properties of complex systems emerge at the edge of chaos. Such systems self-organize—no kind of technique (control) can put them together. They have an unanalyzable, holistic dynamic of their own. The Frankenstein myth is all about the folly of trying to put a human being together out of bodily parts. Many a Newtonian organization has created a bureaucratic Frankenstein's monster with its emphasis on top-down control, tight structure, and imposed plans or solutions, and its obsession with efficiency. Like the creature in Mary Shelley's novel, such organizations have their own way of getting out of control.

Old Paradigm		New Paradigm
Reductive	versus	Emergent
Isolated and controlled	versus	Contextual and self-organizing
The parts completely define the whole	versus	The whole is greater than the sum of its parts
Top-down	versus	Bottom-up
Management	versus	Leadership
Reactive	versus	Imaginative and experimental

Table 4. Old vs. New Paradigm 3

The whole shift in management thinking today is toward the networked or knowledge-based organization. Knowledge (as opposed to mere information) is always contextual. The wider the context in which our knowledge operates, the more meaning it takes on and the more leverage it affords. There is also a growing realization that organizations—or divisions within organizations—cannot be isolated from their wider environments. That fish-and-water insight again. Just as in quantum and chaotic physical systems, the futures of creative human organizations can only emerge in a free-flowing (that is, not heavily controlled) dialogue with the wider economic, political, social, and ecological environments. This again requires a new kind of trust, a trust in the emergent properties of complex situations. And trust requires infrastructures where emergence can unfold, infrastructures that allow the organization to tap into its own collective intelligence, that part of itself that is larger than the sum of its parts. I will discuss this in connection with dialogue structures later on.

EITHER/OR VS. BOTH/AND

Old paradigm science is a science of either/or. Founding itself on Aristotle's logic, which argued that a statement is *either* true *or* false, Newtonian science argues that something is a wave or a particle; a particle is here or there, now or then. Newtonian physical systems are linear. They follow one smooth path from A to B. We all learned in high school geometry that the shortest path from A to B is a straight line.

Either/or logic and linearity are part of the whole Western paradigm. Historians of science feel it is no accident that modern science arose first in the monotheistic countries of the West. We are the culture of one truth, one God, one way. We admire a leader who "knows her own mind" or "keeps his eye on the ball" and sees clearly one vision to pursue. We applaud a young student or athlete who sets out on career preparation with "single-minded dedication." In education, in politics, in military strategy, and in business we seek to find that one best way to do things. We debate about it; we go to war over it; we kill people for it. In his Scientific Management theory, Frederick Taylor argued that there is always one best strategy for any company to pursue. The whole point of discussions, brainstorming sessions, and strategy meetings is to find that best strategy and then to pursue it ruthlessly.

Clearly, there are times when decisiveness and certainty about the best way forward are an advantage. In our goal-oriented, problem-solving culture, it seems the only advantage. Yet we all know that there is a downside to too much single-mindedness and certainty too early on. We speak of "blinkered idealism" and people who "can't see the woods for the trees." There are metaphors about horses that "get the bit between their teeth." Common sense tells us there are times when caution, open-mindedness, or even a little bit of healthy uncertainty may be more appropriate, but there is little in the philosophy of Western culture, Western science, or Western management to support these qualities.

In our Newtonian organizations, both political and corporate, there is a constant and seemingly unresolvable tension between the individual (the particle) and the group (the wave). How do we foster the initiative and creative qualities of the individual while at the same time develop the cooperation and team qualities of the group? Western liberal individualism is atomistic. It stresses the crucial importance of the individual and is suspicious of the group. The eighteenth-century French philosopher Jean-Jacques Rousseau, like Karl Marx after him, saw the advantages of the group, or the collective. Both were suspicious of individuals and wanted to limit their rights. It is well-known Asian countries often have poor human rights records and limited individual creativity, but their capacity to work in teams, to dedicate themselves to the common good, and to tap into a kind of collective energy and intelligence often puts the West to shame. It is a significant competitive advantage for some Asian industries. A quantum organization or a quantum society would see the need to foster a more synchronistic, co-creative balance between the needs and rights of the individual, and the needs, values, and vision of the whole.

QUANTUM SYSTEMS ARE BOTH/AND

The new science of the twentieth century is radically different from the either/or paradigm. Quantum entities are *both* particle-like *and* wavelike at the same time, *both* here *and* there, *both* now *and* then. They are both point sources of action situated precisely in this place in space and this moment in time and wavelike fingers of potentiality present everywhere in space and time simultaneously, interconnected members of other systems. The particle-like aspect is the hereness and nowness of the entity—its actuality. But the wavelike aspect represents all its pregnant potentiality.

In quantum systems, we saw, relationship creates further possibility. A quantum whole C is larger than the sum of its parts A + B. Each quantum "individual" has a *further* group potentiality. A quantum organization would seek to capitalize on this insight. It would build infrastructures that bypass the old individual-versus-group dichotomy, infrastructures that allow individuals to flourish both as individuals and as members of larger creative groups. Such leadership would not be wholly top-down control, but at least partly bottom-up learning, sensing the emergent and self-organizing possibilities of the group.

There is a famous character in quantum lore who expresses the both/and nature of quantum reality. This is Schrödinger's Cat, the mascot of the new science. Schrödinger's Cat has been put into an opaque box along with a fiendish device, a radioactive source that can trigger the release of either food or poison. (See Figure 4.) Common sense would tell us that if the device releases food the cat will live, and if it releases poison the cat will die. But radioactive sources are quantum devices, and Schrödinger's Cat is a quantum cat, existing separately and simultaneously in several places. So the device releases *both* food and poison, and the cat is *both* alive and dead. (Until we look at it, but I'll keep that part of the story for a later time.)

Inside the box, unobserved, Schrödinger's cat is both alive *and* dead.

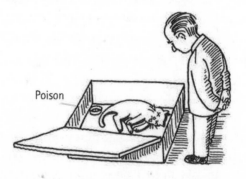

If we open the box and *look*, the cat is dead.

Figure 4. Schrödinger's Cat

The story of the quantum cat is also a metaphor for the way that quantum systems evolve. When a quantum bit wants to get from A to B, it doesn't follow just one path. On the contrary, it throws out an infinite number of possible paths—these are called *virtual transitions*. Each path represents one possible best path from A to B, a "feeler toward the future." In fact, in quantum reality, B itself is not yet sharply defined. B is still part of a future scenario yet to emerge. So infinite possible paths strike out from A toward an uncertain or ambiguous B, mutually defining the future as they interfere with (get into dialogue with) each other. This allows the whole system to be creative in responding to its own uncertain future. In the end, B will emerge, and one of the infinite paths from A to B will emerge as the "right path."

A quantum system's many paths from A to B remind me of the ethos behind Shell Oil's "scenario planning." Scenario planning is a strategy device that gets leaders to imagine many possible futures for a given situation and then in turn to imagine the best strategy for handling each. This way, it is assumed, Shell will be ready with an action plan for any eventuality. The strategy worked brilliantly in the 1970s oil crisis. One of Shells scenarios was that the Arab countries would turn off the taps. Shell was the only oil company that had a contingency plan ready for this "impossible" situation. It made a profit; the other companies lost heavily.[16]

When an organization settles on "one best path" from A to B, it commits all its resources and energy to a strategy that may not be best, that may even be a mistake. When it sets a tightly defined B as its goal, that B is the best it will ever get. Quantum systems are creative precisely because they play on the uncertainty of both means and ends. Infrastructures that allow an organization to do the same would greatly contribute to its creative flexibility and to its ability to thrive on external uncertainty.

Both quantum and chaotic systems are nonlinear. Quantum systems evolve in quantum leaps, radical jumps from one definite state to another with nothing but feelers of potentiality in between. Chaotic systems can be massively perturbed by the slightest input. In linear systems, a large effect requires a large cause. Small causes have almost no effects. The famous "butterfly effect" shows how this is untrue for nonlinear, chaotic systems: the mere flap of a butterfly's wings in Beijing can result in a massive tornado in Kansas City. The implication of both quantum and chaos sciences is that no input or disturbance is so small that it can be safely overlooked. No part of a system is insignificant. Production engineers have found to their horror that the very slightest defect in one small part can escalate to disturb a whole manufacturing process. Consultants working with companies have commented on their surprise to find how much the janitors and tea ladies, never mind the secretaries, know— expertise that is overlooked because it is thought insignificant.

CHILD'S PLAY

Both quantum feelers toward the future and chaotic nonlinearity remind me of the human imagination and of children's play. In our imaginations, we do not restrict ourselves to one possible scenario. Sometimes we imagine three or four different outcomes or activities simultaneously. That is why imagination is part of the creative process. When children play, they seldom have a fixed goal nor are they much bothered about the reality of their dramas. They throw out experiments in every direction, and are thus much more creative than adults. As adults, we lose our capacity for play. We fear the make-believe and replace it with the definite "real" goal, the practical solution. In our schools, we teach children to *concentrate*, to narrow down the options and focus on definite learning goals (usually exams). In our organizations, we expect employees and managers to "focus on the job." We like directors to come to meetings with plans, reports, and vision statements.

I attended a meeting of the global team handling Marks & Spencer's women's fashions division. Five divisional directors attended, along with Andrew Stone, their managing director. The meeting was opened by one divisional director saying that none had brought formal reports. "We know," he said to Stone, "that you don't like these. Instead, we'll just throw out a few ideas and try to share our excitement about some new product lines." For two hours the four men and one woman spoke of the possibilities they imagined. They passed model bras around the table, proudly displayed new shirts, and tried on foolish-looking hats. They were like children playing with objects drawn out of a treasure chest, enjoying themselves and what they were doing. Their sense of fun was palpable. The women's fashions division at that time was Marks & Spencer's *most* profitable division.[17] The creative play at its source successfully excited the market.

Body language, styles of dress, tones of voice, personal tastes, metaphors—these are all part of our ambiguous and playful communication. Each carries several messages simultaneously and facilitates the unfolding of emergent meaning and possibility in a strategy meeting. Such richness is lost in an e-mail communication, a crisp fax, or the deadpan tone of a director's formal report. It is lost whenever people in meetings are formal and stiff. Leaders who lead with heavy top-down authority or fear lose the playful potential of those whom they would lead. They lose their *own* playful potential. It may not be too strong to suggest "Just jump in and see what happens" as a maxim for the quantum organization.

HEISENBERG'S UNCERTAINTY PRINCIPLE

The executive director of menswear at Marks & Spencer opened a senior strategy meeting to discuss revising the global code of ethics by saying, "It's really good we're confused about this. If we thought we knew what we're doing here we'd cock it up. We need some uncertainty to give us room to think."[18] This man, in his late fifties and with little formal education, had probably never given the new science a thought. But his leadership style went straight to the heart of quantum thinking.

Mechanistic science was about *knowing*. Its style of knowing depended upon isolating elements of systems and focusing on them. Its central achievement was a gloating promise to have delivered answers to all nature's questions. At the end of the nineteenth century, Lord Kelvin, the president of Britain's prestigious science academy, the Royal Society, advised his best graduate students to avoid physics as a career. "There is nothing new to be discovered in physics now," he said. "All that remains is more and more precise measurement."[19] The old management culture, like the old science that inspired it, relied on a quest for focus, certainty, and control. It stood to reason, according to the popular wisdom of that culture, that the more a leader knew about a situation and the more tightly he/she could structure any possible contingencies, the better the outcome he/she would achieve. Mechanistic managers like answers, things they can manage (the Latin root of manage is *manus*, the word for "hand," the root of "hands-on").

The most important principle of the new science focuses our attention on the importance of *not knowing* everything about a situation. Indeed, on the impossibility of knowing everything. According to Heisenberg's Uncertainty Principle, those who would create structures, design strategies, or make decisions are forever destined to grasp at shadows in the fog—and a good thing it is too!

In quantum science, the constantly shifting and contextual properties of things come in pairs of "complementary variables." So a particle moving through space will have position and momentum variables, it will have x and y variables, z and z' variables, and so on. But the Uncertainty Principle tells us we can only know one member of a pair of complementary variables at a time. If we set out to measure the position of a particle, for instance, its momentum will become fuzzy and indeterminate. Alternatively, we can choose to measure the momentum if we wish, but then the position will elude our grasp. We can never know both position and momentum. This has enormous implications in both science and business.

THE QUESTIONS WE ASK

The first big implication of the Uncertainty Principle is that the questions we ask in any situation determine the answers we get. And the answers we don't get. Whenever we interfere with a quantum system—by questioning it, by measuring it, by focusing on it—we pluck out one aspect of the system from the many-possibilities whole, and we lose all the other associated possibilities. We see only what we look for.

Light, for instance, has the possibility to be both particle-like and wavelike, but as with Schrödinger's Cat, we can never catch it in its double act. With the cat, when we open its box it is *either* alive *or* dead; with light, when we measure it, it is *either* particle-like *or* wavelike. If a scientist asks a particle-like question, that is, designs an experiment in which a beam of light is measured at only one slit in a barrier screen, the light will hit the detector as a stream of particles.

If, on the other hand, the scientist asks a wavelike question by allowing the light passing through two slits in the barrier unobserved, the light will hit the detector (a screen) as a wavelike interference pattern. This experiment, known as the Two-Slit Experiment, is the most famous in quantum science. (See Figure 5.)

If you allow a stream of photons to pass through two slits unobserved, you get a wave.

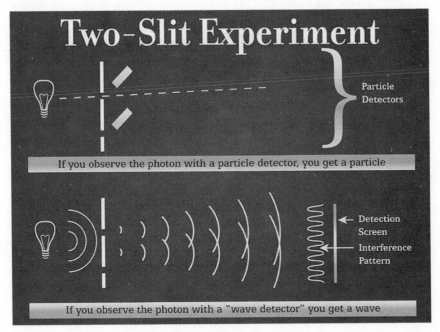

Figure 5. Two-Slit Experiment

Similarly, a corporate recruitment officer might ask a prospective employee a series of "particle-like" questions. How old are you? What is your employment history? Your marital status? Your educational background? And so on. Such questions will produce a lot of facts that the recruitment officer can write in a report, but when the prospective employee leaves the room, the officer will have precious little idea about the kind of person who just walked out. If, on the other hand, the recruitment officer uses a more "wavelike" approach, simply spending time with the prospective employee, chatting, exploring personal interests, perhaps lunching together, the session will generate a strong sense of the interviewee as a person—but very few facts.

A senior member of a European consultancy firm expressed how his team is in danger of being caught out by the Uncertainty Principle. Referring to the corporate fixation with bottom-line results and how this affects the way consultants lead clients through change processes, he said, "As consultants, we know that we cost a lot of money, so we just *assume* that we should deliver our clients big monetary savings as a net result. If, however, we thought that what the client wanted was a fundamental culture change, with less immediate emphasis on quantifiable, short-term gains, we would use a very different approach and put a wholly different change process into play."[20] The assumptions consultants make determine the results they will get for their clients. Different assumptions would mean different results.

Anytime we act on a quantum system, we change it. Our questions, our assumptions, our prejudices, our beliefs—in short, our paradigm—determine how we will act, and therefore what changes we will bring about.

LOOSER STRUCTURE

The second big implication of the Uncertainty Principle is the message it gives us about structure, about how tightly it is wise to structure situations and our approach to systems. In the laboratory, the scientist's experimental design provides the structure for the activity. But it also dictates the outcome of his/her experiment, as in the Two-Slit Experiment with light. The particle-detecting structure (observed at one slit) dictated that light would show itself as a stream of particles. It can be the same in business, sometimes with disastrous results.

Heisenberg's Uncertainty Principle

"We can focus on the position or on the momentum of a particle, but never on the both."

When we focus on one aspect of a situation we abstract that aspect out from the whole, and we lose its associated possibilities.

When we interface with a quantum system we change it.

During the course of one two-day session I spent with a group of senior operations managers at the aforementioned European consultancy company, the theme of structure arose time and again. Initially, the team believed that structure was essential both to their consultancy work with clients and to their own company identity. "If we didn't have structure," asked one member, "what would happen to our identity?" By structure here, he meant a standardized methodology for dealing with clients, a recognizable style of approach, a curriculum for training new members of the company, and so on. Another team member voiced the shared view that a consultant's main job with a client company was "to go in and implement new systems and processes."[21] That is, give the company a *formula* for how to improve. This formula is arrived at by the consultant during the period of analysis, the initial period of breaking the client company's problems down into their constituent pieces, and then drafting a project goal. Analysis→ Project Goal→ Implementation Plans = Go In and Do It.

"The trouble with this," one of the managers recalled during our discussion, "is that it can go badly wrong. The CEO's focus may be wrong. I remember one case where we accepted a project goal with a company. The project goal succeeded beyond all expectation. But the company failed to realize the expected financial benefit. Its original focus had been too fragmentary."[22]

A project goal is a structure. According to the Uncertainty Principle, any structure results in outcomes that preclude other outcomes. By the end of our two-day session, the consultancy team members came deeply to question their initial reliance on structure. A three-hour dialogue session focused on the identity of the company had not raised one mention of structure. Rather, the group decided the company's real identity lay "in the way we think, and in our energy."[23] As for imposing structures on clients, they came around to realizing the real success of their young company rested more on a spirit of co-creativity with those clients. Listening to the clients, feeling their way forward toward various possibilities in dialogue with the clients, *feeling* the situation in which they were being asked to intervene. None of this had anything to do with structure. On the contrary, tight structure would have made this style of consultancy impossible.

A business consultant, at his/her best, can be one kind of "servant leader." I will discuss the servant leader at great length at the end of this book, but just in passing here it is important to say that such leaders lead from within. They lead with listening, with intuition, with gut feeling, and they lead in service to a deeper vision and values than either they or those whom they lead can at first articulate. Such leadership requires a high tolerance for uncertainty, for ambiguity, and for loose structure that allows the dynamics of a situation to play itself through. Heisenberg's Uncertainty Principle, and its larger implications, sums all this up. At some point, any leader must make decisions, must impose structure and put strategies into play. But to do so with an awareness of cost is to do so in a different way and with a different sense of timing. As the Marks & Spencer director said, "We need some uncertainty to give us room to think."

ACTUALITY VS. POTENTIALITY

Old paradigm science is concerned with the "here and now," with things it can see and touch and measure. Its focus is on actuality. The new science has discovered that much that is interesting or valuable about physical systems lies hidden, is beyond our grasp, or is yet to unfold.

This potentiality aspect of the new science is perhaps the most difficult for people in our culture to grasp. Facts are, after all, facts. Let's stick to them. A bird in the hand is worth two in the bush. If you are a Newtonian scientist, you trust what is before your eyes. You trust substances that you can capture in test tubes, subject to analysis, and describe on graphs bordered by Cartesian coordinates. Likewise, as a Newtonian manager, you trust quarterly returns, solid figures you can send to your stockholders. You trust results. You know an employee is busy when you can see papers shuffle and hands move, when you can measure the number of hours the employee has spent at the desk.

We know from the latest brain science—and, if we reflect on it, from our own experience—that we do our most creative thinking when the mind is not busy. When we concentrate on a particular mental task, the mind focuses the bulk of its energy on that task. This is effective for achieving the goal in sight, but it fragments the unity of our consciousness. We make fewer sideways (lateral) associations. The focused mind cannot extend down into the deep pool of unitary consciousness from which things are seen in a broader perspective. These associations and broader perspectives emerge only when we take our minds off some particular task. When we relax, when we sleep, when we get up from our desks and walk down the hall to the coffee pot, this is when we suddenly see the whole picture, when things fall into place. Many of us have had the experience of solving a problem by sleeping on it. This is because during sleep the mind reunifies itself. Deep-sleep awareness makes contact with the ground state, or full potentiality, of consciousness. If, at work, we feel we must always be seen to be busy, then we are not allowing our minds to tap into that vast pool of creative potentiality.

In quantum science, as we saw, any attempt to grab hold of and measure a system collapses all the manifold potentiality of the system into one actuality. Heisenberg's Uncertainty Principle told us that anything we can say about a quantum system is only a part of the story. Facts aren't always just facts. Understanding depends upon how we look at facts, upon what questions we have asked in arriving at them. Birds in the hand are all very well, but in grabbing any one of them we destroy the pattern of the whole flock. Sometimes that pattern might have contained information or beauty of value to us.

IMPORTANCE OF GOOD METAPHORS

Sometimes metaphors are the most powerful way to understand difficult concepts. In his book *Finite and Infinite Games*, James Carse has arrived at the perfect metaphor for expressing what business needs to understand about actuality versus potentiality. Actuality, the here and now that is in front of our eyes, is the stuff of what Carse calls a "finite game." "Finite games," he says, "are played for the purpose of winning. They are played *within* boundaries."[24] Leaders who go for bottom-line results, companies that measure share value in terms of tangible assets or that invest their research budgets in technology for the given, are playing a finite game. When Shell describes itself as "an oil company," it is playing a finite game. When consultants narrow their task to doing what the client wants, to pleasing the client, they are playing a finite game. And when healthcare systems invest endless funds in interventive medicine to cure illness, they are playing a finite game. All finite games have in common the acceptance of a limited playing field.

Potentiality—that unlimited pool of infinite, unfolding possibility, those things on which we can't yet quite focus, that won't neatly fit into boxes—is the stuff of what Carse calls an "infinite game." "Infinite players," he says, "play for the purpose of continuing play (i.e. for sustainability). Infinite game players play *with* boundaries."[25] A leader who goes for growth instead of immediate bottom-line returns is playing an infinite game. A company that finds some way to measure the value of its *intan-*

gible assets—its software, the creativity of its people, the power of its deep vision, employee and customer loyalty—and that invests a good portion of its research funds into research for the unknown is also playing an infinite game.

When consultants place what the client wants in the larger context of what the client needs, they are playing an infinite game. And when healthcare systems invest less in the never-ending cost of interventive medicine for illness and more in quality-of-life support for health, they are playing an infinite game. All infinite games have a couple of things in common: they are played on an unlimited field, and they are sustainable.

SUBJECT/OBJECT SPLIT VS. PARTICIPATORY UNIVERSE

Old paradigm science divides the world into subjects and objects. The scientist is detached from the environment. The world is "out there." New paradigm science is participatory. The subject (the scientist) is "in the world," where involvement helps to make the world happen.

Western culture has always been dualistic. It divides the world into subjects and objects, minds and bodies, spirit and matter. The Newtonian universe is a material universe, made of cold, brute matter that simply is as it is. Newtonian scientists are detached observers who look at their world, weigh and measure it, and do experiments on it. They stand back from nature and study it. Newtonian technologists use nature; they manipulate and control it. This attitude has been a large factor in today's environmental crisis.

Newtonian organizations divide the world into the organization and its environment, the organization and its market. They seek to manage (control) that environment and to exploit the market. Natural resources are just that, resources to be used. Customers are out there, and they too are to be managed. Their tastes are to be manipulated through advertising and availability, their dissatisfactions stoked up, their expectations set. Such organizations make a sharp division between management and labor, between those who make decisions and those who are expected to follow them passively or to react through their official agents. As the senior manager of one global electronics plant reminded me, "It is the business of management to manage and of unions to react"—like Newtonian billiard balls bashing into one another. God forbid they should, as I had suggested to him, sit down and dialogue with each other. At an American communications company, employees are described as "most valued resources"; at a Swedish financial services company they are "intellectual capital."[26] Such mechanistic language reinforces mechanistic behavior and learning structures.

PRIVATE AND PUBLIC LIVES

In Western liberal democracies, we make a sharp split between the public and the private. This follows from our Western notion of a split between mind and body. In our Newtonian organizations, this split underlies a sharp division between the world of work and the employee's conduct at work, and the world of private life. Newtonian employees (including managers) bring to work only those aspects of themselves deemed directly relevant to the job, those aspects that have to do with dealing efficiently with the job, fulfilling the clauses of the contract under which they were hired, aligning themselves with the goals, values, and concerns of the company. They relate to their superiors, subordinates, and colleagues with these goals in mind. Anything else belongs to private life and is no concern of the organization for which the employee works. This *anything else* includes personal relationships and their accompanying joys and sorrows, children's needs and illnesses, outside passions and interests, personal idiosyncrasies, personal pain, and personal values. The very modern Newtonian organization has a counseling service where such things can be discussed, if necessary (and in private), so they cause less distraction to the employee's work effectiveness.

A senior manager at Shell Oil told me, "When I am at home for the weekend with my family, we go for walks in the country. We talk to each other; we meet with our friends. I love my children; I care about nature.

But when I go to work on Monday morning, I am expected to leave all that outside the door. My job is about making money."[27] Yet this man's actual job is in the human resources division of his company. He describes loneliness as his greatest problem at work. He feels that he can't give all of himself to his job.

A senior member of the managerial team of the European consultancy company described returning from a three-week holiday with his family. "I realized," he said, "that we have all the priorities wrong, and this is damaging. We focus only on the quality of work, not on the quality of life. But now I realize that if you focus more on quality of life, you improve the quality of work."[28] A Newtonian organization does not make room for these insights. An employee's quality of life is a private concern.

In new paradigm science, it is impossible for observers to distance themselves from what they observe. Both are mutually co-defined parts of the same holistic system. The questions quantum scientists ask, the experimental apparatus they design, play an *active*, *co-creative* role in the result that emerges. We saw this with the Two-Slit Experiment about light. A "particle question" evokes particles; a "wave question" evokes waves. Reality is not something out there but rather a constantly evolving drama in which human beings are partners.

IN QUANTUM PHYSICS, SUBJECT AND OBJECT ARE ONE

The common Newtonian notion that organizations or those who lead them simply act upon or react to their surroundings is an illusion, an illusion with crippling effect. In the words of Fons Trompenaars (*Riding the Waves of Culture*), "Organizations do not simply react to their environment as a ship might to waves. They actively select, interpret, choose and create their environments."[29] CEOs don't simply *act on* employees, customers, the community, the market, and the ecology. All are members of a *living system* whose many parts influence and mutually define each other. Likewise, consultants are not just outside experts called upon to diagnose and cure the ills of a company. Any attempt at such allegedly objective observation will of necessity bias both what they see and the results they get. Students of organizational behavior have noted this about the questionnaires management and consultants ask employees of companies to answer. The questions themselves elicit one kind of response. Different questions produce quite different answers, and thus a quite different picture of employee interests, concerns, and attitudes. This is a participatory universe. There is no "out there." The world does not make us. *We make the world.* This is a crucial insight of the new quantum worldview.

Neither, we know from all the new sciences of this century, is there any basis for the many dualisms of Western tradition. We know now there is no radical split between mind and body. Our state of awareness and ability to think is affected by the health of the body; the health of the body is affected by our psychological state. Our character is affected by our genetic code, but also by the material and social environment in which those genes flourish. Consciousness behaves differently from matter, but both are patterns of energy on an underlying reality. I firmly believe there is no more basis for a sharp distinction between public and private, between the selves we bring to work and the selves we share with our families and friends. This distinction is an illusion created by mechanistic structures and attitudes, and dissolves with their dissolution.

At Motorola I spoke with a secretary who had worked for years on the shop floor of the components division. This division was run mechanistically. Her boss played by the old rules. "If one of my children got sick," she said, "my boss didn't want to know. I had certain hours I had to be in and a job I had to do, and he didn't care what was going on at home. I hated him, and I hated the job, and I did just what I was required to do and no more." Later this woman worked as a secretary at Motorola University, the training side of the corporation. "My new boss is completely different. He always smiles in the morning and asks how I am. He asks after the husband and the kids. When one of the kids is sick, he tells me not to come in to work. I adore him, and I'd do anything for him."[30] Now she puts in extra hours, does things outside her job description, and has volunteered for a training course to become a conference organizer. She works with her whole person, and both she and the job are growing.

In his Scientific Management theory, Frederick Taylor described employees as *passive units of production*. But in this participatory universe, no one can be passive. Every action that we take, every attitude that we harbor, every thought that we think reverberates throughout the universe's many interconnections. The least of an organization's employees has the potentiality to be a responsible agent, and thus to bring creativity to the job. Many are now being required to do so. At Shell Oil, a member of the Leadership Council commented, "It used to be that you knew you would have a job for life and eventually settle at the right level of seniority. All you had to do was what you were told. But that's no longer enough. Today, every one of us has to reinvent the job as we go along."[31] That kind of challenge goes beyond doing a job with efficiency. It requires an engagement with meaning.

VACUUM VS. QUANTUM VACUUM

In old paradigm science, the universe is a still, cold, and silent place. Black emptiness fills the space between visible objects. Newtonian scientists are preoccupied with the objects, with their observation, manipulation, and control. They think that objects are all that is. Newtonian organizations and Newtonian leaders concentrate on *doing*, on setting goals and achieving results, on technique.

New paradigm science sees that the universe is a vast pool of seething potentiality, an interwoven pattern of dynamic energies that convey information. There is no emptiness. Objects are just surface manifestations of a deeper, underlying source. Quantum or complexity scientists are preoccupied with hidden patterns, with unseen connections, with synchronicity and evolution. They are filled with the adventure and excitement of *becoming*. New paradigm organizations are rooted in their vision. Their leaders focus on *being* as well as doing. They are rooted in the future as a way of managing in the present.

Quantum science tells us, as I have mentioned, that everything in the universe is energy as information. *Things*, objects on which we can focus—rocks, trees, stars, buildings, animals, ourselves—are all specific, recognizable patterns of incarnate energy and information. The matter of which these things consist comes and goes, like the water molecules that flow through the funnel of a whirlpool, but the patterns persist. In human beings, the matter that composes our bodies, the molecules of water and fat and protein, is exchanged entirely within every seven-year period. The neural connections in our brains alter every second. And yet we remain recognizable over the years as the individuals that we are. Our overall *patterns* change only slightly.

Organizations, too, are persisting patterns of dynamic energy and evolving information. That is why they have character, personality, a recognizable style over the years even though their employees and even their CEOs come and go. Andrew Stone described the 60,000 employees of Marks & Spencer as the individual particles in the company's brain. In other conversations with me, he spoke of the company's ongoing personality, of its instinct over the years for choosing leaders with different styles or visions because they are the leaders needed at that moment.[32] The company itself, its persisting pattern, is larger than, and somehow functions above and beyond, the actions and conscious decisions of all its individual parts—the CEOs, the board chairmen, the employees, the shareholders, and so on.

A SEA OF POTENTIALITY

In physics, when we recognize that every existing thing is a pattern of dynamic energy, questions arise: What are these patterns of energy patterns *on?* On what is the information of the universe *written?* The answer is the quantum vacuum. As described by the new physics, the whole universe consists of energy, and the ground state of that energy, the still, unexcited state of source energy, is the quantum vacuum. An Eastern philosopher might describe it as "the Infinite that is the background for the whole." Here in the West it is more difficult to understand the true nature of the quantum vacuum because we take "vacuum" to mean empty. But the quantum vacuum is only empty of *things* and *qualities*. We cannot see it or touch it or measure it, but it is not empty in itself. On the contrary, the quantum vacuum is full with all the potentiality latent in the universe. The quantum vacuum is *full* of everything that ever was, is now, and ever will be. The concept of such "full emptiness" is common to Eastern thought. As the poet in the Indian *Isha Upanishads* describes it,

> There is an endless world, O my brother
> And there is a nameless Being of whom nought can be said.
> Only he knows who has reached that region:
> It is other than all that is heard and said.
> No form, no body, no length, no breadth, is seen there:
> How can I tell you that which it is?
> Kabir says: It cannot be told by the words of the mouth,
> It cannot be written on paper:
> It is like a dumb person who tastes a sweet thing—how shall it be
>   explained?[33]

The quantum vacuum, then, is an equivalent from twentieth-century physics of the Hindu Brahma or the Chinese Tao. It is a concept similar to the Buddhist *Sunyata*, the Void. It is what the Western psychologist Carl Jung would call "the Self" that is the source of ego self. In physics, it is the ground state and source of our world and of human existence. Existing things—ourselves, our thoughts, our decisions, rocks and trees, and all physical things both living and nonliving—are "excitations," or waves, on the still pond of the quantum vacuum. To *ex-ist* in the original Latin literally means "to stand out from," and that is what existing things do. They stand out from the quantum vacuum. That still pond of energy provides the ultimate vision for the universe's unfolding. It is the source of all vision and value as we know them.

In the most literal sense, human organizations are self-organizing systems written on the quantum vacuum. They, too, are "ex-isting" things. And just as each individual existing thing is one finite or limited expression of the infinite potentiality of the universe as a whole, so each human organization is rooted in and is a finite expression of that pool of vision that nourishes the whole of creation. The vision of an organization drives the organization. It is expressed in its style of leadership, in its style of doing business, in the basic values that inspire its spoken and unspoken code of practice.

VALUES THAT DEFINE

At Marks & Spencer, which began as a small, family-owned business, those values are still rooted in the basic values of the Jewish spiritual tradition. Judaism is a religion that celebrates the sanctity of community life. For a good Jew, it is a holy duty to supply the needs of the community. A butcher, a baker, or a haberdasher is a holy man just as much as a rabbi. Today's very modern and very secular and frequently non-Jewish directors of the M&S global concern still speak privately among themselves of satisfying their customers' wish to feel happy about themselves, of turning out products that put smiles on people's faces. In their 1981 book *The Art of Japanese Management*, Richard Pascle and Anthony Athos point out that Japanese firms like Matsushita Electric list as core company values things like fairness, harmony and cooperation, courtesy and humility, and gratitude.[34] These, of course, are core spiritual values of the Buddhist tradition.

Newtonian organizations seek their identity in technique, products, and structure. Their core values are profit, efficiency, success, and perhaps excellence (in the service of profit). They seek customer loyalty, and, where necessary, customer "satisfaction." They are, to return to the words of James Carse, playing a "finite game,"[35] a game played for the purpose of winning. New paradigm organizations (and some of these are very old, very established firms) draw their focus, their energy from a deeper pool of vision and more-lasting values. They see themselves as part of some larger tradition. Organizations like Marks & Spencer and Matsushita don't shun profit, success, efficiency, and so on. But these mechanistic values are realized as by-products of deeper spiritual values.

CHAPTER 5

LEADING AT THE EDGE

However it may storm and rage
I thank it,
Because it is cold, and cruel, and ruthless
And yet gives peace.
Become as free as the sea,
Surrender utterly to the sea,
Surrender to uncertainty as the only certainty.

—**Par Lagerkvist,** *Pilgrim at Sea*

While writing this book, I spent a week at a seaside pub on the North Cornish coast. As I sat in the pub's glassed-in conservatory, in front of me I had a view of the stormy winter sea thrashing itself against the rocky cliffs, white spray filling the surrounding air like fog. Behind me, inside the pub, men were playing billiards, bashing the hard balls against one another with their cues. I felt I was sitting at the edge between the uncertain and turbulent quantum world and the deterministic world of Newtonian physics.

The turbulence of the sea, the sometimes tempestuous unpredictability of the weather, the precarious balance of the planets in the solar system, the whirlpools that form in streams and rivers, the ebb and flow of blood through our bodies, and the beating of the human heart. These are all examples of chaotic systems poised at the edge. They are balanced between stability and instability, between predictability and unpredictability. They possess structure and yet at every moment may transmute that internally into new structure. They do work and serve a purpose, but they are not fixed on any goal or locked into any set rhythm and thus are always open to adapting to change. They are sometimes called "open dynamic systems," "self-organizing systems," or "dissipative systems."

A few years ago at the Volvo Car Corporation in Sweden, engineers redesigned the car development process. The old engineering groups were tightly structured, intricately planned, and centrally controlled. Each group member represented a specific function and participated strictly in that role, giving the entire group a regular, determinate structure. The groups were organized hierarchically to deliver the desired products. Then the company started from scratch with a new idea. Engineers worked together on loosely organized, collective teams, and other professionals were brought in as well. Subteams worked within larger teams. Individual engineers were encouraged to move around from one team to another or to another subteam within the team. Not just the chairs, but even the desks of the engineers were put on wheels. Said Anna Nilsson-Ehle, Volvo's vice president in charge of change management at the time, "We didn't know what we were going to get out of each team until we had the team. Their way of working surprised us and them. But it worked!"[1] Nilsson-Ehle was inspired by quantum physics. She took pride in boasting that in this exercise, Volvo was a corporation poised "to think at the edge." With the new process in place, both corporate creativity and productivity increased, and with them corporate profitability.

At Marks & Spencer, the then managing director Andrew Stone discouraged his managers from coming to divisional meetings with formal reports. "Just come with your ideas and your enthusiasm, and let's see what happens."[2] A spirit of play predominated at these meetings. And yet serious things got done. Decisions were taken, and product lines emerged. The retail market is chaotic, driven by the whim of fashion, economic fluctuation, uncertain competition, social and political instability, changes in the buying power of different age groups, demographic shifts, cross-cultural influences, links between taste and wider cultural shifts. For well over a hundred years Marks & Spencer has thrived at the edge of chaos. The company has a genius for choosing leaders and leadership styles that are right for the moment.

In chaos theory, *the edge* is not a precipice. It is not something we can fall off, like the edge of a table or the edge of a cliff. Being "at the edge" is not the same as being "on the edge," or "over the edge." Being at the edge is a risky and exciting place to be, but in a different sense. In chaos theory, the edge is the border between order and chaos, the point at which self-organization arises from a meeting of stability and instability.

We have all seen natural systems poised at the edge, but we have not been aware of the dynamics unfolding before our eyes. Take the simple case of standing on a bridge watching the flow of a river or stream. Upstream, the water is smooth, flowing evenly without perturbation, scarcely a ripple on its glassy surface. Then just beneath us, the water encounters some twigs or rocks. At this point its surface parts and the water forms itself into a series of whirlpools. The whirlpools dance around the obstructions, constantly changing their sizes and shapes but always maintaining a distinctive, coherent pattern. Then, just beyond the whirlpools, the water fragments completely into white turbulence.

Where the water upstream is smooth, it is in a state of order. And its structure contains information. In nature and in computing systems, information is nothing but structure we can access. An ordered structure contains a certain amount of information. A simple structure contains less information than a complex one. There is, for instance, more information in a human fingerprint than in a simple drawing containing only a few lines, more information in the hologram of a jungle scene than in a black-and-white photo of the same. But however simple or complex the structure, if it is ordered, the information that it contains is fixed. Reliable, accessible, but ultimately finite. Order means reliability, predictability, and control. But it also means limitation.

The chaotic state of the water, where it is fragmented into white turbulence, may contain information, but if so it is useless to us. Its structure is either so complex or simply so nonexistent that we can't access it. A system that is totally chaotic is a system totally out of control.

At the point where the river meets the stones or twigs and forms itself into whirlpools, it is poised delicately between order and chaos, between being in control and out of control. This is the point at which its water molecules self-organize into a new, coherent pattern. A whirlpool is nature's most simple example of a self-organizing, open dynamic system. Such systems create *new* order, manufacture *new* information. They are neither in control nor out of control but poised delicately between the two, adaptive and creative. The river's whirlpools change their size and shape. Their inner structure is in dialogue with their environment, as they wrap themselves around the stones or twigs, but it remains recognizable as the pattern of a whirlpool.

We are surrounded by such self-organizing systems. We *are* such self-organizing systems! Each of us is, essentially, a self-organizing pattern of dynamic energy. Indeed, according to the most advanced physics, quantum field theory, everything that exists is a whirlpool in the quantum vacuum—the ground energy state of the universe. The solidity that we take for granted about ourselves, the resistance we feel when we thump our arms or legs with our supposedly solid hands, is just a transient phenomenon, an illusion of corporeal identity. Seven years ago, not a single molecule of which my body is made today was any part of me. Molecules come and go from my physical system at every second. The air molecules that I breathe in are breathed out within seconds. Most of the water molecules that I drink are passed out within hours, the food molecules within a day or two. Some of these substances that I take in become muscle, fat or protein molecules, brain cells, and these remain part of me somewhat longer. But within a seven-year cycle, every molecule has been exchanged.

What persists about me during and beyond those seven years is a self-organizing pattern. It is the pattern that my distant relatives recognize when they see me after several years, not the molecules circulating within it. And, like the shifting boundaries of the whirlpools dancing around the obstructing rocks, my own pattern changes and evolves over years. I both am and am not the five-year-old child my great-aunt from Toledo, Ohio, once held on her knee. I both do and do not resemble my teenage photograph, my wedding photos, and so on. The same is true of corporations and other human organizations. They are patterns that have persisted over the years. The successful ones, the sustainable ones, are patterns that have evolved.

All biological systems, from the simplest bacterium to things as complicated as ourselves and our organizations, are self-organizing patterns of dynamic energy poised at the edge of chaos. Their proper name is *complex adaptive systems*, and they are, for all practical purposes, living quantum systems. This is the secret of life's ability creatively to adapt to changing conditions. And it gives lie to the previous, old-paradigm belief that all balanced systems tend toward stability.

THE FALLACY OF STABILITY

Even the most forward-looking companies find themselves trapped in a belief in the importance, and if not the inevitability, then the desirability, of stability. This is one Newtonian assumption that dies hard. In economics, in politics, and in business we still live with the paradigm of law-abiding, separate working parts that will, if left to themselves, reach a state of equilibrium. This is the guiding assumption of laissez-faire capitalism, inspired by the Newtonian economics of Adam Smith. And if the system doesn't stabilize itself, then checks and balances meant to dampen down any positive feedback must be built in—like the cybernetic control of a central heating system whose thermostat kicks on and off as necessary to keep room temperature stable.

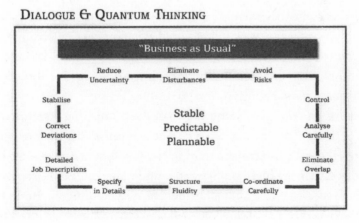

Figure 6. Business as Usual

At a global communications company based in the United States, one of the architects of the new leadership renewal program spoke to me for over an hour about the new physics, chaos and quantum theory, and the important lessons these hold for companies. Yet when he showed me the new course plan for leadership development, its central focus turned out to be the crucial importance of stability. "All systems tend towards stability," blared out from the page. The new leadership program, among other things, has been designed to enshrine this value. This is the *business-as-usual* paradigm illustrated in the figure.

"Business-as-usual" in this very mechanistic way of looking at things, whether the business of business or the business of Newtonian science, is about reducing uncertainty and eliminating disturbances, and therefore about avoiding risks and structuring any fluidity. It is about dampening positive feedback, influences from within or without that might rock the boat.

When I queried this juxtaposition of an interest in the business implications of the new science with a goal of maintaining stability, the global communications executive used the example of the human immune system, how it supposedly stabilizes itself to fight off disease. But this is precisely what the immune system does *not* do. The alien viruses and bacteria that invade our bodies mutate constantly, always trying to outsmart the immune system's defenses. The only way the immune system can stay one step ahead of its enemies is to be poised at the edge of *instability*, ready to evolve in any direction required at a moment's notice. Instability underpins the immune system's flexibility, its adaptability. It is the same with most of our biological functions, including creative thought and most of our learning ability.

California biologist Walter Freeman did pioneering research on the role played by chaos in our sense of smell. Freeman's work was actually conducted on the olfactory system of rabbits,[3] but the structures of the olfactory system are highly conservative and remarkably consistent across the whole spectrum of mammalian life. The nerve endings in the olfactory bulb, the brain's center of smell, are delicately poised between stability and instability. When we sense a familiar smell, one that the olfactory bulb has already wired into its recognition system, the firings of the various nerve endings quickly settle into an ordered state. Existing wiring can deal with existing information. But when the olfactory nerve endings are exposed to no odor, or to an unfamiliar odor, the nerve endings fire irregularly across all possible frequencies and amplitudes, poised to respond quickly to any change in input. This chaotic state allows the olfactory bulb to rewire itself to deal with new information.

Similar research has been done exposing the role of chaotic instability in human visual processing, and this has led scientists to speculate that chaos plays a crucial role in many human learning processes, as well as in concentration and decision-making. It is precisely because the nerve endings at our neural junctions (synapses) can fire across large spectra of frequencies and amplitudes, feeling their way toward the most stable patterns, that the brain can wire and rewire itself in dialogue with experience.

So the infant's brain is poised at the edge. Chaotic instability in its initial neural firings enables the brain to adapt to the physical and cultural conditions in which it finds itself. It is this chaos that allows the brain to be nature's most effective "learning organization," and children its most effective practitioners.

Children are such successful open dynamic systems, such effective learning organizations, precisely because they are not yet wired up. We have seen that in our culture, it takes roughly eighteen years for young people to lay down sufficient neural connections to deal with the usual challenges they face in coping with the world's complexities. During that time, each child's growing mind is poised at the edge, driven by curiosity and using play, imagination, and mistakes to learn and wire itself according to necessity. During this period of growth, the young brain uses huge amounts of energy and requires a compensatory amount of rest and sleep.

Young corporations wire their growing brains in much the same way, combining a rich mix of vision, experimentation (play!), imagination, curiosity, chaos, mistakes, and learning in laying down the style, habits, and infrastructures of the expanding company. These young corporate brains are flexible, sometimes a little unsteady. They make mistakes, and the ones that succeed learn from them. There is a great deal of literature on the role "creative mistakes" have played in the developing careers of some of industry's leading entrepreneurs. For instance, as John Micklethwait and Adrian Woolridge observe in their 1996 book *The Witch Doctors*, "[Jack] Welch was first noticed at General Electric in the 1960s because he ran a plastics plant that blew up. As a young entrepreneur, Richard Branson spent a night in a police cell after smuggling records into Britain from France. Rupert Murdoch nearly went bust on several occasions at the beginning of the 1990s, Babe Ruth may have been best known for his home runs, but he also set a record for strike-outs."[4] It is well-known that the Hungarian financier George Soros, who has made billions by playing the uncertainties of the stock market, has also lost billions.[5]

Soros named his main investment fund "The Quantum Fund." He did so, he said, because of the insight Heisenberg's Uncertainty Principle gave him into the inherent instability in free markets and open societies—societies that allow free expression, dissent, and a recognition that many points of view should flower because all points of view are somewhat flawed, and certainly limited. In Newtonian science, there is an assumption that the observer and the observed are independent. A Newtonian physicist can measure a system with an instrument from any vantage point in space and time and always get the same result. Reality is "out there." Adam Smith's Newtonian laissez-faire economics assumed the same about markets and customers, about prices, supply, and demand.

In consequence, Soros pointed out in the February 1997 *Atlantic Monthly*, classic economic theory "has managed to create an artificial world in which participants' preferences and the opportunities confronting participants are independent of each other, and prices tend toward an equilibrium that brings the two forces into balance."[6]

But quantum mechanics and a more honest appraisal of human behavior show us otherwise. According to Heisenberg's Uncertainty Principle, the observer and the observed are inextricably linked. If a quantum scientist asks a particle question, a particle answer emerges from his/her experiment. As noted in Chapter Four, a wave question results in a wave answer. Soros extended this to economic activity, where he saw prices and preferences, values and preferences, preferences and demand as inextricably linked, and the whole unstable mix as poised at the edge of chaos.

"In financial markets," he argued, "prices are not merely the passive reflection of independently given supply and demand; they also play an active role in shaping those preferences and opportunities. This reflexive interaction renders financial markets inherently unstable."[7] If, for instance, most investors think a stock will be attractive to other investors, the price of the stock will jump. This is an instance of "positive feedback" leading to instability.

Open societies and laissez-faire markets are poised at the edge of chaos. Hence their creativity but also the necessity of some centrally controlled checks and balances and the temptation of totalitarian regimes to impose total central control. Total freedom, lack of all checks and balances, risks chaos. Total control in a quest for imposed and therefore reliable equilibrium costs freedom and inevitably results in a system that runs down from a lack of its own internal, creative instability—as "closed systems" do in nature. Nature works with an uncertain system of positive and negative feedbacks, and the negative feedbacks don't always keep the positive ones in check. It is massive, chaotic fluctuations that push evolution forward. This is the paradox of "leadership at the edge," and there is no set formula (as in Newtonian physics!) for getting the balance right.

We face the same paradox in our creative thinking processes and the design of our corporate infrastructures. A learning, creative brain uses more energy than the whole rest of the body put together. Out of the box, at-the-edge thinking uses as much energy per unit of time as a game of rugby football. If we were creative all the time, we would get exhausted. So our brains are designed to conserve energy as well as use it. The whole point of wiring up all those neural connections in childhood is so that we can use them later reliably and at least semi-automatically. Habit can be a wonderful thing! Reliable corporate infrastructures, hierarchies, habits, and chains of command can make leadership a lot less stressful. Second- and third-generation corporate leadership can (or at least *used* to be able to) do a good job sailing the ship with sound managerial skills.

By about the age of eighteen, it *used* to be possible for most—it is still possible for some—adult brains to slow down. But going onto automatic pilot, relying on the learning and lessons of the past, relying on training, habit, and precedent—on competence—only works if the environment in which we have to function and thrive is the same environment as the one in which we wired up our brains. But for a vast number of adults today, for most corporate leaders, such environmental stability is itself a thing of the past.

A WHOLE CULTURE AT THE EDGE

In his recent and devastatingly powerful account of life in the twentieth century, *The Age of Extremes*, British historian Eric Hobsbawm points out that there has been more change in the past fifty years, globally, than since the Stone Age.[8] Transportation and communication, of course, have been revolutionized, and with them social and economic expectations and possibilities. When I was an undergraduate at MIT in the early 1960s, we had one mainframe computer on campus, and it occupied a huge room. Only the most science-fiction-minded of our professors envisaged the desktop PC and the information revolution that would follow. Top executives at IBM certainly didn't! Only a handful of today's top executives are comfortable with this revolution, and most billion-dollar-company information technology systems are underemployed or not fully applied. They have been slotted in, as an afterthought, to company infrastructures designed to block, or at best not to use, the free flow of instantaneous information.

But not just travel and communication have changed beyond recognition in this past half-century. In this new millennium, with our social, religious, and family institutions all up for reinvention. Both domestic crime rates and corporate and political scandals expose the fragility of our moral code, the general lack of moral conviction, moral common sense, and leadership. Technological breakthroughs like genetic engineering have outpaced our ability to use them wisely.

Along with his remarks on the inherent instability of laissez-faire market economies, George Soros mentions this crisis of values and its own contribution to general cultural instability.[9] Adam Smith and his contemporaries could take stable societal values as a given, and could rightly assume that a set of moral principles outside the market mechanism would help to keep that mechanism itself at some equilibrium. This is no longer true. Now, says Soros,

> As the market mechanism has extended its sway, the fiction that people act on the basis of a given set of non-market values has become progressively more difficult to maintain. Advertising, marketing, even packaging, aim at shaping people's preferences rather than merely responding to them.... Unsure of what they stand for, people increasingly rely on money as the criterion of value. What is more expensive is considered better. What used to be the medium of exchange has usurped the place of fundamental values.... The cult of success has replaced a belief in principles. Society has lost its anchor.[10]

At the same time, and on another level, the identity and identity-conferring power of the nation-state have greatly diminished. Globalization has destroyed the meaning and usefulness of national boundaries so rapidly that politicians cannot keep pace. A new global culture rich in universal values has yet to emerge. Space and time themselves must find some new meaning.

It has been a hundred years since Nietzsche announced the death of God,[11] and finally, today, we are face-to-face with that reality. Nietzsche didn't mean specifically the death of religion, but rather the death of our whole cultural framework, the end of our paradigm. It is terrifying, but it is also filled with infinite opportunities. The death of one paradigm usually heralds the birth of another, and those who inherit the new one often wonder what all the fuss was about. But ours is a generation at the edge, a generation poised (or torn!) between the old, dying paradigm and the ambiguous outlines of the new one waiting to be born. The neural connections we grew in childhood won't carry us through our turbulent adult years. Ours is a generation that must wire and rewire our brains, that must invent new categories, new concepts, new patterns, new organizational structures, new leadership. Those of us with children experience this daily in the difficulty of making up the rules as we go along. As Nietzsche pointed out, we can no longer get by just following given values. We have to create new ones.

Those leading companies find their jobs demanding in a way never experienced before by second- and third- and fourth-generation managers. Managing an existing system is no longer enough when no system can afford to be stable. Leadership at the edge requires all the poise, the gut instinct, the risk-taking, the wide-ranging imagination, and the creative mistakes of the child, the artist, or the founding entrepreneur.

The book in which Nietzsche announced the death of God was called *Thus Spoke Zarathustra*. The book opens with the people of a village gathering in the village square to watch a tightrope walker perform his act. According to the story, the tightrope walker must walk a rope stretched between the Towers of Certainty. He doesn't make it. In the book, the tightrope walker falls off and is killed. Nietzsche shakes his head with sadness and says, "He wasn't ready yet."[12] Now, a century later, that is the trick every one of us is called upon to perform.

In some of the training seminars I run with a partner, we offer people taking the course something called "the concept café." This is an evening dinner at which each of the participants is asked to read some famous quote or poem and reflect on its implications for his/her personal and working lives. One of the quotes we often use is by the Irish poet Arthur William Edgar O'Shaughnessy, a poem called "The Music Makers." O'Shaughnessy's poem was written to describe the creative role of poets and other artists, people who in any culture live and work at the edge. Today it seems to apply to most of us:

> We are the music makers,
> And we are the dreamers of dreams. . . . Yet we are the movers and
>   shakers
> Of the world forever it seems. We, in the ages lying,
> In the buried past of the earth,
> Built Nineveh with our sighing, And Babel itself with our mirth;
> And o'erthrew them with prophesying
> To the old of the new world's worth; For each age is a dream that is
>   dying,
> Or one that is coming to birth.[13]

AT THE EDGE OF THE MANAGEMENT/LEADERSHIP PARADIGMS

Much of this book is about paradigms and their impact on business thinking and corporate infrastructures. O'Shaughnessy's poem is about the death of an old paradigm and the birth of a new. In earlier pages I have focused on surfacing the extent to which business and management theory are in the grip of Newtonian thinking, and how we might shift that to a new perspective offered by quantum thinking. Taken at this simple level, I seem to be offering readers my own Towers of Certainty, and the task of moving from one to the other. I have something much more difficult in mind, but let's focus for a moment on the two towers, the choice between Newtonian management and quantum leadership. What would it look like in detail?

The Newtonian paradigm, we saw earlier, describes a world that is simple and law-abiding. It is a world framed in certainty, a world we can control. The quantum paradigm, by contrast, describes a world that is complex and chaotic, a world that is uncertain. Any attempt to dissect the complexity or to regulate the uncertainty with hands-on control reins in, or even destroys, everything that is rich, interesting, and creative about a natural self-organizing system.

In Table 5, I have constructed a chart that puts the features of these two contrasting paradigms in management and leadership terms. The left-hand column takes the features most prominent in Newtonian physics and sums them up as a management theory. This is very familiar territory. It is straightforward Taylorian Scientific Management that we can find in any MBA textbook.

Taylorian management stresses the values of certainty and predictability. This is a corporate world governed by inner laws and hands-on control, a world where blueprints and five-year plans are inviolate. This is goal-oriented, results-oriented "management by objectives." It is a world of hierarchy, where power emanates from the top or from the center. (This can be quite explicit, as in the plant manager's statement quoted earlier: "It is the business of management to manage and of unions to react."[14]) Just as Newtonian physics sees the atoms as passive units of matter operated upon by universal forces, Taylorian management sees workers as passive units of production, subject to the goals and control of management. Employees are company resources—"human resources"— like coal or iron or silicon chips. Employees are most easily controlled, and give their maximum productive output, if divided into separate labor functions. Remember Adam Smith's pin factory. Lines of command and rules of control are inflexible. Organization is rule-bound, heavily bureaucratic. Where Newton argued that there is one absolute perspective on space-time, a God's eye view of the universe, Taylor argued that there is a single point of view in management thinking, one best way for any company to proceed. We can discuss, and we can brainstorm, but the ultimate point is to find the one best way forward. Where Darwinian biology extended Newtonian thinking to the importance of competition between species, to survival of the fittest, Taylor stressed the inevitability and the benefit of competition between companies and between teams and divisions within the same company. Competition keeps us on our toes. It weeds out the weak.

Newtonian "Scientific" Management Stresses	Quantum Management Stresses
Certainty	Uncertainty
Predictability	Rapid change unpredictable
Hierarchy	Non-hierarchical
Division of labor or function fragmentation	Multi-functional holistic (integrated)
Power emanates from top or from center	Many interacting centers of power
Employees passive units of production	Employees co-creative partners
Single point of view one best way	Many points of view; many paths from A to B
Competition	Cooperation
Inflexible; heavily bureaucratic control	Responsive and flexible; hands-off
Efficiency	Relationship, meaning, and service value-driven
Top-down (reactive)	Bottom-up ("experimentation")

Table 5. Management-Leadership Chart

Like Newton's machines, the prime value of Taylorian companies is efficiency, the most output for the least input. Even in very recent years, this led to the ultimate Taylorian practices of downsizing and reengineering. And finally, like those billiard balls in the void, Taylorian companies are "reactive." They bounce off changes in the environment, changes in the market, changes in the competition. They *react* to changes; they don't initiate change.

The right-hand column of Table 5 is very different. It is also less familiar and more open to question and further suggestion because I made it up myself. I have constructed a chart of quantum leadership emphases by trying to do a Taylor with quantum concepts. I have consciously matched key quantum physical ideas to aspects of leadership in an attempt to outline the key points of a new leadership paradigm. This right-hand column has emerged from my work and conversation with companies over the past several years. Most of the quantum characteristics are things I have noticed companies needing, qualities they might benefit from developing, or qualities that leaders themselves within companies have been struggling to articulate. A few of the qualities in this right-hand column are very familiar because they have become buzzwords of the "new management," though many of the company people with whom I work feel these buzzwords are more often talked about than implemented or deeply thought through.

With its Uncertainty Principle and indeterminism, a quantum paradigm in leadership would certainly emphasize uncertainty instead of certainty. It would see uncertainty not as a pitfall but as an opportunity. "We need some uncertainty here to give us room to think," as the Marks & Spencer manager said.[15] Similarly, quantum leadership would take onboard the rapid changes and unpredictability that confront business today but would see these not so much as, or not *just* as, a problem but as an opportunity. Quantum organizations would not just learn to tolerate or to survive rapid change and unpredictability. They would learn to thrive on them. To do this, they would be less concerned with hierarchy, develop many interacting centers of power and decision-making, and create more responsive and flexible, more hands-off infrastructures within the organization. Those Volvo car-making teams are an example of this. So are some of the most prominent features of the Visa credit card company, which I shall discuss in Chapter Eight.

Quantum physics recognizes that we live in a participative universe in which living beings are co-creative insiders. We help to make reality happen. The observer is always *inside*, always *a part of*, the observed reality. None of us can avoid our active role in the makeup of things. "The buck stops here." In a quantum organization, employees are not passive units of production. They are not even "intellectual capital" or "human capital," to be invested as the company feels wise. Employees *are* the company. Even the most humble employee has a personality, a way of interacting with fellows, a point of view, a talent that, if unleashed, can help to create the very fabric of the company. Some recognition is given to this with all the talk about "empowerment," but I have encountered some cynicism among those supposedly empowered. Too often they feel it means being asked to shoulder more work or more responsibility for less reward or recognition. Genuine empowerment means redesigning the infrastructures within which people interact with each other and with the company as a whole.

Where Taylor felt certain there was one best path for a company to follow, one best way from A to B, quantum leadership would recognize the value of surfacing and considering *many* points of view. Quantum systems follow many paths in getting from A to B, and sometimes they arrive at D or E or F instead of B, which may be a pleasant surprise. Quantum leadership is less goal-oriented and more process-oriented. More concerned with what might emerge from putting ideas or processes or teams together than with blueprinting in definite expectations in the original design. It taps into the energy the Volvo manager described: "We didn't know what we were going to get out of each team until we had the team. Their way of working together surprised us and them. But it works!"[16]

Where the Newtonian (Taylorian) company divides itself into competing divisions and divides the market into competing companies, the quantum organization, inspired by the holistic, interacting, co-creative nature of the physical universe, sees the gain to be had from cooperation. Divide C into A and B, and all we have is A and B. Put A and B together in a cooperative, holistic unit, and we get a C that is larger than the sum of its parts. As I earlier quoted, Managing Director Andrew Stone said, "At Marks & Spencer we have learned that our competitors are also our suppliers and our customers."[17] Competition is a win-lose situation. Cooperation can be win-win.

Increasingly in management circles there is much talk about meaning and service, about value-driven companies. Too often things like TQM, valuable in themselves, are taken on by Western companies for the real motive of increasing efficiency. Reliable service can be interpreted as yet another competitive device, a way to earn the loyalty of the market. And values can be mistaken for those things that appear in vision statements. Quantum physics, with its contextualism and observer participation, necessarily raises questions of meaning and value at a more profound level.

On a quantum view, a company's community, its customers, its environment are as much in the company as the company is in or surrounded by them. (The fish is in the water, but the water is also in the fish.) There can be no hard-and-fast boundary between service to the community or service to one's customers and the community's or the customers' service (loyalty, financial support, employee provision) to the company. When Motorola and Marks & Spencer contributed to local education programs and local education budgets, they served both the community and their own future employees and customers. When Motorola flooded a closed Chinese society with cellular phones, the company cocreated the very (more open) environment in which it would function. It was selling communication, not just telephones. Quantum leaders are not just their nine-to-five ability to command and control. They are their whole history, their whole character, their deepest personal visions and values.

And for similar contextualist and holistic reasons, a quantum organization realizes that it cannot just react to its environment or to events. Top-down control is not just insufficient; it can be damaging. Bottom-up experimentation and flexible infrastructures and reward schemes for risk-taking are crucial to a company's own creative adaptation to the changing environment and to its creative co-creation of that environment.

NOT EITHER/OR BUT BOTH/AND

Quantum physics has not superseded Newtonian physics. It does not make it wrong or even less valuable. On the contrary, quantum physics contains the truth of Newtonian physics within itself. If we want to build a bridge or put a man on the moon, it is still Newtonian equations we will use to do our calculations. It is just that, given the newer quantum perspective, we now know that Newtonian physics is valid only over a certain narrow range of experience. For larger systems, we need relativity theory; for smaller ones, quantum theory. One day, undoubtedly, there will be a further physics that will incorporate quantum physics and relativity theory within its own still-larger perspective. There is no limit to the recontextualizing vision of expanding science.

By the same token, there is nothing wrong with the left-hand column of Table 5. There are times when it is appropriate to be certain, to have definite goals, to control situations, to provide structure, and to do all the other things called for by Taylorian management theory. It is a useful management approach for much that same part of experience handled by left-brain activity, the brain's logical, analytical hemisphere. But the brain has a right hemisphere, too, that is more intuitive, and like the right-hand column of Table 5, it comes into its own in quite different situations. There are situations in which it is better to let the imagination run, not to pin ourselves down or limit ourselves to definite goals, not to control or constrain things too tightly. Any company that wants to stay in business has to worry about its bottom line (efficiency), but a sole concern with that can limit growth, expansion, risk-taking, experiment, and vision.

We have seen that our brain works so creatively because our serial and parallel thought processes are integrated by a third kind of thinking that is poised between order and chaos. The brain is also designed to use both its left and right hemispheres in unison, and these are joined at the corpus callosum and by the integrating 40 Hz "quantum" field that sweeps across the brain. If this dialogue between the two hemispheres is broken, as is sometimes done to treat very bad epilepsy, our field of consciousness splits and each hemisphere is less effective. Similarly, so-called normal, conservative science limits itself to working within a paradigm, but then all it can do is ratify that paradigm. It is revolutionary science, working at the edge of paradigms, that moves knowledge forward. Quantum thinking can see the strengths and limitations of various paradigms, and can create entirely new ones.

My real point in drawing up the Management-Leadership Chart shown in Table 5, then, is not to offer two Towers of Certainty, one superior to the other. It is more to offer the vision of what "leadership at the edge" would look like, leadership that is aware of different paradigms, leadership that can assess the worth of a given paradigm for a given context and choose between options. And leadership that can invent new paradigms when necessary. Both/and, not either/or.

Marks & Spencer had two very different sorts of leaders at the top of the company, their different styles likened by some observers to Newtonian and quantum. Sir Richard Greenbury, the former chairman, was a more orthodox manager, a command-and-control, let's-get-the-job-done sort of leader. As we have seen, Andrew Stone, one of his four joint managing directors, was much more at home with a quantum style of leadership. The two men's leadership styles clashed. There was friction between them, yet mutual respect. Outsiders attributed the success of Marks & Spencer at the time to its ability to have both those very different leadership styles working in partnership. Similarly, Andrew Stone had thirteen directors reporting to him, three of whom are on the main board. They often disapproved of his leadership style and of the decisions he made. Every week Stone invited those three critics to his office for a "bitch session." They shouted at each other, they were rude, they surfaced their grievances—and then they all worked together as a team more effectively.[18]

Individuals are not all the same. Some personality types are more at home with uncertainty and ambiguity than others. Some have a higher threshold for chaos than others. Some like to be creative, to think and act out of the box. Others panic if expected to do so. Some, in short, prefer left-column, Newtonian management, others right-column, quantum leadership. "Leadership at the edge" also means being able to get the best out of both these types, and to use the strengths of each for the company as a whole.

PART II

THREE MODELS OF ORGANIZATIONAL STRUCTURE AND LEADERSHIP

In his book on the world in the year 2020, British financial writer Hamish McRae forecast that within the next quarter-century such "old motors of growth"[1] as land, capital, and natural resources would become less crucial to national and corporate economic success. Instead, he argued, future success would depend more on "qualitative features" like the quality, organization, motivation, and self-discipline of people. These, in turn, I believe, hinge crucially on our working concept of the human self/individual, and the importance of the personal qualities of both the employees and leaders of business organizations.

Our concept of the self includes things like our personal identity and personal boundaries—what is inside or outside of the self? How much of "me" is really me? For how much of myself am I responsible, and how much is beyond my control? How much is within the control of my genes, my upbringing, my education, my training? How does one individual self-relate to another or to a group or an organization? Do we need to manage or control these relationships, and if so, how? What damages or nourishes the self, and thus what motivates it? From where does the self derive its own sense of self-worth and responsibility and its wider notions of meaning and value? How do I, as an individual self, assess the worth of others? Do I derive my authority, my ability to act and to choose and to make decisions from qualities within myself? Or do I seek authority, wisdom, and discipline from outside myself—from parents, society, religious or political bodies, or corporate organizations?

Such questions are vital to organizational theory and practice. Organizations are human organizations, and they organize people—human selves. Organizational theory is based on a culture's answers to questions about the self. The success or failure or organizational practice depends upon how closely these answers fit the reality. If we think people are constituted and motivated in a certain way, we will create laws, rules, expectations, and organizational structures accordingly. If people are not in fact like our concept of them, the structures may well fail—and/or damage the people they organize. At best, inadequate or inappropriate structures will limit or distort the human qualities they had hoped to organize.

It is the central thesis of this book that the thinking structures and processes of the human brain are the natural prototypes of human organizational structures that we evolve or design. There are three kinds of structures in the brain, each responsible for a different kind of thinking. We saw in Chapter Three that serial, one-on-one neural tracts, or neural conglomerates that behave like this, embed our logical, rational, goal-oriented thinking, our problem-solving, how-to thinking. Parallel or neural network-like structures embed our associative thinking, the emotion-centered, body-centered thinking with which we recognize patterns, learn skills, form habits and emotional associations, and store tacit knowledge, knowledge that we can't communicate through rules and manuals. Neural oscillations, perhaps quantum in origin, integrate our serial- and parallel-thinking processes and form a third kind of brain structure/cognitive process. These are responsible for our creative, insightful, reflective thinking, for our ability to create new concepts and new patterns, to challenge our assumptions and change our mental models, to adapt to rapid change and radically new situations.

Each of these three brain thinking structures also underlies, I believe, a quite distinct model of the human self and its potentialities. These three models of the self lead, in turn, to three different models for human organization and for control and development within organizations. This next section of the book will be devoted to exploring these, their infrastructures, and their leadership.

In neuroscience, we saw, the serial and parallel structures for thinking are well-researched and well-understood. Both have been successfully modeled as types of computing systems. One-on-one, like neural tracts are the model for serial processing PCs. Parallel neural networks are the model for parallel processors, or neural network computers. Broadly speaking, the two associated models of self and their accompanying models of organization are also familiar. Both have been written about extensively by sociologists and organization theorists, though seldom as coherent models of self and organization, and never in association with underlying brain structures.

One familiar model of self and organization is the dominant Western model. This model describes an individualist self-organized in a rule-bound (or law-bound), contractual, and often bureaucratic structure. The other familiar model of self and organization predominates in the East, particularly in Confucian society. This model describes a self that is contextual and relational, defined wholly or largely in terms of associations—household, extended family, village, work community, and so on. This self is organized in complex and ambiguous networked structures bound by habit, custom, and tradition. The two models have been described succinctly by Chinese sociologist Fei Xiaotong as "the two basic types of society." "One type of society," writes Fei in his 1992 book *From the Soil*, "forms as a natural result of people growing up together, and has no other purpose than being simply an outgrowth of human interaction. The other type of society is that which has been organized explicitly to fulfill goals. . . . The first is an example of organic solidarity and the second an example of mechanical solidarity."[2]

I have found this book invaluable. It makes the difference between Eastern and Western societies (and hence familiar Eastern and Western organizations) very clear, and was crucial to my own insight that a society's model of the self underpins its theories of organization.

As stated clearly by Fei's use of words, the Western model is mechanistic. It is a Newtonian, atomistic-particle model. Indeed, Fei uses the metaphor of Western individuals seen as isolated straws that can be gathered up into organizational bundles. The Eastern model is wavelike, holistic, every individual ambiguously interwoven with many others. Fei uses the metaphor of Eastern individuals being like stones dropped onto the still surface of a lake, each radiating a pattern outward and the various connecting patterns overlapping and influencing each other.[3] Sociologists usually associate the atomistic Western model with large, anonymous urban societies, and the Eastern model with more close-knit, community-oriented agrarian societies. The whole basis of Fei's Confucian sociology is that the Chinese are essentially a peasant people rooted to the land. Even those who have migrated to large urban areas keep their traditional landed patterns of association.

In organization studies, small new companies still led by the inspirational founder are often compared to networked agrarian societies. Everyone knows everyone else; formal rules are less important than customs, relationships, and associations; new ideas and new products evolve through inspiration, cooperation, trial and error; and the personality and vision of the founder-leader somehow suffuses and guides the whole network. These small-company infrastructures tend to be informal and flexible. But such small companies, if they grow and succeed, usually evolve in the second and third generation into large, anonymous, bureaucratic organizations of the Western type. Something is gained on the level of scale and organization by this transition, but the personal, inspirational, and associative qualities of the small company are usually lost. Infrastructures become more rigid, adaptation to change less easy. A new kind of leadership is demanded.

Inspired by the new science of this century, particularly quantum science, and by the creative thinking structures in the brain, I envisage a further, third model of the self and an accompanying third model of organization. I call these the *quantum self* and the *quantum organization* because of their similarity to quantum physical systems and processes. This third model has the both/and qualities of particle (individualist) systems and wave (networked) systems and the further qualities found in the creative thinking and organizational potential of our distinctively human brains.

CHAPTER 6

THE WESTERN MODEL:
THE NEWTONIAN SELF AND
THE NEWTONIAN ORGANIZATION

The billiard ball was Newton's metaphor for the atom, the smallest possible bit of matter. As described in his mechanistic physics, each atom (billiard ball) was isolated in space and time from every other. The atoms bounced about in a void, connected to each other by forces of action and reaction, their movements determined by iron laws of motion that assured universal order and predictability. Each atom was circumscribed by a hard and impenetrable boundary. None could get inside another. When they met, they experienced collision, and one or both was knocked off its course. The billiard ball has become a familiar metaphor for the Western self. The game of billiards works just as well as a metaphor for the Western organization.

THE BILLIARD SELF

Atomism is much older than Newton's physics, dating back to the ancient Greeks. And the atomistic unit of the self is as old as Christian theology. The Christian soul, too, was portrayed as a discrete entity, a small bundle of holiness placed inside us by God and different from everything else within us or about us. This soul preceded the body and its personal ego and survived both. It was what was essential about us, what mattered, what was worthwhile. And just as Newton's atoms of matter were related to each other and to the larger scheme of things through universal laws of motion, so these atomistic souls were manipulated and controlled by universal forces of Good and Evil, the love of God and his angels, the temptations of the Devil. Souls had no direct relationship to each other. Any interrelation was mediated through universal moral law. Each soul was essentially alone, utterly unique, and in direct relationship only to the Godhead. Salvation or damnation was thus decided according to universal moral principles.

As we saw in Chapter One, Newtonian atomism influenced modern Western concepts of self and society through Sigmund Freud's scientific psychology and through John Locke's liberal individualism. The Freudian self, like each atom in the void, is tragically isolated, a self to itself but just an object to others. This self is imprisoned within hard boundaries, impinged upon from below (its behavior determined) by the dark forces of instinct and aggression latent in the id. And it is manipulated from above by the codes and expectations of parents and society, the superego. There is nothing essentially good about this Freudian self. (Freud was not religious.) The self is just the determined result of its instincts and experiences, and left to itself it is quite selfish and unloving. Society's survival (social control) rests on the expectations of the superego and on the ability of universal moral and social laws to enforce these.

Even before Newton, the social philosopher Thomas Hobbes formed his view of the self in response to mechanistic notions of the universe. For the Hobbesian self, life was "poor, nasty, brutish, and short" because individuals, the atomistic units of society, were driven by greed and self-interest. Left to themselves, without adequate social control, such individuals would tear each other and society to pieces. No friend of freedom, because freedom meant a lack of control, Hobbes conceived of a firm social contract that would ensure order through strict legislation and enforcement. Following Newton, liberal political philosopher John Locke took a kindlier view of human nature and thus the potentialities of freedom. But Locke, too, felt that the atomistic individual was the basic unit of society and that some form of social control had to legislate the behavior of and relationships among these individuals.

In liberal democracies, following Locke's model, we divide selves into public and private aspects and society itself into a public domain and private life. Through discussion, reflection, legislation, and soon, individuals (or at least majorities) agree upon those things to be shared, and thus controlled, by the public domain and its social contract (constitution, laws, and codes). Everything not included in the proper concern of the public domain is considered private, and individuals should be the sole guardians of their own private lives. Western democracies differ about the scope, size, and power of the public domain, but all agree on the distinction between public and private and the rights of the individual to be protected against too much intrusion.

The sanctity of individual rights emphasizes the burden that Western societies place on privacy and the private self. My real self, the real me that I care about and can reveal when I let my hair down at home, is unique and private. It has boundaries that no one dare invade. Boundaries, indeed, that no one *can* invade, even if they wished. "Each of us is alone," wrote the British novelist and intellectual C. P. Snow. "Sometimes we escape from solitariness, through love or affection . . . [but] each of us dies alone."[1] This private self is in need of some control, but it should be self-control.

My public self, by contrast, includes those aspects of myself I have agreed to share and control over which I have agreed to legislate away. Or perhaps my society has determined that I have to legislate them away, but if so, only in so much as all others have done so too. My public self is universal, general, the aspects of me that everyone else also possesses, and their control is subject to universal laws and principles that are the same for all members of my society. The boundaries of my public self, too, are sharply defined, and neither my most intimate partner, my neighbor, nor the state must violate them.

Western organizations, like Western societies as a whole, organize and control their members on the basis of firm boundaries and formal rules that are universal for all members of any given category. Any such organization, whether business or social, has criteria for membership. Those who don't meet the criteria are excluded, but just as important, those who are included exclude much of themselves from the organization. Membership in any Western-style organization, even an intimate organization like a nuclear family, requires the member to commit only some part of the self to the organization and its rules. "Nobody can own my soul." "The only organization to which I belong is me."

Indeed, the identity and stability of typical Western organizations are ensured by excluding the individual, unpredictable, private concerns of members, those things that can't be summarized in general rules. People can belong to the same bridge club for twenty years, and know little more about each other than styles and strategies for playing bridge. Big companies modeled on Newtonian (Taylorian) principles don't want to know the personal problems and family obligations of employees. Local government and healthcare bureaucracies don't function well with exceptions, with cases that can't be universalized. Most of us find such bureaucracy tedious, and can easily feel alienated within our organizational systems, yet most Western people also find security in the rules and boundaries that divide public life from the private and feel threatened if these are eroded.

Two of the big companies for which I have worked in recent years, a communications company and an oil company, have been involved in transformation programs that attempt to increase personal involvement and personal expression at work, particularly at the managerial level. During one of the communications company workshops, a senior manager commented, "All this talk about being a particular type of person and joining the company 'community.' I feel the company is trying to invade my personal space, trying to take over my identity."[2]

At the oil company, another senior manager made a similar comment. "To me, this company has always been a job. Now I feel they are trying to buy my soul."[3] Such comments sharply conflict with others made by managers who feel isolated at work, who suffer because they can't bring "themselves" to work. Indeed, the same conflicting comments might have been uttered at different times by the same managers. This is the tragic paradox of the Western self isolated by choice and yet alienated by that isolation. Lonely, yet unwilling to commit to those more full-fledged intimacies that would defeat loneliness.

This same paradox lies at the heart of corporate debates about loyalty. Employees want a more loyal commitment from their companies to job conditions and security, but they don't want to give all of themselves to the company. Corporations want a greater loyalty from their employees, but they don't want to concern themselves with the "personal problems" of those employees. One of the big corporations for which I have worked has made greater employee loyalty a central theme of its transformation process. "We put a lot of time and money into training people. We expect some loyalty in return." In the next breath, the CEO of this same corporation said, "Don't look to us for lifetime employment. It's a rough world out there, and you're on your own."[4]

Newtonian physics grew out of this Western split between soul and body or mind and body, between the public and private spheres of the universe. Newton concentrated on material bodies, the physical properties of the universe that all material things have in common, that is, the "public sphere." As a scientist, he had no concern with souls, the "private sphere." The Newtonian ideal was the machine, the clockwork universe that relies solely on its formal rules (the laws of motion) to operate. Following Newton, the machine—seeing human beings and human organizations as machines or parts of machines—became the wider cultural norm.

The Newtonian machine consists of separate and replaceable working parts, each of which is included because it serves a function. The machine itself has been built according to blueprint to serve a function. A good machine is one that works efficiently, each part working in harmony with the others to achieve the desired result, but this never happens organically. The separate parts of a machine work in harmony because they are subject to control. If the machine is a sophisticated cybernetic device like a central heating system, such control is programmed into the machine through an internal system like a thermostat. The great universal clockwork machine is controlled by universal laws of motion. Simpler machines are controlled externally through a human controller.

BILLIARDS AND ORGANIZATION

Frederick Taylor's Scientific Management theory looked to the Newtonian physical model. Both Taylor's vision of the organization and his notions about the role of human beings within an organization were mechanistic. Newtonian business corporations are machines that were designed to make profit through the sale of some product or service. Their separate employees and separate divisions are organized and controlled according to impersonal (public sphere) rules, by the constraints of a contract—and rules and contracts are designed with efficiency in mind. Those things not having to do with the employee's work function are outside the job description, and thus outside both the company's concern and the employee's company responsibility. The boundaries are rigid. The ideal employee in the ideal bureaucracy is replaceable, having a skill that has a market elsewhere or that the company can replace as need be. Such employees work most efficiently when given machinelike functions to perform.

Similarly, relations between Newtonian organizations are impersonal, rule-bound, or defined by formal contract, designed to exclude consideration of the idiosyncrasies or personalities of the entities with which they are contracting. If an oil company makes a contract to sell so many million gallons of fuel to an airline, it doesn't want to have to concern itself with whether the airline changes its CEO, or whether that CEO has an unfaithful wife or a sick child. Similarly, it is not the oil company's contractual concern whether the airline suffers a series of fatal crashes and goes bankrupt. That is what insurance is for.

The assumption in all Western, Newtonian organizational models is that the organization consists of separate parts bound together insofar as is necessary or desirable through universal rules or centralized control. Information flow and learning within such organizations are mediated through the negotiated, rule-bound structures that make up the organizations' internal and external contracts. If I want to inform my Newtonian colleagues of some decision I have made, or of some change in procedure, I should do so through proper channels. If I need to have a job done, I should seek assistance from a designated authority.

The advantage of goal-oriented, rule-bound Western or Newtonian organizations is that they can be efficient and reliable. Their clear boundaries make membership unambiguous. Every procedure and every role is specified and pinned down in its place. Every employee knows exactly what is expected every day—and what is not. So long as procedure is followed and proper channels used, information can flow smoothly to those parts of the organization where it is directed. But there are disadvantages. Just as rules don't accommodate exceptions easily, these organizations are inflexible. Turning them around to deal with the unexpected takes time and thorough reprogramming. Indeed, most procedures take a lot of time. As an Indian employee of Delhi's state power company complained, "Every time I want to spend five dollars, I have to fill out fifty pieces of paper and wait three months for clearance."[5] And where proper channels or existing procedures don't cover the situation, such organizations can suffer a "learning disability"—as happens all the time in companies where one division has benefited from some new educational or consulting technique, or even from a "creative mistake," but no infrastructure exists for communicating this to other divisions.

The structural model for our Western, Newtonian organizations is the serial thinking process in the human brain. Like the separate parts of an organization, the brain's neural tracts behave as though they consist of separate neurons firing one-on-one to other separate neurons. Each individual firing pattern is orchestrated by a program (a set of rules), and this in turn has been learned for the purpose of solving some problem. Those neurons not involved in the program for solving the problem in hand are superfluous to the process. If a new problem arises, the serial thinking process cannot handle it until supplied with an alteration to its program. Thus it is efficient and reliable, but rule-bound and therefore inflexible. On its own, serial thinking can't deal with complex data or rapid changes. Its neural circuits can deal only with a few inputs and outputs at any one time. This, for instance, is why PCs—modeled on serial thinking—can't deal with pattern recognition. Patterns are too complex.

In the human brain, serial thinking does not function in isolation. It is only in our mechanistic, cognitive-science models of thinking that it does so. Taking the structures of serial thinking alone as the central model for organizational structures is distorting the whole ball game. In the real brain, serial, parallel, and quantum (creative, insightful) thinking structures are integrated and work in tandem to generate our uniquely human thinking processes. In the same fashion, the uniquely complex human self functions as a dialogue between the public and private aspects of that self, however high the wall our distorted models of the self may build between the two.

The Newtonian universe, we know, is bound inexorably to the law of entropy. All those rule-bound, well-organized conglomerations of separate particles are destined to slow down and fall apart. All Newtonian systems are fated to certain death in a cold and silent universe. Yet complex, adaptive living systems manage to beat the odds. Real brains manage to rewire themselves throughout life. Both have their own dynamic of spiraling complexity, adaptation, and growth. Nature is telling us there is a better model for organizations than Newton's, a better model for thinking than rule-bound, goal-oriented thinking in isolation. "Management by objectives" is not a good model for management, and there are certainly better models for leadership.

CHAPTER 7

THE EASTERN MODEL: THE NETWORKED SELF AND THE NETWORKED ORGANIZATION

"Chinese managers like to boast that, in contrast to their legalistic western peers, their businesses are based around negotiating relationships, not contracts. The chief assets of an overseas Chinese business are usually its guanxi [or connections]."

—John Micklethwait and Adrian Wooldridge,
from *The Witch Doctors*

I would like to begin with a tale of two conferences. I was invited to be a keynote speaker at each. The first was organized by a Western oil company and held in a large American city. I was told in advance what I was expected to speak about, for how long, and how much I would be paid. Three weeks before the conference opened I received a detailed agenda for the whole session, broken down into forty-five-minute segments punctuated here and there by lunches, break-out sessions, and coffee breaks, all of definite length. Each speaker was described and a tight program of the planned speech offered in advance. The thoughts that would be "processed" during each break-out session were specified. A preconference manual supplied every table and diagram to which speakers and facilitators would refer. The conference was supposed to be about transformation and out-of-the-box thinking!

The second conference was organized by a Japanese retailing billionaire and held in Kyoto. Vague quasi-invitations to speak had been arriving at my home for months before an actual date was finally set and a plane ticket offered. Two weeks before I was due to leave for Japan, I realized I knew nothing about the conference. What was I to speak about and for how long? To what size audience? Who else was speaking? What would I be paid? What was the conference about? In answer to my urgent fax asking these questions, the host's Korean assistant wrote back saying, "Don't concern yourself with these matters. This is going to be a Taoist conference. We will just all meet and see what emerges. We will have some good meals and make some good friendships. Then we will see what we can agree about." This conference has continued in peripatetic fashion for a year subsequently. The Japanese businessman, his Korean assistant, and I have dined together in three world capitals and continued to "develop our friendship." I think they are concerned about the nature of the self and have some vague plans to institute a new form of education. The details have yet to emerge.

THE WAVELIKE SELF

The Japanese don't have a specific word for "self." They are concerned with relationships, and what we Westerners call the "self" is, for them, a matter of who is related to whom and in what larger social context. Nobel Prize–winning Japanese physicist Leo Esaki, who has spent his life working for IBM, compares Japanese society to a state of superfluid helium. Every particle is related to every other to such an extent that boundaries don't exist and the parts share the identity of the whole. The Chinese sociologist Fei Xiaotong, as I wrote earlier, compares Confucian society to a complex pattern of interlocking waves, each fanning outward from some stone (individual) dropped in one of the many centers, but all so intricately entangled that no clear boundary can be discerned between the waves caused by one stone and those of another. "Everyone stands at the center of the circles produced by his or her own social influence. Everyone's circles are interrelated. One touches different circles at different times and places."[1]

In Confucian society, probably the purest example of the "Eastern model," the wave description of selfhood is at its most extreme opposite from our Western, particle model of the self. In Chinese culture, I am defined by my relationships, but I have many different kinds and circles of relationships, and thus the boundaries of my own identity are quite ambiguous and contextual. With my parents I will have one way of conducting myself, with my children another, with my wider kinsfolk still another, with neighbors, members of my community, or my state still more. I can't fully articulate the set of moral principles that guides my life because I have many such sets of principles, each applicable in its own context. A Western notion of universal moral codes makes no sense in such societies.

"In these elastic networks that make up Chinese society," writes Fei, "there is always a self at the center of each web. But this notion of the self amounts to egocentrism, not individualism."[2] In individualist, Western societies, the whole is made up of its parts and each part has its tightly defined identity circumscribed by boundaries. In its public aspect at least, every part (every individual) is equal to every other. Every individual has the same rights and obligations within an organization as anyone else with the same organizational status or function. In Chinese society, my self is always at the center of my circle, but I have many circles, and the characteristics, obligations, and codes of each circle define who I am and how I should behave. I have no universal rights, only contextual obligations. Fei adds, "The boundary between public and private spheres is relative—we may even say ambiguous."[3]

In the West, even my most private relationships are bound by contract. Some aspects of my behavior are bound by a specific contract; all other aspects are not. My obligations are limited by the terms and boundaries of the contract. In the Chinese networks consisting of circles within circles, there can be no hard-and-fast boundary to my obligations nor any limit to those relationships that might share my blame if I err. Improper conduct toward my mother-in-law reflects badly on the way my mother raised me, which reflects badly on the way her teachers and parents educated her, and so on. Everyone is responsible for everyone else. In the introduction to *From the Soil*, Fei quotes this stark example from "The Myth of the 'Five Human Relations' of Confucius":

Cheng Han-cheng's wife had the insolence to beat her mother-in-law. This was regarded as such a heinous crime that the following punishment was meted out. Cheng and his wife were both skinned alive, in front of the mother, their skin was displayed by the city gates in various towns and their bones burned to ashes. Cheng's grand uncle, the eldest of his close relatives, was beheaded; his uncle and two brothers, and the head of the Cheng clan, were hanged. The wife's mother, her face tattooed with the words "neglecting her daughter's education," was paraded through seven provinces. Her father was beaten 80 strokes and banished to a distance of 3000 li. The heads of family in the houses to the right and left of the Chengs' were beaten 80 strokes and banished to Heilongjiang. The educational officer in the town was beaten 60 strokes and banished to a distance of 1000 li. Cheng's nine-month-old boy was given a new name and put in the county magistrate's care. Cheng's land was to be left in waste "forever." All this was recorded on a stone stele and rubbings of the inscriptions were distributed throughout the empire.[4]

In the West, we wonder whether parents should be held at all responsible for the behavior of their delinquent children!

WAVES AND ORGANIZATION

The Confucian model of the contextual, relational self is perhaps the most pure, as I said earlier. But throughout Asian societies, including India, this basically more wavelike model of self has underpinned group-oriented, networked, and, most commonly, family-based companies. Because Asian societies differ so much more among themselves in their social structures than Western ones, any hard-and-fast generalization comes unstuck. Japanese companies are very different in many respects from the large family networks of the overseas Chinese, and both are different from some of the star companies in Taiwan and Singapore. India has superimposed Western-style bureaucracy and management techniques in business onto an essentially networked, family-oriented society, not infrequently ending up with the worst of both worlds. But my purpose here is simply to draw a distinctive contrast between particle-like Western models of self and organization and wavelike Eastern models, regional variations notwithstanding.

Among the overseas Chinese, the networked self has formed the basis of large, complex, and ambiguous networked organizations very reminiscent of the neural networks found in the brain's parallel thinking structures. Like neural networks, everything and everyone seems to be connected to everything else. The connections within the networks are informal and pretty much organic—they grow in response to conditions, opportunities, and local constraints much as neural network connections grow in response to experience. In this sense, both are flexible and adaptive. Both can learn. The size of the neuron bundles joined in a neural network varies with requirements, just as the ambiguous boundaries of family and kinship that underpin Chinese business networks expand and contract to suit needs.

On the downside, in both neural networks and Chinese networks, flexibility is limited through the crucial importance of habit, familiarity, and tradition. The brain's parallel connections function best with repeated experience. Chinese businesspeople are most comfortable with relations of trust, and trust itself is reliable because of the tradition-bound nature of Chinese social relations. Stability in these communities is achieved through reinforced familiarity, custom, and discipline of the self. And they're a bit claustrophobic. "The more linkages one maintains," says Fei, "the more intensively one is wedged into an existing social order and is committed to the status quo."[5] Thus where bureaucratic Western organizations can get fossilized by rules and procedures, networked Eastern organizations can be just as weak at dealing with unexpected change.

The brain's parallel processing structures—those used for tacit knowledge, skill acquisition, and pattern recognition—work cooperatively and locally. They are the structural prototype of agrarian societies and small groups anywhere in the world, groups that function well because everyone knows everyone else, most important knowledge is shared, responsibilities and necessary tasks are shared, and power is distributed according to tradition. Such societies need few formal rules because familiarity and the weight of group expectation keep most people in order.

As a young child in the early 1950s, I had a personal experience with these close-knit groups. I was raised by my grandparents in a small country town in America's Midwestern farm belt. The town's population was only two hundred adults, all of whom worked in the local pickle factory, in the few local shops, or in jobs servicing local farms. Everyone in the town knew everyone else, knew their children and kept an eye on them, knew their health problems, their marital difficulties, their small scandals, their achievements, and their contributions to the community.

Both my grandparents belonged to a number of small groups that met in the town. Both belonged to the "True Blue Society" of the local church, the group for church members over fifty years old. My grandmother belonged to the local teachers' association and to the Ladies' Grange Society, a group of town and farm wives who met to plan local farm-centered events and to raise money for local charity. My grandfather belonged to the Elks and to the local branch of the Ohio Justices Association, a group formed by justices of the peace from nearby towns. Nearby, my great-grandfather was the ward chairman of the local Democratic Party, and a small group of party members met regularly in his sitting room. We all belonged, of course, to our own large, extended family, to the circle of my grandparents' fourteen siblings, their children, and grandchildren. All lived within a fifteen-mile radius of our town, and some subgroup of us met at least once a week to spend Sundays and important family occasions together.

My grandparents and I were seldom alone in our house except when we slept. There was always a flow of townspeople or relatives meeting in our sitting room, gathered at the large kitchen table, or grouped around the bed to which my grandfather was confined much of the time with heart trouble. Our house and our lives seemed always at the center of the extended lives of the various groups who passed through and stayed awhile. There was constant, ongoing conversation (about local and national politics, about religion, about town events or town policies, about what the local grocery store should stock and what it was charging) that sometimes reached high-pitched argument but was always lively. My memories and the meaning of my childhood are inseparable from memories of all these people, their activities and conversation.

In the West, when people moved from small rural communities to large, impersonal cities, a different social structure was imposed, and the small groups broke up. My parents' generation moved to the nearby city and took assembly-line jobs in factories. Church attendance and local society memberships dropped off among family members, and so did our family get-togethers. Where my grandmother had belonged to an education association whose members never counted the hours or the energy they devoted to their teaching jobs, my mother joined a teachers' union and fought for better pay and conditions. Teaching became a job instead of a vocation. The cousins of my own generation then moved to other cities or other countries, wherever their jobs took them. I never see them, and I don't know their children's names. Rule-bound, bureaucratic organization and its imposed, impersonal mobility became the norm. The local and diverse meaning structures of the small groups and the small community to which my family had traditionally belonged were lost. Our personal lives are the poorer, but so are our working and political lives. Aspects of life that were all of a piece now happen in compartments.

Bureaucracy and rural, Eastern-style community life are by no means mutually exclusive. There was no society on earth more bureaucratic than the Confucian Chinese, and much of this survives today. Just go through the rigors of applying for a Chinese visa! But as China observers note, the difference between Western bureaucracy and Chinese bureaucracy is that we take it seriously, whereas the Chinese have found a million ways around it. If the Chinese want to get something done, they ignore the local functionary and go instead to the best friend of a fifth cousin twice removed.

Despite the durability of overseas Chinese business networks, observers wonder whether Western-style compartmentalization might not be the fate awaiting them in the modern world. The networks work stunningly well on a local scale, but can they translate their formula to large and complex global markets? Can Confucian family traditions and unquestioned respect for the authority of elders allow sufficient upward mobility for the talented young and the challenging? Looking back to the brain's parallel thinking structures for a clue to answering such questions, I would think not. Neural networks can adapt sufficiently to recognize unfamiliar but existing patterns, but they cannot create new patterns. The ever-strengthening connections between neurons require the weight of habit, of repeated experience, that is, of familiarity. There is no place in a neural network for the maverick neuron that wants to experiment with some new sequence of firing. In consequence, the thinking generated by these networks is more inductive generalization than true insight. It doesn't give rise to new hypotheses or new paradigms like those found in the work of creative (maverick) geniuses like Copernicus, Beethoven, Nietzsche, or Edison.

Japanese companies have succeeded where Chinese networks may fail. There are countless instances of global Japanese corporations competing successfully in complex international markets. Indeed, they thrive on them. Yet the Japanese wavelike model of the self takes its toll on these companies as well. Decisions are taken (control exercised) not by dictatorial fiat, as in many of the Chinese family networks, but by consensus. That is the Japanese tradition. And consensus takes time. Consensus and concern with the good opinion of the group are also uncomfortable with difference, with the swashbuckling, maverick entrepreneur whose apparently mad ideas may bring about great leaps forward. Just as neural networks in the brain are best at small adaptations to existing structure, Japanese industry has made its fortune on clever adaptations of Western inventions. Even many of its successful management techniques were adaptations of Western ideas like those of W. Edwards Deming, where the Japanese genius was to see the applicability of something their more hidebound Western colleagues could not fit into the existing system. Their successful application of fuzzy logic was again a wise application to technology of a Western mathematical breakthrough that Western industry could not appreciate. It didn't fit the rules. But Japan still looks in vain for its own Bill Gates.

Western particle-like models of the self and Eastern wavelike models have thus given rise to quite different organizational structures, each with its own strengths and weaknesses. Like serial thinking structures in the brain, atomistic Western societies are individualist and rule-bound. They recognize a unique personal self, but regard it as isolated. The inevitability of conflict between so many independently functioning parts (individuals) is brought under control through formal rules and contracts, each of which has a universal quality—everyone is equal within the terms of the contract. Everyone has the same rights. A sharp division is made between the public and private aspects of the self, and organizational stability is assured through excluding the private, the turbulence of emotions and associations. Boundaries are rigid, and organizations try to organize only those qualities that are predictable and thus controllable. Leadership of such organizations is mechanistic-straightforward command and control backed up by the authority of the rules.

The wavelike models of the self that predominate in the East, like neural networks in the brain, envision the self as wholly embedded in relationship. The emphasis is not on how to control conflict but rather on how to achieve cooperation. Boundaries between individuals and between the public and private spheres of individual identity are ambiguous, elastic. Thus networked organizations are more adaptive, expanding and contracting their boundaries, evolving their strategies in slow, organic stages. Control, or stability, is maintained through reinforced familiarity, custom, tradition, and self-discipline. Leadership style varies from one Asian culture to another, but the underlying basis of leadership is tradition, and therefore consensus.

In the brain, the serial and parallel thinking structures perform very different functions. The logical, rule-bound serial structures are necessary for practical, goal-oriented thinking. They make it possible for us to do mental arithmetic, to plan journeys from a timetable, or to devise a budget. The associative physical and emotional parallel structures handle tacit knowledge, skills, and patterns. But like both Western bureaucracies and Chinese networks, both rely on stability. One is rule-bound, the other habit-bound. Both are weak at dealing with unexpected change. They seek to dampen down or to exclude the unexpected. And neither, on its own, is creative. Serial thinking works within an existing program; bureaucratic organizations work within the rules. Parallel thinking is reinforced through repeated experience. It recognizes existing patterns. Networked organizations rely on habit and tradition.

We have seen in earlier chapters that when our brain needs to rewire itself—when it needs to make a creative breakthrough, do some out-of-the-box thinking—a third kind of brain structure comes into play to integrate the other two. The brain's third kind of thinking suggests there may be available to us a third model of the self and a third model for organizational structures, a model that allows organizations to function at the creative edge. Based on quantum thinking, I want now to look at the quantum self and the quantum organization.

CHAPTER 8

THE QUANTUM MODEL: BRIDGING EAST AND WEST

The idea of a quantum self is a new model of the self derived from the characteristics of the new science, particularly those of quantum physics. I first introduced it twenty-five years ago in my book *The Quantum Self*. I believe this new model of self can transcend the divide between the classic Western and Eastern (or rural) models and can underpin a new theory of organization and leadership.

The nature of human consciousness and human creativity is at the cutting edge of scientific inquiry today. The majority of mainstream cognitive scientists still believe that both will ultimately be explained in mechanistic terms. We have, they say, a "mind machine" inside our heads. One day, they believe, we will have computing machines that can do anything we can do, probably better and faster. But there is another school of scientific thought that believes human consciousness can never be mimicked by machines. In principle, they say, mind is not machinelike. These scientists look for the origins of consciousness and creativity in brain processes not described by Newton's physics.

Many believe these more creative mental processes are quantum in origin, that quantum physics literally makes possible the characteristics of the human self—humor, grief, relationship, creativity, a sense of meaning, understanding, free will, loyalty, commitment, and so on. Personally, as I discussed at length in *The Quantum Self*, I back quantum theories of mind.[1] But these theories are still speculative, and we needn't wait for the scientific evidence to come in. It is sufficient for purposes of this book that all these interesting features of human thought and behavior are *quantum-like*. They function *as though* arising from quantum structures or processes in the brain, whatever their true foundation. As I mentioned in an earlier chapter, the new branch of cognitive science called "quantum cognition" has produced hundreds of research papers detailing the similarity between human thought processes and quantum mechanical processes. That is sufficient to support my goal here is to find a new conceptual structure for organizations.

So far, we have seen two diametrically opposed models of the self and their effect on organizations. The particle model of the self, so important to Western management theory, is modeled on Newtonian science. This Newtonian self, like the science that inspired it, is seen as atomistic, determined in its behavior, fragmented into separate parts circumscribed by rigid boundaries, and isolated from its environment. Newtonian organizations are rule-bound, exclude private, unpredictable aspects of the self, divide functions and structures, and they, too, are isolated from their environment. These organizations function very much like the brain's one-on-one like neural tracts, which give us logical, rational, rule-bound, how-to thinking. This is our "first kind of thinking." It gives us our "mental intelligence (IQ)."

The Eastern, wave model of the self, lying at the heart of networked Asian organizations (and small rural communities worldwide), is modeled on the complex patterns made by countless intersecting waves. Like waves, the networked self is seen as essentially relational and contextual. A person is his or her relationships. The boundaries of this self are elastic and ambiguous, and relationships between selves are governed by local custom, habit, and tradition. Networked organizations rely on personal contact and personal bonds, trust instead of rules. They make little or no distinction between the public and private spheres of life, are complex in structure, and they learn from and adapt to their environment through trial and error. Networked organizations function very similar to the brain's neural networks, which give us tacit knowledge and the ability to learn skills and to recognize patterns. This is our "second kind of thinking." It gives us our bodily "emotional intelligence (EQ)."

In the brain, as we have seen, logical (serial) thinking and networked (parallel) thinking are integrated through a third kind of neural function, synchronous neural oscillations binding different parts of the brain. These are 40 Hz oscillations, oscillating at forty cycles per second.[2] They are also known as "gamma waves." These enable our intuitive, insightful, creative, and reflective thinking, the kind of thinking with which we challenge our assumptions and change our mental models. The kind of thinking with which we radically rewire our brains. This third kind of thinking gives us our "spiritual intelligence (SQ)," our intelligence rooted in meaning, vision, and value. It allows us to use our whole brains. I have argued that organizations need it (need infrastructures that make it possible) to use their whole brains. We need it to rewire the corporate brain.

I've called our third kind of thinking quantum thinking because of its similarity to quantum processes. I want now to use the central features of quantum processes to discover features of a quantum self. Then we can discuss how to organize and lead quantum selves in a quantum organization.

FEATURES OF THE QUANTUM SELF

Quantum science and, indeed, all the new sciences describe a physical world that is holistic, indeterminate, or at least unpredictable, and self-organizing. Quantum systems are particle-like and wavelike at the same time; they have *both* individual *and* group properties. They are governed by the Uncertainty Principle, which thrives on ambiguity, yet when we focus on or measure them we can pin them down precisely (though only partially). Unlike isolated Newtonian systems, quantum systems are always in and part of each other and their environment; quantum observers are always part of what they observe. Quantum observers evoke, or cocreate, reality.

We human beings are physical systems, too, and fully part of the physical world. Our bodies, certainly, and most likely our minds, obey the same laws as everything else in this universe. At the moment, the best physics we have for describing this universe is quantum physics. "I," ultimately, am a quantum system. As such, my self should have the following qualities:

- The quantum self is both/and. It has both a unique, particle-like individual aspect and a shared, relational, wavelike group aspect. I am "me," my genes, my history, and my unique experience, but I am also all those others with whom I live and work and share experience and to whom I relate. Neither my private, individual self nor my public, relational self is more important or more primary. Both are just facts, and to be interesting and to be used for my own and my community's maximum benefit, they must be integrated. A quantum society or organization would have infrastructures that nourish both the private self and the public self, and which allow them to nourish each other.

- The quantum self is holistic and contextual. The wavelike, relational boundaries of the quantum self extend, in principle, across the universe. My self is interwoven with and defined by everything else that exists. I am in nature; nature is in me. I am a part of all others, and all others are a part of me. I am not just my brother's keeper. I am my brother. I am not just a natural system, but natural systems are affected by me, and I by them. My body is made out of stardust; my mind emerges in dialogue with the four forces of the universe and the laws that define them. It may be a further natural force. Even my particle-like inner boundaries change, adapt, and re-form in dialogue with my environment and my experience. As the new science of epigenetics has shown, my genes themselves are active or inactive in different environments. My self is integrated and dynamic, each part, each sub-self or sub-personality, affected by and affecting every other. "I" am a whole chorus of conversations in harmony.

- The quantum self is self-organizing. It is at the edge, poised precariously and yet creatively between order and chaos. The quantum self has no hard limits, no set, definable boundaries. It has constraints (such as the force of habit), but it is not determined. It has a genetic code, but this is always choosing what parts of itself to express. It has a character, but this is always being molded. The quantum self is always reinventing itself, always rewiring its brain. "I" am a dynamic pattern, an open, dynamic system, a whirlpool. I have no soul in the sense of some little box inside me or some discrete part of my brain that can be registered on a CAT or a PET scan. My soul is a continually self-organizing process, a channel between me and the ground state of reality. It is expressed through all of me, through my thoughts, my emotions, my bodily feelings, and my body language. All of me and all of my experience has a soulful, a sacred, dimension. This includes my work experience.

- The quantum self is free. It is constrained but not determined by any genetic material, by any past experience, by any environmental conditions or conditioning, or by any given neural wiring in its brain. The quantum self's boundaries are elastic and in flux, subject to a creative uncertainty. Its neural connections are constantly being rejigged and rewired anew. The quantum self is an active agent in the world, not a passive victim. It is a self that chooses, and through its choices it chooses itself and its environment. It makes the world.

- The quantum self is responsible. It is in and part of the world with which it interacts. The quantum self lives in a participatory universe, and it actively participates in the unfolding of that universe. It is an active agent of reality, a cocreator of the world in which it lives. The questions that I ask, the thoughts that I think, the emotions and fantasies that I harbor, the decisions that I make, and the actions I take mold the world and others around me. I am a stone dropped into a pond that sends ripples outward in every direction. I am the world. If that world is to be a different place, it is because I will make it different. If something needs to be created, I must act as a midwife to its creation. The buck stops here.

- The quantum self is a *questioning* self. Heisenberg's Uncertainty Principle shows us that the questions we ask give us the answers that we get. The questions *cocreate* the answers. It questions the rules, questions the boundaries, and it questions its own assumptions and mental models. The quantum self is like the fish that jumps above the fishbowl and has the greater perspective to see where it's come from. This "meta-perspective" on its own thinking processes and assumptions is the secret of its creative and transformative edge.

- The quantum self is spiritual. It is steeped in meaning, vision, and value. The quantum self is an excitation of the underlying quantum vacuum, a ripple on the pond that represents the ground state of reality. The quantum vacuum is the soul of the universe, the "mind of God," and each quantum self is a thought in the mind of God. Each self represents one of nature's, or God's, potentialities, one of the many of the unfolding universe's infinite paths from A to B. I have a destiny, a necessity to ask questions of meaning about my path and a need to be driven by meaning. I am fated always to ask, "Why?" and "What for?" And, "Couldn't it be otherwise?" and to seek and to create answers.

These are the features of the self that a quantum organization must nourish and harness. These are the needs and potentialities for which there must be corporate infrastructures in any organization that wants to use all of its human potential and all of its brain. Indeed, as we shall see, in some fashion or other these qualities of the quantum self are qualities that a quantum organization must itself possess.

EIGHT FEATURES OF A QUANTUM ORGANIZATION

In Chapter Four, I applied eight principles of the new science to leadership. I think those same principles can give us the basic thinking we need to see the most important characteristics of a quantum organization. Each organizational feature also suggests infrastructures that can employ the full potentialities of the quantum self and of quantum thinking. These are infrastructures that should assist flexible and creative adaptation to new global, societal, and market potentialities and enable organizations to thrive on ambiguity and rapid change. Let's briefly review the eight main features of the new science, and apply them to organizations.

1. The new science is holistic. The whole organizes the parts and every part is related to and partially defined through every other part. In quantum physics, relationship helps to create further facts, new realities. Events always happen in a context.

   - *The quantum organization is holistic.* Most large corporate organizations now find themselves in a global context. Even more local ones realize that small shifts within local markets or local societies are felt throughout the world. Stock market jitters in Tokyo are reflected in London and New York within hours. Drought conditions in one South American country affect coffee prices worldwide. The manufacturing processes of individual industries depend upon environmental conditions and natural resources. In turn they have a direct and lasting effect on the global environment. The success or failure of any one company depends upon the activities, successes, and failures of other companies, never mind those of political systems and national economies. The corrupt behavior of a few corporate individuals can ruin millions of lives and destabilize international institutions. We saw this with the 2008 global financial crisis.[3]

     Mechanistic notions that the corporate world consists of isolated units each ruthlessly pursuing its own self-interest cannot cope with this interlinkage. Neither can a model of the individual corporation that divides itself into isolated divisions and functions set to compete against each other. Cobbled together out of separate, uncoordinated parts and yet impinged upon from every direction, mechanistic systems have become unwieldy and unstable. Old models of conflict and confrontation must give way to new models of dynamic integration. These must protect the integrity of individual concerns while drawing them into a larger working whole.

     The quantum organization will have infrastructures that encourage and build on relationships, relationships between leaders and employees, between employees and their colleagues, between divisions and functional groups, between structures themselves. It will also be aware of its environmental context, human, corporate, societal, and ecological, and will build infrastructures that encourage exchange and dialogue with these. Nothing is really too far afield to be outside the corporate brief.

2. Quantum and complex systems are indeterminate or at least unpredictable. They are poised at the edge between order and chaos, between particle-like states and wavelike states, between actuality and potentiality. Their indeterminacy makes them flexible, ready to evolve in any direction.

- *The quantum organization must be flexible and responsive, at the edge.* Ambiguity, complexity, and rapid change increasingly dominate events both inside and outside the corporation. The corporate environment is evolving—and so must the corporation. Shifting boundaries of responsibility and identity, experimental modes of living and working, new information sources and new technological systems all demand flexible response. Mechanistic patterns of fixed functional or individual roles and rigidly organized structures for management and control inhibit the potential latent in human response, imagination, and organization.

  The infrastructures of a quantum organization should be like a blend of waves and particles. They should be like movable walls, like the Volvo car-building team with desks on wheels.[4] They can rest in one place when needed, but can also move. Quantum infrastructures should be less like constructions made out of Meccano or even Lego and more like plasticine, which can take any shape and be changed at will. Quantum infrastructures can adapt to the shifting and sometimes contradictory needs of individuals and teams, the corporate need to be sometimes mechanistic and sometimes organic, the complementary and sometimes conflicting need to be both local and global, both competitive and cooperative.

3. The new science is emergent and self-organizing. The newly emer-

gent whole constructed through relationship is always greater than the sum of its parts. Chaotic and quantum systems are creative, always generating surprise and increased complexity. They ensure sustainability by the constant mining of potentiality.

- *The quantum organization must be bottom-up, self-organizing, and emergent.* There is the potentiality for something deeply radical in new corporate thinking. We have seen the limitations of heavy, top-down hierarchies and structures of control imposed by theory, tradition, or boardroom authority. They are inflexible in the face of change and waste the creative, spontaneous resources of the quantum self.

    The infrastructures of the quantum organization must nourish human and organizational creativity. They must enhance inner mobility and personal responsibility and facilitate the free flow of information and ideas. There must be spaces in the organization without boundaries, relationships without fear. The parts (whether individuals, teams, functions, or divisions) must be free to rearrange themselves. Some decision-making must be relocated among front-line workers and front-line managers. (As a Volvo manager told me, "We didn't know what we would get from the teams until we had the teams. But they worked!"[5])

4. The new science is both/and rather than either/or. Matter consists of waves and particles, and has the potentialities of each. Quantum systems follow many paths from A to B; adaptive evolution proceeds through multiple mutation.

    - *The quantum organization will thrive on diversity.* The old vision of one truth, one way, one expression of reality, one best way of doing things, the either/or of absolute, unambiguous choice must give way to a plural way of accommodating the multiplicities and diversities of societies, markets, and individuals. Either/or must make way for both/and. "My way" must give way to shared vision, shared opportunity, and shared responsibility that recognize the validity of many paths from A to B. As

Einstein said, there are as many perspectives on the universe as there are observers, and each adds something.

A quantum organization will have infrastructures that mix levels of responsibility, adapt to assorted educational, professional, and functional backgrounds, and decentralize power and decision-making—infrastructures that really do "let a thousand flowers bloom" and never bring out the pruning shears of ideological purity. Diversity will not be imposed through mechanistic, politically correct appointments and directives, but through infrastructures that create a climate of dialogue.

And a quantum organization will have *both* structure and the free-flowing lack of it, *both* some directive organization from "the top" and the freedom of bottom-up self-organization.

5. Heisenberg's Uncertainty Principle tells us that when we interfere with a quantum system, we change it. When we structure an experiment, we influence the results. The questions we ask partially determine the answers we get.

- *A quantum organization would be like a jazz jam session.* In a symphony orchestra, each player concentrates on one instrument and one segment of the score, and the conductor constructs the whole out of these parts. Conductors' interpretations differ, and thus so can the sound of an identical symphony played by different orchestras, but the whole is always the sum of its parts, and the essential score doesn't change. In a jazz jam session, players are often expert at different instruments, and there is no set score and no conductor. There is an evolving background theme, an emergent whole that organizes the parts, but the composite sound is always a surprise.

  Newtonian companies create roles and sell products. Both roles and products are like a musical score that constrains production and dictates infrastructures. Goal-directed thinking, if successful, achieves its goal but seldom anything more. Managers or consultants who assign tasks, if successful, get those tasks performed, but never know what else individuals or the organization *might* have achieved. A quantum organization would create infrastructures where different questions can be asked, different goals considered, different products or functions imagined. Roles would be less fixed, employees encouraged to play different instruments and to experiment with the score. Quantum leaders would see themselves as holding the space where the background theme can emerge. They would set the vision and embody it through their person. Quantum selves are designed to thrive at the edge. A quantum organization would have some infrastructures that allow the free play of uncertainty.

6. The new science has discovered that much that is interesting or valuable or creative about systems lies beyond the present moment, beyond our immediate grasp, and is waiting to unfold. Complex patterns called strange attractors lie sleeping within chaos. The goal toward which a quantum system evolves has yet to emerge. Both quantum and chaos science are about potentiality more than actuality, about the what *might* be rather than the what *is*. The new science dares to dream. It is *playful*.

   - *A quantum organization would be playful.* Our tightly structured, results-oriented organizations are so serious, so frightened of failure. They want successes they can measure, successes they can predict. But neither nature nor children learn that way. Nature evolves through making lots of mistakes. Most mutations are a mess. Ninety-nine percent of all species that have existed no longer exist. Nonlinear systems have to run through chaos before breaking through to complexity. Children play and learn by making mistakes. They take risks, but they don't even see them as such. When a young child builds a tower of bricks and it falls down, the child laughs with delight. Not because children love destruction, but because the child has learned something from the catastrophe. The next tower will benefit, and so will the child's brain. That's how it wires itself. When asked why he had so many creative ideas, the twice

Nobel Prize–winning scientist Linus Pauling replied, "Oh, I just have a lot of ideas, and throw away the bad ones."[6]

A quantum organization would have infrastructures that encourage play and reward structures that recognize the value of taking risks. It might offer awards for the wildest idea or the most creative mistake of the week. It would recognize the value of wasted time or unstructured time, of nondirective conversations, of long lunches and faces gazing into space, of dream time.

7. Quantum physics describes a participatory universe. The observer is part of the observed reality. The observer is a cocreator who helps to make that reality happen.

- A quantum organization would be "deeply green." Ecologists recognize a difference between normal ecology and "deep ecology." Normal ecology worries about the earth's natural environment. Deep ecology interests itself in the earth as a total system, a system with a human, meaning-centered dimension that is in symbiosis with its nonhuman but life-centered dimension. A quantum organization would be deeply ecological about its environment. It would be concerned with its human environments, internal and external, and with its societal, cultural, and natural environments. Mechanism assumes a sharp dichotomy between human beings and the rest of creation, between culture and nature. Newtonian organizations use their environment; they exploit their resources, both human and natural. The quantum vision is different.

  Just as the quantum self is in nature, and nature is in the quantum self, a quantum organization lives and breathes its environment. It is in and of its environment. It accepts responsibility for its own co-creation of that environment—for the co-creation of its people, its surrounding society, the global community and global values, and the earth's environment. Quantum organizations would consider the importance of "deeply green" questions: What is work for? Do individuals exist to serve corporations and economies, or do corporations and economies exist to serve individuals? Business leaders are world leaders. And quantum leaders know that they make the world they live in.

8. Quantum field theory tells us that every existing thing is an excitation of the quantum vacuum. That is, it tells us that every existing thing is but one actual expression of the universe's manifold, infinitely unfolding potentiality. The quantum vacuum is the vision at the heart of the universe, and existing things exist to give birth to aspects of that vision.

- *A quantum organization will be vision-centered and value-driven.* A Newtonian organization sells products. It does its best to meet present demand or to manipulate demand, to manipulate public and market taste to want its products. It tries to create situations of scarcity, situations of discontent. It feeds on modern society's illusion that personal and spiritual emptiness can be filled with a *thing*. Often the market fails or ceases to respond. The customers become bored or jaded; the company that has tried to satisfy them fails.

  A quantum organization would recognize that people seek meaning, that we transcend our frustrations and our limitations with dreams. Living systems are evolutionary systems, always reaching beyond themselves to new possibility. Customers want to envision new possibilities, dreams, and meaning. A quantum organization would seek to give its customers possibilities, dreams, and meaning. Not cynically, like the worst of the ad men, but genuinely because the leaders of quantum organizations are themselves driven by deep vision and a need for meaning. (They are *servant leaders*!) Such leaders encourage infrastructures that bring the private, meaning-centered side of their own and their employees' lives together with the public, work-centered and goal-oriented sides.

  Coca-Cola has been selling much the same product for nearly a century. McDonalds hamburgers are the same in every city and every culture. But neither company is really selling consumable items. Both are selling dreams. Coca-Cola used to sell the dream of the stable American family of the 1950s, with all its members secure in their roles and material prosperity. Today Coca-Cola sells wind in your hair and rain on your face, raw sensuality, the feeling of being at the edge. McDonalds sells the American way of life for each culture to interpret in its own way. Virgin sells youth and iconoclasm. British Telecom sells the easy of communication. Volvo sells Scandinavian solidity more than cars.

Dreams and visions can evolve in dialogue with the culture. They can adapt to needs and aspirations. Or they can tap deeply into those levels of human meaning and value that transcend culture and the aspirations of the moment. An organization that can channel these can both creatively adapt to and cocreate taste and need.

Many of the qualities I have listed in the preceding pages as features of a quantum organization are familiar. Business change agents have been talking about some of them for years. But they seldom come about. I hope that by describing them within the context of the coherent conceptual framework offered by the new science, they take on some added power to shift corporate thinking.

PRACTICING QUANTUM INSIGHT

I don't know of any perfect, existing quantum organizations. Perhaps they are an idea, an archetype, or an ideal toward which we can strive and through which we might improve on the present state of things. But there are some well-known organizations that have definite quantum features, organizations that have incorporated (sometimes consciously, sometimes not) quantum insights in their infrastructures and styles of leadership. Throughout this book I have referred to the Marks & Spencer example. Here, I want briefly to discuss two others.

West	East
Conflict and control	Cooperation
Self (the personal) wholly excluded and isolated; interactions grounded in universal principles	Self (the personal) wholly embedded and contextual; no universal principles
Stability achieved through excluding the self and the emotions, and organizing only the predictable and controllable aspects of relationships	Stability achieved through reinforced familiarity and discipline of the self
Rigid boundaries	Ambiguous boundaries
Dictatorial leadership	Consensual leadership
Rule-bound	Habit-bound
Mechanical	Organic

Both
Rely on stability
Weak in dealing with unexpected change
Seek to dampen down or exclude the unexpected

Table 6. Self and Organization, West and East

Volvo's Car-Making Teams

I discussed these Volvo teams a bit in Chapter Four. They were an experiment in response to a challenge.

Volvo production lines had for years been turning out cars that looked similar externally, but internally were very different. Few components were universal. This situation kept production costs high and limited market appeal. The ideal, the company came to feel, would be just the opposite, to produce a wide range of cars that looked different externally, but shared many internal components. They felt that getting engineers from different functions to work on teams would be the answer.[7]

The mechanistic work model that Volvo earlier considered was hierarchical and highly structured. Assign people to different groups, give each group a clear task and clear set of boundaries, and have all the groups supervised from above as in Figure 7. This model assumed the company already knew the detailed need for outcome from each group.

Volvo's Hierarchical Model

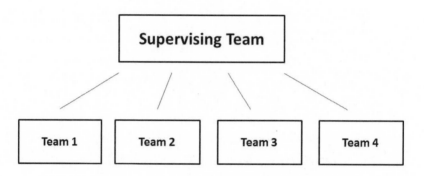

Figure 7. Volvo's Original Hierarchical Model

After exploring both internal and external experiences, doing some reading on quantum physics and other new science theories, and reflecting on the unstructured or loosely structured nature of companies being run successfully by what some Volvo executives call the "Nintendo generation,"[8] the management had a learning breakthrough. They saw the learning and evolutionary value of uncertainty, of saying "I don't know," of taking risks, and they wanted to design infrastructures that could support these. The first step was envisioning a new learning model and beginning action on a small scale, as illustrated in Figure 8.

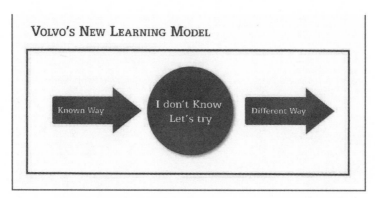

Figure 8. Volvo's New Quantum Learning Model

With this learning model in mind, those with the task of designing the new teams drew what they privately refer to as "some quantum circles."[9] They conceived twelve team modules, one for each of twelve crucial design features—chassis, seats, steering, and so on of their various models. Engineers who once worked on different models within different functions, and who thus had a loyalty to diverse components, were now out together on teams and asked to conceive universal components. Smaller teams were formed within the twelve larger teams, and members of both large and small teams were given the freedom to move from one circle or sub-circle to another. As I said earlier, even parts of their desks were put on wheels. No supervisory head team directed the various teams. Instead, a team of managers kept the various working together teams together by ensuring communication and a common overall vision of goals and concepts. The whole thing—sketched in Figure 9—is dynamic and self-organizing. And it works.

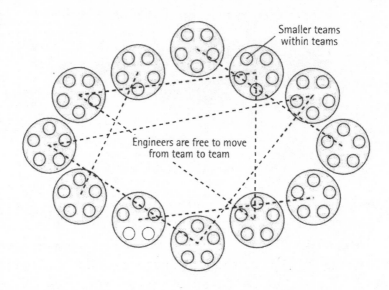

Smaller teams
within teams

Engineers are free to move
from team to team

Figure 9. The Volvo Circles of Circles within Circles

Visa's Federalism

Dee Hock used to be a vice president at a Seattle bank that licensed BankAmericard, one of the world's earliest credit cards. BankAmericard was successful at first, but an ensuing credit card orgy driven by competing banks led to financial chaos. Bank of America held a crisis meeting of its licensees, the result of which was a committee set up to find a better model. Dee Hock was made chairman of the committee, and both the method he conceived for arriving at a new model and many features of that new model itself are quantum. They were inspired by the new science, by chaos theory and biological systems. Hock was fascinated by these concepts, and he wrote and spoke prolifically about the development of Visa and their effect on it. The information and quotes cited here appeared in the October-November 1996 issue of *Fast Company* magazine, "The Trillion Dollar Vision of Dee Hock," by M. Mitchell Waldrop.[10]

Hock felt the first step toward developing a new credit card model had to be vision, getting the vision right. "Unless we can define a purpose for this organization that we can believe in, we might as well go home. . . . Far better than a precise plan is a dear sense of direction and compelling beliefs. And that lies within you. The question is, how do you evoke it?" His committee spent over a year just on this issue. Any company that Hock has touched since must go through a similar initial and prolonged dialogue phase. (See Chapter Twelve.) As MIT's Peter Senge described it, Hock used that period of dialogue to "blow up the whole organization, dissolving power relationships, everything."

In conceiving Visa, Hock felt that there had to be a working balance between competition and cooperation. The new credit card would be issued globally by myriad local banks, each of which would want to serve its own customers with competitive terms and conditions. At the same time, the card had to be a global currency, with certain universal features available only through cooperation. I call this giving the organization particle-like (local) and wavelike (universal) features. Dee Hock calls it "chaordic," poised between chaos (competition) and order (cooperation).

Hock wanted the Visa organization to be "invisible," its structures so flexible that no one could "tell who owns it, where it's headquartered, how it's governed, or where to buy shares." He conceived a nonhierarchical, bottom-up power structure modeled on the American federal system. As M. Mitchell Waldrop describes it in *Fast Company* magazine,

> The organization must be adaptable and responsive to changing conditions, while preserving overall cohesion and unity of purpose. . . . The governing structure must not be a chain of command, but rather a framework for dialogue, deliberation, and coordination among equals. Authority, in other words, comes from the bottom up, not the top down. The US federal system is designed so authority rises from the people to local, state and federal governments; in Visa, which contains elements of the federal system, the member banks send representatives to a system of national, regional and international boards. While the system appears to be hierarchical, the Visa hierarchy is not a chain of command. Instead, each board is supposed to serve as a forum for

members to raise common issues, debate them, and reach some kind of consensus and resolution.

In the language of this book, that is a quantum vision of the networked organization.

CHAPTER 9

QUANTUM CASE STUDY: HAIER GROUP, CHINA

"The answer is to overturn all that was once believed reasonable and rational."

—Zhang Ruimin, CEO, Haier Group, China

Zhang Ruimin was in high school during the Chinese Cultural Revolution. He was sent to work in a factory and eventually became a supervisor. "I saw many employees in the factory who had good ideas, but they were discouraged or reprimanded for thinking for themselves. Eventually they just stopped thinking and did what they were told. I vowed that one day I would lead a company where people were encouraged to think and innovate."[1] Today Zhang is CEO of the Haier Group, known globally as one of the most radical and inspiring companies in the world. Zhang is known in China as "the philosopher CEO" (he is said to read two books a week), but the love and respect bordering on reverence that his employees feel for him might almost merit the title, "the guru CEO." He is certainly one of the world's most interesting and innovative CEOs.

Many people reading the outline of this book, or hearing me speak about quantum leadership in my public lectures to business audiences, have said they find the ideas I set out exciting and inspiring, but they doubted such ideas could ever be implemented on a large corporate scale. It is widely recognized that several small start-ups, especially Silicon Valley start-ups, have begun with the kind of radical management thinking I advocate, but as they grew larger, they morphed into traditional, Western management structures. In this case study, I want to offer a detailed portrait of the leadership philosophy, company culture, and management structure of a company that has implemented its radical philosophy on a large scale, with considerable success. (Though there are still problems, as I will highlight later.)

Haier began as a provincial Chinese fridge manufacturer but now operates worldwide, with 60,000 full-time employees and many more "online staff" who are not employed but provide services through one of Haier's many platforms. Haier is now one of the largest white goods manufacturers in the world, supplying the largest share of the world's market for domestic appliances.[2] Since its transformation experiment into a would-be quantum company under the leadership of CEO Zhang Ruimin, Haier has excited the interest and attention of several Western business leaders, business school professors, and business magazines for its "radical, innovative management style."

In late June 2015, I was invited to visit Haier's global headquarters in Xingdao. I spent three hours in a one-on-one personal discussion with CEO Zhang, interviewed several of the new independent business unit leaders, met with senior managers of the strategy department, and addressed 300 of Haier's top leadership cadre. The visit was one of my greatest learning experiences.

At the beginning of our personal meeting, Zhang said to me, "This is the century of quantum management. All the old management theories went out of date in the last century. Western management looks to me like *quantified* management rather than *quantum* management."[3] From my conversation with him and other Haier leaders and employees, I could see that Haier has *implemented*, in its philosophy and actual company structure, many of the ideas that I suggest in this book. Zhang told me that it was his reading of my books and familiarity with my quantum management theories that had inspired his company transformation program.

Haier's philosophy is that every employee is a leader, every employee a potential entrepreneur. Quoting the ancient Taoist philosopher Chang Tzu, Zhang says, "No matter how much power or ideas a leader has, he cannot compete with 10,000." Zhang often quotes from the Chinese classics, his favorite works being the *Tao Te Ching*, the *I Ching*, Sun Tzu's *The Art of War*, and the works of Confucius.[4]

"There are no bosses at Haier," adds the head of one business unit.

"The customer is boss."[5] The company culture supports this with an active encouragement for all employees to think for themselves, for them always to lead with questions and experimentation, by nurturing the transformation from employee to entrepreneur. The Haier term for this is the cultivation of a "Maker Culture." Every employee is a "Maker." This is a corporate (partial) implementation of the quantum principle of a "participatory universe" in which every observer cocreates reality and takes responsibility for the world.

In addition to a culture of questions and experimentation, Haier *tries* to cultivate a culture of humility and service. The Haier culture can to some extent be described as a "Servant Leader culture" driven by the first five of the positive motivations described in Chapter Eleven of this book: exploration, cooperation, situational mastery, personal mastery, and service. Haier's service is to the customer, through its constant and varied communication with customer needs; the employee, through its ambition to turn every employee into an entrepreneur/maker; the community, through its wide and ambitious community training programs and community stores that function as package delivery posts; to the planet, through its Green Energy initiative; and to future generations, through its Project Hope program to build and equip new schools in poor rural areas of China.[6]

In its actual structure, Haier has done away with the traditional pyramid structure of power from the top filtering down through the ranks of middle managers to employees. In its place, it has created a platform structure. Senior leaders have become platform leaders, and middle managers have been turned into independent entrepreneurs running their own small business units, each of which deals directly with its own customers in sensing the need for and providing boutique products directly to those customers. This is in keeping with Zhang's dictum, "Never follow one way." No customer need, no matter how seemingly unlikely, is ignored. In one famous example, rural farmers complained to their Haier service contact that, when they washed potatoes in their Haier washing machines, the machines clogged up with dirt and ceased to work. Instead of replying that washing machines were never meant to wash potatoes, the business unit responsible referred the problem to the designers at R and D. The result was production of a machine that would wash both vegetables and clothes. The independent citizen who invented the part that made this dual action possible and suggested it to Haier has earned over RMB 250,000 in royalties from Haier.

A platform manager in the company will serve the needs of independent, self-organizing business unit teams within a market sector such as cleaning or kitchen devices, helping to develop a business plan, connect with R and D, and access venture capital. Other platform managers support business units whose "customers" are internal—other business units needing manufacturing, supply chain, IT or legal services. Each business unit, in turn, has anywhere from five to nine team members, and is headed by its own CEO. "Why so small?" asks Zhang. "In theory, the connectivity of a ten-man company is the square of ten. If there are one hundred people in a micro-organization, the connectivity will be too large to handle." The individual business units do their own market research through personal customer contacts and develop their own products. Zhang calls the units "self-organizing micro-ecologies" because, like quantum self-organizing systems, "they are in dialogue with the external world." The business units make and keep their own profit, while at the same time benefiting the company as a whole, which can own shares in individual business units in return for venture capital, and which collects fees for the use of services such as IT systems.

Haier's proliferation of independent business units are like "quantum feelers towards the future (*virtual transitions*)," each exploring and mining the potentiality latent within an infinite field of customer needs. Inspired by Heisenberg's Uncertainty Principle, Zhang calls them "energy balls," systems that display a different potentiality in response to each different situation. Unlike most traditional companies that invest the bulk of their resources in a single product or product range and then suffer a sharp drop in profits or market expansion when demand is exhausted or levels out, the Haier business units are constantly reinventing the future. "One of the biggest things that differentiates Haier from other companies," says Zhang Ruimin, "is our ability to remake and overhaul ourselves. Many companies' ways of thinking and operating have ossified and become hard to change, especially their organizational structures. At Haier we can make quick changes." This constant reinvention contributes to Haier's ongoing sustainability and constant expansion that thrive on the uncertainty and rapid change of market requirements and new technology. They thrive at "the edge of chaos."

Crucially for constant exploration and experimentation, the independent business units are allowed to fail. "In the beginning," says Zhang, "we told our employees in the self-organizing business units it wasn't a big deal if they failed, that it was meant to be a process of trial and error." If a business unit does fail, the team dissolves and the members return to the pool of talent available to re-form around other new ideas.

Haier's culture of innovation and Makers does not stop at the borders of the company itself. Indeed, Zhang believes in a "borderless world," and in consequence the Haier company has no borders. New ideas or essential support services may come from outside the company. In this sense, it is an example of quantum holism and entanglement in action.

"Haier serves as a platform for any member of the community who has an entrepreneurial idea or service relating in any way to enhancing the value or quality of any Haier product," Vice President Diao Yunfeng told me. "So *anybody* can be an employee or designer for Haier." Following a principle made familiar in the West by companies like Uber and Airbnb, Haier's transport and distribution platform services 60,000 delivery trucks owned by individual drivers who earn money by delivering goods to their customer destinations. The platform is open to companies other than Haier, so even rivals' goods are delivered by these drivers, who can take advantage of this "superposition of opportunities" (the platform's algorithms will even calculate efficient routes for multiple delivery demands). As in the case of the washing machine that now washes vegetables as well as clothes, any member of the public can submit an invention to Haier or develop a business idea using the company's platform. This extends to cooperation with other companies, even competitors.

"This borderless philosophy has meant opening up many areas that were previously closed off or untouchable," explains Zhang. "For example, when dealing with new patents in the past, new technologies and products were kept strictly confidential until the products were unveiled. Nowadays, we make users and even competitors part of the R and D process. For example, in the research and development of the Haier 'cordless home appliance,' we invited industry competitors from across the globe to participate."

In describing Haier's radical transformation from traditional company to a culture of Makers, and the transformation of his own role as a traditional CEO at the head of a pyramidal power structure to the servant of his employees, Zhang sums up the philosophy that is helping to make Haier a quantum company:

> What does it take to transform from executor to head of a team of entrepreneurial Makers? What do they want? What kind of freedom do they need to achieve this? In answering these questions, we have signed away three major rights, namely the decision-making right, HR rights, and distribution rights. I think, no matter how great the company is, it boils down to these three rights of management. With these rights signed away, what will remain in the hand of management? Only the right to serve.

HAIER'S FUTURE DEVELOPMENT

Zhang's structural transformation has taken Haier a long way toward becoming the quantum company he envisions. In the following ways, the Haier system accords with the basic principles of Quantum System Dynamics:

> The Haier system is designed to thrive on uncertainty, rapid change, and unpredictability;
> The system consists of a collection of self-organizing, non-hierarchical networks;
> Power emanates from many interacting centers and from the periphery;

The system celebrates many points of view and many ways of getting
   things done;
System structures are flexible, with hands-off supervision;
The whole system is bottom-up experimental, and entrepreneurial;

But in some important ways, these quantum features of the company's new organization have created the danger of a fragmented
company culture. This could explain outside criticisms that the platform
structure is inefficient, and may be a contributing factor in Haier's current
market struggles.[7] I firmly believe that we cannot achieve successful
structural transformation without an accompanying, compatible cultural
transformation. At the present time, Haier is a company with a quantum
structure, but it can do more to move beyond a Newtonian culture.

Quantum management stresses the importance of cooperation over
competition, but in the new Haier structure the individual business units
are motivated by their own success more than that of Haier as a whole.
When a would-be leader of a new business unit is developing the idea,
the platform manager brings together other business units within that
market sector to help put in place the new business plan. But once the
plan is good enough to secure initial funding and the new CEO recruits
a team, they become the unit of success or failure. The performance of
other business units will not affect their financial success and reputation.
This fragments collective creativity and discourages the cross-fertilization
of ideas. Quantum thinking teaches us that the whole is greater than the
sum of the parts. With its approximately 300 independent business units
each going its own way, there is a danger that Haier could be a collection
of parts without a strong enough sense of the whole.

Quantum systems are superpositions of multiple potentialities, many
possible paths from A to B, but, crucially, all these potentialities are
entangled. They interact with each other, and it is this existential dialogue
that leads to creative evolution. The separate Haier business units are not
"entangled." What could Haier do to encourage a shared company "conversation," or spirit of dialogue between the fragmented business units?
Zhang Ruimin himself does meet each week with a selection of twenty or

thirty business unit heads, but more could be done to encourage dialogue groups or even cultural dialogue opportunities where people from the individual units meet each other and share ideas. Facilitating dialogue is itself a valuable service, and Haier could benefit from a platform manager focused on serving this need among the independent business units.

A perennial buzz phrase in Silicon Valley is to speak of a "water-cooler culture." This idea was inspired by the earlier-mentioned study done several years ago at Xerox to see how the company engineers spent their working time and what habits were most effective. An anthropologist hired to accompany a Time and Motion expert noticed that, when gathered around the company's coffee breaks for short breaks, engineers swapped ideas and shared useful shortcuts they had discovered. The apparent "timeouts" at the coffee breaks, we saw, actually boosted the effective use of time and enhanced shared creativity.[8] Today, Silicon Valley companies break down silos with "hackathons," bringing together a diverse group of employees to tackle a specific problem during an intensive period of collaboration (which usually involves ordering in take-away food and staying up all night). There may be no direct cultural equivalent for the coffee breaks in Chinese companies, and all-night, intensive problem-solving sessions may work better for coding software than for developing a new domestic appliance, but Haier could do more to encourage social and professional mingling between members of the separate business units.

Ironically, Haier's strong new "Maker culture," where every employee is encouraged to be a maker and a leader, is also in danger of creating a selfish culture where everyone is just "on the make." "There are a lot of egos here. People are too much out for themselves," one platform manager complained to me. "Everyone just wants to get the best that he can for himself."[9] There is a strong culture of service to the customer, but not a culture of service to each other or to the wider company as a whole. No culture of giving oneself for the whole and for the best of what only the whole can offer.

Self-interest is a negative motivation, and as we shall see in Chapter Eleven, nothing good can ever come from negative motivation. Furthering creative motivation is a worry at Haier. "One of our great problems," a company vice president told me, "is motivating further creativity in the business units once they've had their one good idea."[10] More cross-fertilization of ideas would serve that need, but that would require a company conversation and a company culture driven by higher vision and values that are not currently as evident as might be desirable at Haier. There is, to be sure, a strong culture of personal creativity, but little vision of shared creativity or a service ethic about how shared creativity might serve the company as a whole, and beyond that, wider society and future generations.

Zhang Ruimin himself is a remarkable man revered for his strong personal vision and values. Service to others and to the wider community is one of his driving ideals. He is a leader who does "walk the talk," and at the moment his personal example inspires a love for him that creates a sense of cultural unity in the company as a whole. But Zhang is in his midsixties, and he won't be leading Haier forever. Only a vibrant and unified company culture driven by co-creative internal dialogue, a shared sense of belonging to something larger than one's own self-interest, and a passion for service that matches its unmistakable passion for personal creativity will sustain the company's current success under the leadership of a less charismatic CEO. Haier today is a quantum company in the making, but there is more work to be done.

PART III

QSD:
QUANTUM SYSTEMS/
STRATEGY DYNAMICS

CHAPTER 10

QUANTUM SYSTEMS DYNAMICS

I argued at the very beginning that the central assumption of this book is that many organizational systems are broken or face challenges they do not know how to meet. And I argued that I believe all the problems or challenges confronting organizations are problems or challenges of thought. If leaders could change their thinking, they could change themselves and fix their organizations.

Organizations are systems made up of human beings, who have not only thoughts but also have purposes, motives, values, and biases. All these things impinge on the nature and content of our thinking. And like human beings, corporate/organizational systems have "brains." It is through its brain that a corporation organizes itself internally and also how it interacts with information, demands, and opportunities in the outside environment. My mission has been to help leaders rewire their own and their organization's brain. The name that my colleague Chris Wray and I have given to the whole body of work devoted to this end is Quantum Systems Dynamics and Quantum Strategy Dynamics. This follows from our conviction that both human organizational systems and human thought processes mirror the systems and processes described by quantum mechanics.

Quantum Systems Dynamics considers in detail the working elements of a human system, the nature of a specifically human system, and seeks to identify the most effective intervention strategies for getting the system to operate in the most productive and sustainable way possible. Quantum Strategy Dynamics considers the brain as a system of thought processes and seeks to identify the most effective intervention points for getting an individual leader or team within an organization to reframe situations and problems and thus to make effective decisions.

At the purely simple scientific level, of course, human beings are biological systems, or living systems. But science today understands that living systems are very special systems, with quite unique qualities that distinguish them from most nonliving systems. If we want to understand best how to work with human systems, we need to look at the latest science that describes all living systems. This takes us into the realms of complexity theory and the complex adaptive systems that it describes.

In the 1960s, science moved away from its obsession with the simple to a celebration of the complex. Newtonian scientific theory describes systems that are simple. Such systems are linear, predictable, controllable, isolated, and consist of separate working parts into which the system can be broken down for analysis. The whole is just the sum of its parts. Newtonian systems models have been, and in many cases still are, applied to human systems like the market or business organizations. Without realizing it, most companies are still using simple, Newtonian business models, often with disastrous consequences.

In addition to simple Newtonian systems, two other kinds of classical systems have come to be understood. These are "complex systems" and "simple adaptive systems." Unlike a simple system, a complex system has many parts, and these interact. To understand the system, we have to understand these interactions—like the many parts that go to make up an automobile and the way their interaction gives rise to motion. Such mechanical complex systems are nonadaptive—they do not learn, do not evolve. The individual component parts of the systems do not alter through their interaction with each other or with the environment. Unfortunately, most "systems thinking" in the corporate world is modeled on these kinds of nonadaptive systems. That is why the usual brand of systems thinking has not been able to deliver deep transformation.

By contrast with mechanical simple or complex systems, a simple adaptive system, though existing in isolation and having very few parts, can adapt, or evolve. Darwin's model of genetic mutation described such a system, where a single gene sometimes undergoes a random mutation. The environment in which the gene is located is at first unaffected, but the gene itself, and so the whole organism, is altered.

With the rise of complexity science some forty years ago, it became clear that living systems can follow a very different kind of evolutionary pattern. In looking more closely at how life operates in its environment, complexity biologists discovered a further kind of system known as a "complex adaptive system." These systems have many interacting parts and are in constant creative dialogue with their environment. They live at the edge of chaos. When the environment presents the system with a crisis, the whole mega-system (organism plus environment) *and* the elements within it "co-evolve."

These complex adaptive systems are nonlinear, they are unpredictable, attempts to control them are destructive, and they cannot be broken down into separate, more simple parts. A living system poised at the edge of chaos has to be seen as a whole, and that whole is greater than the sum of its parts. Where Newtonian simple systems are designed by blueprint or according to Newton's three laws of motion, complex adaptive systems emerge through self-organization. Where Newtonian systems are the same in all conditions, never subject to any internal change, complex adaptive systems creatively explore their own futures as they adapt to and evolve within an environment to which they are internally sensitive. And where Newtonian simple systems are stable, complex adaptive systems can be radically unstable, their instability allowing them to thrive at the edge of chaos.

The edge of chaos itself represents a new, third kind of order in the universe. Any system, if not disturbed, will settle into a small number of its possible states, which are stable. These stable states in any field are called "attractors." (Our motives are attractors in a field of meaning.) If the system is challenged or disturbed too much, it can spin off into chaos, where there is no discernable or predictable order. But when complex adaptive systems are presented with a crisis, they are drawn to the edge of chaos. This is a point between order and disorder. The elements of the system are just ordered enough to be in a number of semi-stable states, but these are easily upset by the smallest disturbance. When this happens, the system searches in every direction for new attractors to settle into, creating new order and new information in the process. The principles of transformation that the system uses to find its new state are the same as those we will need to shift our motives from old attractors to new ones.

All living things have the capacity to be such systems, from the smallest amoeba to ourselves, our organizations and our culture. We are complex adaptive systems poised at the edge of chaos. Our immune systems are poised at the edge of chaos, as are our heartbeats, much of our brain activity, and certainly our emergent mental activity when we are thinking creatively. Spiritual intelligence is a complex adaptive intelligence poised at the edge of chaos. That is why it can make and break existing paradigms, and dissolve fixed patterns of thought or behavior. It composes its self-organizing patterns of meaning as these emerge in a creative dialogue between our minds and their environment. The brain's many interactive complex adaptive systems interact with the field of meaning.

There are ten distinctive characteristics of complex adaptive systems that give them their uniquely creative mode of operating in the world. Since these are the qualities that give rise to the system's creative evolution, they can be seen as the *principles of transformation* within the system. "Mind" itself, our consciousness and its structured contents, is itself a complex adaptive system that emerges when the brain meets the field of meaning. Thus these principles of transformation are also principles of transformation (learning, evolution) within consciousness. I believe they are the transformational principles (in part) that give SQ its paradigm-breaking/paradigm-making abilities. And they are the transformational principles that will underlie any attempt to shift human motives, and therefore behavior. These ten principles are:

1. *Self-organizing.* These systems have a deep order sleeping within, but this order is a potentiality that then takes on whatever form it will adopt as the system self-organizes in dialogue with the environment.
2. *Bounded instability.* These systems exist only at the edge of chaos, in a zone of instability that falls just between order and chaos. They are described as being "far from equilibrium." If they were wholly unstable, they would disintegrate into chaos. If they were wholly ordered, they would be inflexible and nonadaptive.

3. *Emergent.* These systems are "larger" than the sum of their parts. The whole has qualities and properties that the individual parts don't possess, and this whole emerges only as the system adapts to and evolves within its environment.

4. *Holistic.* These systems have no internal boundaries, no recognizably separate parts. Each "part" is entangled with and impinges upon every other part. The parts are *internally* defined through their relationship to each other and to the environment.

5. *Adaptive.* These systems not only learn as they go. They create themselves as they act to explore their own futures. This adaptation is always in mutually self-creative dialogue with an environment to which they are internally sensitive.

6. *Evolutionary mutations.* Mutations play a creative role in the final emergent structure of these systems' future.

7. *Destroyed by Outside Control.* The delicately poised internal order and balance of these systems are destroyed if we try to impose control from the outside. Their own self-organization collapses, and they revert to being simple or complex Newtonian systems.

8. *Exploratory.* These systems are constantly exploring their own possible futures, and creating themselves as they go.

9. *Recontextualizing.* These systems reframe their own inner development as they recontextualize (relearn) the boundaries and qualities of their environment.

10. *Order Out of Chaos.* These systems create order out of chaos and have "negative entropy." They bring new form into an unformed or unstructured arena. They create new order and thus new information.

In the brain, our thought processes act as a complex adaptive system when we are doing quantum thinking. Thus, in my earlier book, *Spiritual Capital*, I derived the transformational principles of SQ (which leads to quantum thinking) from these transformational properties of the body's complex adaptive system.[1] Nurturing these principles is one of the key elements in practicing QSD, and we will look at them in depth in Chapter

Twelve. If the individuals who make up an organization practice these principles, then the organization itself will become a complex adaptive system—i.e., a "living quantum system."

As the property of holism tells us, everything in a complex adaptive system is interrelated with everything else, every element (individual member) entangled with and defined by its relationship to the other elements (individuals). And because the qualities of individuals are influenced by the motivations from which they act, looking at the motivations that drive our behavior, and how to shift them, is another key element of QSD. In Chapter Eleven I will introduce a Scale of Motivations and discuss each of sixteen positive and negative emotions at play in human beings. Chapters Twelve, Thirteen, and Fourteen describe actual practices that individuals and teams can undertake to become functioning elements of a quantum organizational system—dialogue, meditation, and reflective practice, and a new methodology for decision-making. The materials discussed in these five chapters are, if you like, the "tools" available for transforming an organization into a quantum organization.

CHAPTER 11

THE MOTIVATIONS THAT DRIVE US

Any great shift of consciousness or culture requires first that we understand both the negative consequences of staying where we are and the motivations that have put us there. Why are we here in this predicament now? Just exactly where are we starting from? And then we need to envision the future. What shift are we trying to make? What are its attractive features? And what motivations would we need to get there? This need to understand motivations and how to shift them is critical to outgrowing the crises facing today's business culture.

I believe that four primary motivations drive capitalism and business as we know them today. These are the motivations that form the culture inside which so many millions work. They are *self-assertion* (competitiveness/ego), *anger*, *craving* (greed), and *fear*. The culture is highly competitive, often "dog eat dog," and competitive people reap most of the rewards. There is a great deal of anger because people feel a sense of injustice, a lack of fairness and representation, a resentment that they are just pawns in a larger game. The greed needs no explanation. It is the primary driving force of big business today. The fear comes from a fear of making mistakes, a fear of being told off, a fear of being made redundant. This is the heavy baggage, along with its accompanying attitudes, behavior, and emotional driving forces, that we have to shift.

Such motivations are all negative. They are all associated with what Abraham Maslow described as "deficiency needs,"[1] needs shared with the lower animals that don't in themselves take us to the level of being fully human. These will never take us to the higher level of a quantum organization.

It is easy to see some of the negative consequences that follow from the motives and narrow values of business-as-usual. These include the depletion of resources, ignoring and thereby imperiling future generations, a sense of meaninglessness, and the great stress to which that leads. Many of these consequences contribute to a leadership crisis in this culture, with the "brightest and the best" migrating toward the more idealistic professions. The business world is riddled with corrupt self-interest, fueling both distrust and terrorism. The prominent position of such an amoral business culture driven by self-interest and greed lowers the moral standards of society at large and disheartens the people who work within such companies.

At the same time, acting from higher motivations makes us happier and more stress free. It was Maslow himself who originally suggested that for those people who have achieved basic shelter and livelihood, acting from a wish to increase self-esteem or self-actualization (positive motives) carries much more meaning and contentment than acting from lower motivations like self-preservation, self-assertion, or a desire for more money (negative motives).[2] Acting from higher motivations like self-mastery and service also increases a sense of inner power.

It is easy to envision some of the positive consequences we might expect from a business culture inspired by higher motivations. This culture would steward and renew vital resources, and it would include future generations as stakeholders. Its broader vision and deeper values would inspire participants, replacing much of today's stress with a sense of fulfillment and making leadership within it a higher vocation. Corrupted self-interest would be replaced with dedication, and its deep compassion (*active* compassion) would address the inequality and anger that fuel both terrorism and social unrest. A values-based business culture such as this could raise the moral standards and vision of politicians and society at large, as well as bring more happiness and a more significant sense of meaning to the many individuals concerned.

I will argue in a moment that the higher motivations needed by a critical mass of the business community to ensure these more positive consequences are *exploration, cooperation, mastery, creativity, and higher service.* But to see the implications of this, to put it in context, and to have any notion how to activate such motivations, we need a broader picture of the full range of human motivations and of how we can shift from lower motivations to higher ones.

The study of human motivations is as old as our ability to reflect on one another's behavior. It is a primary quality of our intelligence (IQ as well as emotional and spiritual intelligence) to ask "why?" and motivations are what we describe when trying to explain our own or another's behavior. In the Bible we read that Cain killed Abel because he was motivated by jealousy and envy. The "seven deadly sins" of lust, pride, gluttony, etc. are in fact seven negative motivations that drive our behavior. The Ten Commandments were an early attempt to shift that culture. Freud thought, pessimistically, that all human behavior is driven by the two primary motives of sex and aggression. Various therapists since have tried to counter-balance this by stressing motives like love, altruism, and service.

Abraham Maslow's Hierarchy of Needs was the first attempt to present an organized scale of all motivations, from the most basic to the most lofty. Maslow's scale of needs has been widely used in business ever since. He listed survival as the most basic motivation, then a need for security followed by a need to belong or to be loved. These are his "deficiency needs." For what he called "higher needs," he described self-esteem, self-actualization, and peak experience.

In the years since, Maslow's hierarchy has inspired many attempts to develop motivation theory further, with psychologists, doctors, and scientists like R. B. Cattell, Ian Marshall, David Hawkins, and Daniel Goleman publishing more elaborate lists of motivations and different scales or hierarchies. These particular approaches pretty much correlate with one another. There are many, many others, but still no broad consensus among psychologists about the full range of human motivations nor which to emphasize. I have decided to use Marshall's scale in this book because it has evolved together with my own earlier joint work on spiritual intelligence, and this will prove essential when we come to understand how a motivational shift can happen. Its close correlation with Cattell's list of motives[3] grounds it in experimental psychology. This scale offers a new way of systematically diagnosing the motivational and emotional foundations of where a culture or an individual is now, and then suggests how we can shift the present state to a more desired future one. As we will see, diagnosis is made with our emotional intelligence, and shift occurs through applying our spiritual intelligence.

THE SCALE OF MOTIVATIONS

Ian Marshall was a practicing medical psychiatrist and psychotherapist, with a Jungian background and leaning. His Scale of Motivations was derived from over forty years of clinical observation of patient behavior and response.[4] As we can see, the scale pictured below draws from Maslow's Pyramid of Needs, but extends Maslow's original six motivations to sixteen, eight positive ones and eight negative ones. These are arranged in a hierarchy from -8 to +8 and have the unique property that the positive and negative legs of the scale mirror one another. Thus +3 *power-within/integrity* mirrors and is paired with -3 *craving*; +1 *exploration* mirrors and is paired with -1 *self-assertion*, and so on. This has great implications for how to use the chart, as I will discuss in a moment.

As implied by the numbering, it is better to have a motive of +3 than one of -1, but it is also better to be at -1 than at -4. Our personal effectiveness increases, and our behavior improves or has a more positive outcome as we progress up the scale. A leader driven by *fear* (-4) will adopt far more reactive and defensive strategies than a counterpart who is driven by *self-assertion* (-1). This has clear implications for risk management. *Fear* leads to behavior that is risk averse, or perhaps desperate; *self-assertion* may lead to overconfidence or carelessness.

In fact, not just our strategies, but the even deeper cognitive processes underlying them, alter as we move up or down the chart. It is clear that motivations drive behavior, but they also drive thinking. Each motivation is a whole paradigm, embracing assumptions, values, aspirations, strategies, relationships, emotions, and behavior. It could be said of a paradigm what the philosopher Ludwig Wittgenstein said of a hammer: "If all you have is a hammer, everything looks like a nail."[5] If I have the paradigm of fear, everything looks like a threat. A motivation acts as an "attractor" for our patterns of thought, just as the various-numbered holes on the surface of a pinball machine act as attractors for the silver balls we fire. A person motivated by *anger* (-2) will use a very different decision-making process than one who is driven by *gregariousness/cooperation* (+2). The angry person will be preoccupied with blame and a desire for retribution, and will seek strategies that bring this about. He or she feels set against an opponent or enemy. The cooperative person will be concerned with finding a balanced analysis of any problems and a desire for consensus. He or she sees the other as a prospective partner, and appropriate strategies will follow.

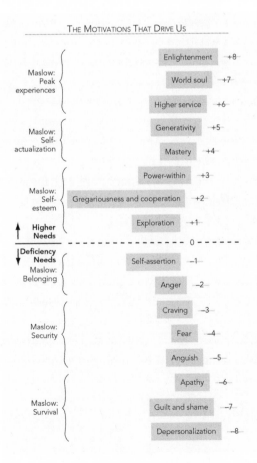

Figure 10. The Scale of Motivations

Therefore any move up or down the scale also represents a shift of outlook and behavior. The visions, goals, and strategies (and therefore the *results* of a corporation or a government or educational system) will be radically different depending upon those organizations' underlying motivations. We can see from this that any growth or transformation process aimed at altering behavior (habits), attitudes, or emotions is bound to fail if it does not address these. *Shifting motivation is the only stable way to shift behavior.* Motivations are causes; behaviors are effects. If we hope to see a shift from self-consuming to sustainable capitalism, we have to find some way to shift the corporate world's present driving motivations of *fear* (-4), *craving* (-3), *anger* (-2), and *self-assertion* (-1), to the more positive ones of *exploration* (+1), *cooperation* (+2), *power-within* (+3), *mastery* (+4), *creativity* (+5), and *service* (+6). This is the momentous paradigm shift envisaged when I speak of creating spiritual capital within a quantum organization.

Seven Steps to Using the Scale of Motivations:

1. See where we are now. What motivations drive us as individuals or as a culture in the present?
2. How do these motivations affect our behavior and strategies?
3. What results do we get?
4. Assess where we would like to be.
5. What motivations are needed to get there?
6. Work to make the motivational shift happen.
7. Reap the behavioral and strategic changes, and consequent desired results.

Steps 1 and 2 require the diagnostic skills of emotional intelligence; steps 4 and 5 will require spiritual intelligence. Step 3 requires a bit of each.

POSITIVE AND NEGATIVE MIRRORING

One further way to make good use of the Scale of Motivations is to make diagnostic use of its positive and negative mirroring. Among other things, this mirroring (of +4 and -4, for instance) allows us to attach weight to the force of a motivation with respect to another motivation. Using it, we can derive by simple arithmetic whether the motivations of one individual or culture can contain those of another, or whether they will be overwhelmed by them in some positive or negative way.

An angry person (-2) can never contain another angry person. They just clash and make things worse. Nor can a cooperative person (+2) have much effect on an angry person (-2). They just cancel each other out. However, an angry person's *anger* state (-2) can be raised by another person who is at least at +3, *power-within*. By the same token, an angry person (-2) can be dragged further down into *fear* (-4) by someone who is motivated by desperation *anguish* (-5). This simple arithmetic lays the foundation for a new kind of motivational dynamics, which I shall discuss more in a moment.

The arithmetic allows us to diagnose our relative position on the chart, and helps us to decide whether we can be of some use to another or to a situation, or whether we are simply threatened by them and need to disengage. This can enable us to evolve a strategy for how to handle the situation.

The positive and negative mirroring of the scale's motivations also allows us to identify what Jung would have called "the shadow" characteristics of any given motivation. Those are the characteristics we choose to disown or to project onto another because we can't bear to own them. The shadow is the "underside" or the "dark side" of a quality or personality trait. Thus *anger* (-2) is the shadow of *cooperation* (+2), damnation (*depersonalization*, -8) the shadow of salvation (*enlightenment*, +8). Jung believed that an individual's or a culture's shadow provides an unconscious energy dynamic that greatly affects actual behavior. Our shadow "haunts" us, and brings unwanted consequences. All the negative motivations on the scale are shadow motivations. That is, they result in self-defeating strategies. From the scale, we can see that the four negative motivations that drive today's capitalism and business ethic mean that capitalism is living out of its own shadow. From there, it has inspired the same negative motivations in at least one of its enemies—terrorists, too, are driven by *fear, craving, anger*, and *self-assertion*.

FINDING OURSELVES ON THE SCALE

Daniel Goleman has described self-awareness ("Recognizing a feeling as it happens") as the "keystone" of emotional intelligence. He says that it is our primary required emotional competency.[6] It is with honest, strong self-awareness that we must find our place on the chart of motivations. Yet this is more easily said than done. Because a motivation supports a whole paradigm—all our thoughts, perceptions, and assumptions—it is very difficult, if not impossible, for most individuals to diagnose accurately their own position on the chart, especially if they are in some negative state. Self-awareness is the most primary competency of emotional intelligence, but it is also the most difficult to achieve.

Most of us live a tissue of lies, or at least illusions, and most of these are about ourselves or our group. Take the case at a global insurance company. This company had articulated its values as the "Four Ts"— truth, trust, transparency, and teamwork. Employees basked in a feel-good factor about these values. They would have placed the company quite high on the chart, probably ranging from +1 to +4. Then one morning a senior executive came into the office and threw a suitcase full of women's clothing around the office. They were his wife's. "He's been screwing her," he shouted, pointing at the CEO's private office. It turned out the CEO had been having an affair with the man's wife. To spend more time with her, he had promoted her beyond her competency to his personal assistant, and they frequently travelled abroad together on business trips. Employees now felt betrayed, and saw the company values as a sham. The CEO's behavior had violated every one of the Four Ts, and most people could now see that the company culture was really motivated by drives at -4 to -1.[7]

People who work with paradigms argue that we can never see beyond our existing paradigm so long as it works. It is when a paradigm breaks down—as in the case of the Four Ts—that its assumptions are exposed as false and we begin to look for a new paradigm. Traumatic incidents like the one above can shake us out of our illusions. A betrayal, a dreadful crisis or failure, a significant loss can increase our self-awareness. Then, too, there are some people who are above 0 on the chart of motivations from whose behavior we can gain a learning perspective on our own. Many people who are at minus positions on the chart nonetheless have glimpses or twinges of higher motivations.

As Daniel Goleman has pointed out, being able correctly to interpret other people's emotions and responding appropriately to them is also an important part of the diagnostic work of emotional intelligence.[8] But we cannot properly interpret another's behavior or emotions if we do not know the true motives underlying the behavior. If we get these motives wrong, the strategies we devise in response to the other will be wrong.

The relationship between teenage children and their parents is a familiar case of misinterpreted motives. Many parents, indeed probably most, relate to their children with motives at +4, *mastery* or +5, *generativity* (loving creativity in the service of a higher cause). They want the best for their children and take an interest in their development. Sometimes this leads to nagging. But teenagers, with a newfound instinct for independence and motivated in this case by -4, *fear* (of being repressed) or -1, *self-assertion*, very often misinterpret their parents' motives as stemming from their own *self-assertion*, -1, *anger*, -2, or *fear*, -4 (of letting their children go). This leads to strategies of deceit and conflict on the part of the children, and often pushes the parents into defensive strategies.

According to David Hawkins (*Power vs. Force*), who constructed his own hierarchy of motivations based on assessing the degree of muscle tension associated with the attitudes accompanying various motivations (kinesiology), 85 percent of us are motivated by drives that score less than zero on our chart. Of the 15 percent who score above 0, only about 4 percent ever get as high as +5, *creativity*. The vast majority, perhaps 60 percent, score between -4, *fear* , and -1, *self-assertion*.[9] We have only to watch the behavior of most public figures, be they in business or politics, to see the alarming truth of this. On the more positive side, Hawkins reckons that the very few who act from higher motivations have a disproportionate capacity to drag the rest of us somewhat higher, or at least to make us aspire to higher motivations. Intellectual historians argue that all the progress ever made by humanity in its 40,000-year recorded history has been made through the leadership of the top 2 percent.

In my view, people or a culture whose motivational drives are below 0 can't really assess themselves or itself (or others!) accurately. They can't listen to themselves because their negative paradigms skew all incoming data and give them blind spots. An increased self-awareness must come from being listened to or by dialoging with others who are themselves motivated by at least +1, *exploration*, or +2, *cooperation*. Thus, even finding ourselves on the chart of motivations requires that we work with others, in dialogue or discussion groups. Conversations with disinterested but caring friends can help us assess some of our behavior, as of course can professional help—therapists, counselors, co-counselors, mentors, priests, or workshop attendance. The practice of 360 degree evaluation from colleagues and peers can also be very effective.

Apart from group work, the most effective method for an individual to reach a higher state of self-awareness is through some sort of meditation practice, for those who can engage in this effectively. Meditation takes the mind beyond the distractions and noise of the moment to a broader level of awareness that notices causes and patterns within events. In a meditative state, I can get beyond my anger to become *aware* that I am angry, and then reach a stage of reflection or insight as to its causes. Also, each of us has a number of barely conscious sub-personalities whose own split-off motivations might help or hinder us. "I" may be angry, though there may be a less accessible aspect of me that feels an underlying *power-within* or *mastery* associated with deep compassion. Through meditation we become conscious of these sub-personalities and are better able to integrate them and their motivational drives.

Meditation transcends the whole level of ego awareness where motivations dwell, and puts the mind more in touch with the deeper level of values that underlie motivations in the first place. As we shall see in later chapters, this can move us from the diagnostic use of our emotional intelligence to the transformational use of our spiritual intelligence. We move from *recognizing* motivations to *shifting* them. The whole of Chapter Fourteen in this book is devoted to a deeper look at the power of Mindfulness meditation.

HOW WE MOVE ON THE CHART

Once we see that we are acting from a lower motivation that has negative consequences, or we are inspired by a person or culture clearly acting from higher motivations than our own, we naturally want to know how to shift our own motivations. How can I get from thinking and acting out of -4, *fear* to at least -2, *anger*, which is at least an improvement on my situation? If I am more ambitious, how can I move from -2, *anger* to +2, *cooperation*? Or how can I prevent myself from being dragged down from +1 *exploration* to -4, *fear*? In short, what are the dynamics of this scale and how does shift happen?

There are two kinds of shifts that might happen to an individual or a culture with respect to the chart. The first is an *external*, and most likely temporary or dependent, shift that can result from the influence of others or the environment. I may be in a state of *fear*, -4, and yet, finding myself surrounded by a group of people who are at *mastery*, +4, I may for a time become more self-confident. As a group, perhaps we can handle the threat. However, I will not really have addressed the underlying causes of my fearfulness and, without the support of the masterful group, may fall back.

As a real case instance of individuals returning to their original motivations and attitudes once divorced from group pressure, we can look at the American GIs who were captured by the Chinese during the Korean War. These men were brainwashed, and happily appeared on television criticizing capitalism and the United States. They had become "good communists." But within six months of being freed and living back in their familiar American environment, every one of them reverted to his earlier patriotic attitudes.

The second kind of possible shift is a deeper, *internal*, and much more lasting shift. This results from examining my original motives, coming to understand the purposes and values that underlie them, and then shifting those values themselves. The consequent motivational shift brings about a paradigm shift. One of the main purposes of the QSD methodology discussed in Chapter Ten is to help a person undergo this internal shift.

We are not yet in a position here to discuss internal, paradigm shifting motivational change. That will require bringing the twelve transformational principles of spiritual intelligence into the discussion, which I shall do in the next chapter. But at this stage, we can see how environment or emotional intelligence influences how we can move up or down on the chart. This external dynamics can be articulated in four basic principles.

Principle One: A negative person or culture cannot help another on the negative scale. Two people stuck at *anger*, -2, will just spark each other off and make each other angrier. Two *assertive* people at -1 will get locked into a power struggle. Similarly, using a negative motivation to make a change in a situation can *only* result in getting to some other negative motivation. For instance, some years ago, Nike allegedly reacted out of *fear*, -4 to customer loss over their sweatshops employing child labor in Southeast Asia.[10] They changed company policy and offered their Asian workers better conditions.[11] But this only brought company motivation one step higher, to *craving* -3. One could conclude they wanted to get profit back on track, and improving the conditions of their workers was just a necessary means toward that end.

Principle Two: A person at -3, *craving*, is just cancelled out by a person at +3, *power-within*. Equality of opposites is not enough to change the motivations of either person. To have the power to raise another up the scale, someone must make what chess players call a "knight's move." That is, it would take someone at +4, *mastery*, to raise a -3 to -2 or higher. This principle usually underlies the philosophy behind dialogue groups or mentoring—the notion that a dialogue facilitator or a mentor (or a workshop leader) is at a higher motivational level than his or her group and can thus raise the game.

Principle Three: An individual at +4 can contain another who is coming from -3, but an individual who is only at +2 can be dragged down by someone who is at -3. Thus a culture or a group higher up on the scale can raise the game for those lower down. This is the point of having priests, good teachers, master artisans, and servant leaders in society. They inspire us upward with their example or vision. But it is also the case that a culture can drag individuals down. Most children, for instance, begin a 0 on the scale in infancy but quickly move on to *exploration*, +1. They begin school filled with a sense of exploration. But much of the educational system is motivated by *fear* -4 or *craving* (for control), -3. This very quickly reduces most children's educational experience to one of -3, a *craving* (for credentials), or worse still, -4, *fear* (of failure).

At a graduate business school in South Africa, an "idealism" survey was done on two groups of MBA students.[12] The first group consisted of young people just fresh out of university. They were found to be very idealistic in their work aspirations. They acted out of *exploration*, +1, *cooperation*, +2, and *power-within*, +3. They hoped to become *masters*, +4 through their MBA work. The second group was made up of older MBA students who had worked in the corporate world for at least ten years. They were very low in idealism, filled with some anger, and quite cynical. Ten years in a corporate culture whose driving motives are -4, *fear*, -3, *craving*, -2, *anger*, and -1, *self-assertion* had dragged these people down to its own level. *If we want to change the motives and behavior of people within corporate culture, we must change the underlying motivations of that culture itself.* I can't emphasize enough that no meaningful transformation can take place in a company without an accompanying cultural transformation.

Principle Four: We can use our emotional intelligence (primarily self-awareness and emotional control) to move up the scale provided this is accompanied by a wish not to hurt others or not to make a situation worse. For instance, if I know that I have a bad temper (-2, *anger*), I can make a great effort not to lose it. Now I am acting out of +2, *cooperation*, or perhaps even +3, *power-within* (self-mastery). But this kind of move begins to take us into the deeper territory of underlying values, and thus of spiritual intelligence. In this example, it is an underlying *value* of not wishing to cause harm that really shifts me to a higher motivation.

APPLYING THE MOTIVATIONAL SCALE

The sixteen motivational states described on our chart are, as I said, "attractors" or whole paradigms comprising behavior, emotions, attitudes, assumptions, values, thinking processes, and strategies. Thus to know the motivation or set of motivations driving an individual or a culture is to know a great deal about their internal state as well as how they will react with and influence their environment. It is to know the individual's or organization's personal or group "psychology" and to be able to predict their approach to action, and its effectiveness.

We can assume from historical accounts of his past and his emotional reaction to Germany's humiliating defeat in World War I, and his own disastrous failure as an artist, for instance, that Adolf Hitler was motivated by *guilt/shame*, -7, *craving* (for power and glory), -3, *anger*, -2, and a good bit of *self-assertion*, -1. These motives were apparent in Hitler's speech and body language, as well as in the aggressive strategies he evolved. If world leaders had been able to see this during his rise to power, they would have had little difficulty believing that his Reich might pose a great threat to surrounding countries and to certain ethnic groups within Germany. Perhaps, seen at an earlier date, this would have allowed allied countries to counter Hitler's threat from a position of *power-within*, +3, or *mastery*, +4. Instead they waited until he began invading Austria and Poland, and then they responded from a position of *fear*, -4. Eleven million people died because they got it wrong.

This extreme example reminds us that no good can come from negative motivations. As David Hawkins puts it, "All [motivational] levels below [0] are destructive of life in both the individual and society at large; all levels above [0] are constructive expressions of power."[13] A person or a culture must be at least +1 to have a beneficial effect on himself/herself or the world. *The crises of capitalism and many of the crises of business are the crises of negative motivation.*

As I describe each of the motivations in turn, I shall do so in their positive and negative, mirrored pairs. Thus we shall move both up and down the scale simultaneously, letting each "shadow," negative motive come just after its positive equivalent. This is important for understanding the dynamics of internal shift when we come to that.

The motives between +4 and -4, the most common, were all picked up by R. B. Cattell's statistical (factor analytic) studies of ordinary people.[14] Beyond these limits is more the territory of genius and sainthood on the one hand, and of psychosis or nervous breakdown on the other. The vast majority of any working population will fall between +4 and -4.

0, *Neutral*: The position of neutrality is not itself a motivation. It is either our starting point as infants or our life-changing crossover point from being driven by negative motivations to acting from more positive ones. It is like the neutral position in a car's clutch system, free and ready to go, but with no direction yet determined. Many of us awaken fresh in *neutral* each morning, before the memories, images, and emotions from the day before rush in to fill our consciousness. It is like the *tabula rasa*, described by the philosopher Descartes—the tablet on which nothing is yet written.

+1, *Exploration*: *Exploration* is associated with curiosity, a sense of wonder, and an open, willing attitude to whatever life throws in our path. It is very common in young children. It reflects a desire to know our way about a scene or a situation, such as that first exploration we do when we arrive at a new tourist or residential destination. These people are in open dialogue with their environment; they look and listen, and they easily engage. *Exploration* is a recognition that we need to know, to learn, to explore, and we need to realize that it will be fulfilling to do so. It involves us in reading books, papers and magazines—anything that will teach us more and allow us actively to engage with our environment. It makes us good students and willing, attentive employees. People driven by this motivation are usually interested in music, art, and film. They love traveling to new places and are enthusiastic to solve new problems or to meet new challenges. They like to know how things work, and they pursue knowledge and learning for their own sake. All their strategies will be bent on reaching out, on extending their skills, knowledge or area of activity. They will be drawn to innovation because it excites them, and they will greet adverse circumstances with a "What can I make of this?" attitude.

-1, *Self-Assertion*: This motivation is associated with thoughtlessness, unbridled competitiveness, too much pride, self-centeredness, and aggression. David Hawkins comments that there is enough energy in this motivation to drive the United States Marine Corps.[15] Like the Marines, these people are always "charging over" some hill, imposing their will and structure on the environment, "taking no prisoners." They are businesspeople who set out to conquer the market and destroy the competition. Their attitude toward learning and knowledge is manipulative. They try to assert what they already know, or they engage in learning as a means to strengthen their already entrenched position. Thus they are not open to learning things that do not further their ends. In the end, this is self-defeating. Self-assertive people have a will to power that brings them into conflict with anyone who has a strong or independent point of view different from theirs. Two self-assertive people or cultures in conflict makes for "war," psychological or real. They are argumentative and averse to dialogue and must have their own way. Self-assertive people are also driven by a need for status and self-esteem of a sort dependent on others. They need the good opinion or open admiration of others. They care how they dress and dress to win further esteem. They will adopt strategies that gain them territory or acclaim or that boost their power. They play to win, and count the scalps of the losers. They can be pleasant, but only if they are getting their own way and receiving enough "respect."

+2, *Gregariousness/Cooperation*: We human beings are social animals. We need to relate to others and usually gain great nourishment from doing so. Some psychologists call this our "herd instinct," but that is very reductive. The bonds that we form with our fellows and culture through our gregariousness are bonds of fierce loyalty often based on shared values as well as shared goals. A gregarious person usually seeks company, preferring it to being alone. He or she likes people and enjoys doing shared social or work-related activities with them. These people make good team members and have a strong *esprit de corps*. But the stronger aspect of this motive is the drive toward cooperation that is required if we are to be with others. This causes us to evolve strategies of pleasing, negotiation, conciliation, and conflict management. Cooperative people are good at seeing the other's point of view, and harbor a natural respect for it even if they disagree. This makes them very good negotiators, but also good at drawing out creative ideas in others. They are good listeners. Gregarious/cooperative people usually seek social occupations and are common among professions like teaching, coaching, and social work. They are the social "glue" of any group or organization, always evolving strategies that would bring people together. Every new relationship looks like a new opportunity. The motives of +1 and +2, taken together, are sufficient for living in a small group, in a static way. But evolution and creativity require higher motivation.

-2, *Anger*: We all recognize anger in others. Angry people are usually very "cold," carefully holding their emotions in check, or very "hot," letting their anger spew all over the place. They feel bad, and they blame someone or something for this. Bad things in life are someone's fault. As David Hawkins puts it, "Anger as a lifestyle is exemplified by irritable, explosive people who are oversensitive to slights and become 'injustice collectors,' quarrelsome, belligerent, or litigious."[16] They are often rebellious just for the sake of rebelling. Angry people seldom feel like cooperating. Where cooperative people seek company and thus the resolution of conflict, an angry person often rejects the group or society. He or she feels spiteful and seeks strategies of revenge. The other is the enemy, and the enemy must be punished or conquered. Vandalism is driven by anger, as is terrorism. Both vandals and terrorists feel overlooked or excluded by society. Their need for self-esteem is threatened or frustrated, and they want to lash out with a claim that their existence (cause, values, etc.) be recognized. Indeed, frustration of one sort or another underlies most anger: love or loyalty that has not been requited, worth that has not been valued, a point of view that has not been heard, a self that has been rejected, denied, or left out. As a business strategy, anger leads to finding some way to beat, destroy, or damage the competition, even if cooperation might have led to a better result. In an executive, it can lead to strategies of finding fault.

British Airways famous "dirty tricks" campaign against Virgin Atlantic several years ago was a strategy inspired by a wish to destroy or damage the competition. BA telephoned passengers intending to fly on Virgin and offered them cheaper fares if they would transfer to BA.[17]

+3, *Power-Within/Integrity*: We usually associate personal power with the ability to move or dominate others: "power-over." But power-over is external power. A person has it because he or she owns something, occupies some position of authority or influence, has a strong body, "is somebody." Those acting from -1, *self-assertion* seek power-over as a means of using others to make themselves feel strong or important. Unless wielded from a higher motivation, most power-over usually creates winners and losers, and the conflict that results.

The only person the man or woman motivated by *power-within* really seeks to have power-over is him or herself. These are people who are centered in themselves, at peace with themselves. They know whom they love and what they value, and they act from this level of love and/or values. They have *integrity* in the strict sense that they are whole people, as well as showing behavior that is filled with integrity. They may also be rooted in their skills, or, if they are athletes, in their well-trained minds and bodies. The very pleasurable sense of "flow" when performing at our physical or mental best is the correlate of *power-within*.

People who have *power-within* are trustworthy. We know where they are coming from and know that that is from a place within themselves that we can trust. They have a recognizable personal style derived from deeper commitments, and they have a strong felt-sense of their own identity. These people can be counted on to fulfill any responsibility they take on. They often act from a sense of responsibility, of loyalty, service, or guardianship (stewardship), though they can say "no" if they disagree. They are more self-directed than other-directed, and think quite independently. Since their deepest motivation is a sense of their own values and direction, they are open to and tolerant of the ways and values of others. They are open to diversity and will often evolve strategies that bring many different elements or voices together. If in positions of power-over (as parents, as executives), their strategy will include empowering others. They will listen to all sides before making a decision, and seldom rush to judgment. Their strategies are usually driven by a quiet (sometimes fierce) determination. They get things done.

-3, *Craving*: The Buddha said that craving is the root of all suffering. Most of the seven deadly sins are sins of craving. Craving expresses itself as perpetual restlessness, a sense of never having enough, of there always being something more to want or need. Driven by a sense of inner emptiness (the exact opposite of *power-within*), these people constantly adopt strategies of grasping. They are greedy people, who are never satisfied. Most feel they "are owed," that someone, somewhere didn't give them what they needed or never gave them a break. They want things, but often they don't think they should have to pay for them. Their greed makes them materialistic if it is a greed for money or things, and it makes them jealous if it is a hunger to be loved. Capitalist greed is a greed for ever more profit, and damn the consequences. Craving makes us jealous because we see in whatever someone else has, something we want. *Craving* is of course the basis of all addictions—overeating, gambling, alcoholism, drug addiction, etc., and the strategies of the craving person are always the strategies of an addict: a quick fix rather than a long-term plan, instant results rather than patient plodding or planning, seeking out feel-good factors or "highs," betraying anything or anyone (including ourselves) that frustrates satisfaction. Craving people may not be trustworthy where the object of their craving is concerned, and they are often deeply irresponsible.

+4, *Mastery*: The man or woman (or culture) that has reached +3, *power-within* is centered in deep personal values. But when our motivation reaches *mastery*, we find ourselves rooted in wider, interpersonal values and skills—especially those of a profession, a tradition, or a system of understanding distinctive of wider thinking or some shared vision. A master stone mason wields with his hammer all the skill and all the power of master stone masons throughout history. He draws on his craft's collective pool of wisdom and skill. A master-level executive leads with an easy air of authority and inner self-assurance. He or she has an *instinct* for good strategies and decisions. There is a sense of inner discipline and of "flow" in a master's behavior and decisions. This is honed by reining in

whim and easy desires or snap decisions through disciplines like meditation or prayer, or through constant practice of a skill or an art. At the level
of *mastery*, we see the bigger picture or are in tune with a larger pattern,
and thus our strategies are more complex and more long-term. We'll seek
long-term objectives and constantly reframe those objectives as we take
in new information. Because we are in touch with a wider pool of potentiality through being grounded in the collective wisdom of our tradition,
we will see opportunities and possible innovations where others don't.
The martial art of Aikido develops *power-within*; Shaolin kung fu, featured in the film *Crouching Tiger, Hidden Dragon*, is more a practice of
masters. The Aikido warrior moves with a sense of personal power, the
Shaolin master with a power "granted by the gods."

David Hawkins claims that very few people in our culture get above
the level of *mastery*.[18] Only eight to ten percent achieve mastery. We find
among them most people who have reached the top level of their profession or craft—senior doctors, higher executives, first violin players
in an orchestra, champion sportsmen, leading (but not great) scientists.
Winston Churchill and Franklin Delano Roosevelt were master politicians; Marie Curie was a master scientist.

-4 *Fear*: *Fear* is associated with anxiety, suspicion, a sense of being
threatened or of being too vulnerable. It is the very opposite of being a
master of the situation. Acting from this motive, I seek always to protect
or defend myself. I see others in my environment as threats or enemies.
I tend to see opportunities or challenges as possible threats (because I
doubt my ability to deal with them). I tend to withdraw from people
(those whom I feel threaten me) or the environment; I become timid.
My body language is defensive, and I avoid taking the initiative or calling
attention to myself. I don't volunteer, and I don't take risks. *Fear* isolates
me from the moment and costs me my spontaneity. Hence the expression,
"frozen with fear." The strategies I adopt will always be reactive and cau-
tious. They will be ones of avoidance and retreat, or they may be passive.
Not wanting to rock the boat or draw attention to myself, I may act so
as to hide my true emotions or aspirations. And I may take unnecessary
precautions to avoid being blamed or criticized. The battery of unnec-

essary tests and procedures ("defensive medicine") for which American medicine is famous stems from this fearful strategy. Driven by *fear*, business executives become risk-averse and closed to any kind of innovation or exploration.

We get to a place with the next eight motivations where we begin to find the exceptional people, either the supernormal especially gifted or the subnormal especially injured or damaged. These are the realms of greatness at the one extreme and of psychiatry at the other. No more than 4 percent of the general population is driven by these higher or lower motives.[19] These are the people whose personalities differ from the normal, perhaps up to the extreme of incipient madness. These include borderline manic-depressive (bipolar) individuals, or those individuals prone to but not actually in schizophrenic breakdown, who are known as schizotypal. There is a well-recognized correlation between this "borderline madness" and creativity. The same qualities that give rise to unusual behavior confer unusual vision or exceptionally sensitive temperament. For such personalities, the risks of great catastrophe are balanced by the chance of great genius.

We don't see many of these people at the positive end, but their presence in a culture is necessary to raise the motivational level of others lower down the scale. Only someone who is at least at +5, *generativity* or at +6, *higher service*, can raise another would-be leader from +3 *power-within* to +4, *mastery*. Such higher motivated individuals are also necessary to raise the motivational level of a culture because it is they who bring in the creativity and freshness of new energy. We will look at a few of these exceptional business leaders in the concluding chapter of this book.

+5 *Generativity*: *Generativity* is a special manifestation of creativity. It is creativity driven by love or passion. It stands in what Martin Buber would have called an *I-thou* relationship to the medium of its output. A painter *loves* color and his art. Einstein said that he loved mathematics, and Isaac Newton felt a great awe and love for the universe he wished to explore. This love or passion gives generative people a sense of playfulness about their creativity. They *enjoy* it and identify with it. The work is the life. It is a famous story that the chemist Kekule dreamt his ground-breaking image of the benzene ring. But it is less well-known that in Kekule's dream, the six carbon atoms that made up the ring were holding hands and dancing.[20] Kekule had a child's sense of fun about his work.

Because their creativity is so closely linked to play, generative people are often generative in many directions. They just spark off creativity and are excited by anything that arouses their interest or curiosity. So their creativity is not necessarily in service to anything. It is just driven by an unbounded love. The strategies they adopt are always strategies of learning or discovery. They are playful strategies—seeing what will happen "if," and delighting in it whatever it is. They readily take risks.

Masters (+4) draw out the potentiality within their shared tradition. They are the leading expressers *of* a tradition. Generative people create *new* traditions, new paradigms. They love and are drawn to the unknown or the unexplored, and their creative gifts allow them to give new shape to the unformed. The German poet Rilke would have called them "the bees of the invisible,"[21] restlessly gathering the honey that becomes the visible for others. Most of the very great names that we remember from human intellectual and artistic history were people motivated by generativity, from Plato to Picasso. Very great scientists like Newton or Einstein were driven by generativity, as are some of today's great businesspeople. Steve Jobs at Apple was one; Konosuke Matsushita who created Japan's electronics industry, Henry Ford, probably Bill Gates, and certainly Virgin's Richard Branson are a few others. Branson is a particularly good example of *generativity* at work because his boyish creativity sparks off in many different directions. He lists "having fun" as one of Virgin's core company values.[22]

-5 *Anguish*: Hamlet's famous soliloquy, "To be or not to be, that is the question," is the cry of an anguished man. Unlike grief or mourning, which is a necessary and healthy reaction to loss, anguish arises from a sense of being lost or helpless for what to do or what to decide. It comes from a sense of blocked potential. Our generative process itself is blocked. We ring our hands and feel despair. We feel stuck, caught in the moment, with little prospect for movement. Anguish often results from incurable tragedy, like having a damaged child, being an athlete who has lost physical agility, or being an infertile woman who had desperately wanted children. Retirement can bring it on, or immersion in a situation that we feel we can't handle. Anguished people have no strategies because their very anguish arises from the fact that they can't see any. Everything seems impossible. This is, of course, an important component of depression. But although the anguished person is suffering, they have not lost all hope, as is the case with -6, *apathy*.

+6, *Higher Service*: Higher service is the motive that drives the servant leader, the highest and most dedicated form of leadership possible. Any great leader serves something from beyond his or her self, but the servant leader serves transpersonal values—things like goodness, justice, truth, the alleviation of suffering, the salvation or enlightenment of others. Any leader serves his/her fellows, his/her community, his/her country or company, but servant leaders ultimately serve their own notion of the highest or most sacred. The best of them serve that longing in the human soul that conjures up visions and possibilities. They have a sense of vocation, of being "called" to serve, and in answering to this they find their own deepest peace, their own destiny. This is *focused* creativity, going beyond +5.

Servant leaders make things happen that others have found impossible; they create new ways for human beings to relate to one another, new ways for companies to serve society, new ways for societies to *be*. The Buddha, Moses, and Jesus were such leaders. In our own times we have had the good fortune to be served by Gandhi, Martin Luther King, Mother Teresa, Nelson Mandela, and the Dalai Lama. But there is no need for such greatness in servant leadership. Any of us can be a servant leader if we act from the motive of higher service.

Servant leaders necessarily deal with power, but they do so through humility and personal surrender. Power is always used to further the good they serve, never to aggrandize themselves. As Jesus said, "Not my will but thine." For the enterprising and very determined personality types who naturally become leaders, such surrender is not easy. Its very possibility is an act of grace.

The strategies adopted by servant leaders will often be bold and large-scale. They will be canny strategies that recognize the best and the worst in people and know how to use both to further the cause. They usually have a panoramic vision of the possible, like Gandhi's dream of Indian independence and the nonviolent path to achieving it or King's dream of a society freed from racism.

The nineteenth-century Indian philosopher Vivekananda described the universe as a gymnasium in which the soul is taking exercise.[23] Vivekananda was one of those who inspired Gandhi's view of "trusteeship," his own particular vision of servant leadership. Gandhi said that when an individual or a company obtains more than their proportionate share of the world's wealth they should become a trustee of that portion for God's people. This is the vision we now need a critical mass of business leaders to adopt if we are to move from capitalism as usual to spiritual capital.

-6, *Apathy*: If Hamlet is the man of *anguish*, Macbeth is the man reduced to *apathy*. "Tomorrow and tomorrow and tomorrow/ Creeps in this petty pace from day to day/ To the last syllable of recorded time/ And all our yesterdays have lighted fools/ The way to dusty death . . . [Life] is a tale/ Told by an idiot, full of sound and fury/ Signifying nothing."[24] Macbeth has seen all his dreams and schemes come to nothing, and now he feels that he is nothing. He is the embodiment of the existentialist philosopher Sartre's "Man is a useless passion." In *apathy* we are overwhelmed with a sense of *anomie*, of having no role to play in life. Where the person of *anguish* suffers because he or she is no longer able to play life's game, the person of *apathy* can't see that there is any game to play. Apathetic people have very little energy, only barely enough to keep going. They show little interest in anything, and often neglect themselves and their affairs. They adopt no strategies because nothing seems worthwhile. This is a very deep form of depression. It may be the norm for Third World people who are just at or only slightly above survival level.

+7, *World-Soul*: Servant leaders at +6 are rooted in their "God," but their calling is to be of service in this world of daily affairs. At the next level up, +7, *world-soul*, a person sees him or herself, others, and nature as parts of the divine made manifest. If habitual, this state may be accompanied by a withdrawal from the world of daily life, as with monks and some artists. These people, perhaps only one in ten million of the population, commune with a world of archetypes and pure forms. They see the world bathed in celestial light (Wordsworth), or are inspired by the voices of angels (the poet Rilke). They have lost the craving to be themselves, the sense of ego, and hence the sense of limitation. They dwell at, or sometimes reach, a level of awareness that transcends space and time and thus have a sense of immortality, of the infinite. Their consciousness has become one with the collective unconscious of our species (and sometimes that of other species), and when they do speak or create works of art it is as though through these utterances we hear the voice of the collective unconscious. Mozart's music was literally dictated to him from this level. He said that he merely wrote down what he heard. Dante's vision of both the Inferno and of Paradise comes from these realms of the divine and archetypal. So, too, does Shakespeare's genius for seeing and bringing to life the disparate points of view in a complex array of human characters. "All the world's a stage, and all men and women merely players," and Shakespeare saw them from the vantage point of a celestial playwright.

Most of us will never reach this mystical level of motivation as a stable state, and indeed would not aspire to do so, but at least 50 percent of us have intimations of it through occasional (or once in a lifetime) mystical experiences of oneness, beauty, peace, or love. We also gain intimations of it through the great works of the geniuses who dwell there, and this is why art, music, and literature are so necessary to the human soul.

For people at +7, motivation is toward celebrating the sacred aspect of the world, and thus toward any strategies that further that cause. Distractions will be painful or indeed beyond being heeded, as these people's calling is to a world beyond the world. Some people enter this realm prematurely, as an escape from worldly problems. Their worldly personalities are often immature or damaged, and many of the great among them have ended their lives in early death or madness.

-7, *Shame/Guilt*: *Shame* and *guilt* fill a person with an almost exactly opposite sense of being to that experienced by *world-soul*. When overcome by the motivations of -7, I feel wholly *apart* from any meaningful or deeper level of reality. Indeed, I feel out of joint with "existence," feel that I have no right to be here, or that my presence in some way makes the world a worse place. I experience myself as a wound or a scar on the face of existence, and may wish to destroy myself. I simply cannot face myself, or go on living with my guilt. Suicide rates are high among people driven from this motivation, often ritual ones. The Japanese tradition of *hara-kiri* results from loss of face (*shame/guilt*), as did the practice of disgraced Roman generals falling on their swords. Judas killed himself out of unbearable shame. People acting from this level have sometimes betrayed their own deepest ideals, and their strategies may be ones of self-destruction—either directly through suicide or indirectly through drugs, alcoholism, or reckless behavior. But violently aggressive or grandiose strategies may result if the *shame/guilt* have resulted from humiliation. Humiliation, too, can result in strategies to harm others, to gain vengeance against them for real or imagined slights, or to find scapegoats who can be blamed for our unbearable pain. We saw that Hitler had *shame/guilt* as one of his driving motivations. We are, here, at the gate of evil.

+8, *Enlightenment/Serenity*: We come at this point almost to a failure of words or images. As Lao Tzu wrote at the opening of the *Tao Te Ching*, "The Tao that can be expressed in words is not the eternal Tao."[25] That small handful of people in human history who have reached *enlightenment* and written about it can only allude, or speak in metaphor. They speak commonly of the total absorption or annihilation of self in "the Absolute" or "the nothingness." The Christian mystic St. John of the Cross described it as,

> All things I then forgot,
> My cheek on Him who for my coming came.
> All ceased, and I was not,
> Leaving my cares and shame
> Among the lilies, and forgetting them.[26]

That the Absolute is described in so many mystical traditions as an emptiness or a darkness follows from our inability to grasp it with concepts or images. As St. John says, "It is a lightsome darkness and a rich naught."[27] The Buddhists describe it (*Sunyata*) as "an emptiness that is full." Even quantum physics has a vision of the absolute ground state of reality with the quantum vacuum. Again, the quantum vacuum is empty only of structure and qualities; it is replete with possibilities. We must "grasp" (be absorbed within them) these naught absolutes in a state of structureless awareness. This state can be experienced in Mindfulness meditation.

It is possible to have experienced *enlightenment* and then to have returned to the world. The Buddha did so, as did those who have written about their experiences. But the return to the world is as an altered person, free of all negative motivations and partially identified with the experienced divine reality. As St. Paul said after his conversion experience, "Now there lives, not I, but Christ living in me."[28] Or we have in T. S. Eliot's *Four Quartets* the thought, "Below, the boar hound and the boar/ Pursue their pattern as before/ But reconciled among the stars."[29] Back in the world, these people live lives of grace. They are at peace with themselves and existence. Though they may pass as quite ordinary, the ordinary is for them exalted by an inner light.

-8, *Depersonalization*: A person who has reached *enlightenment* is all inner light without a physical shell. A person who has undergone *depersonalization* is an empty shell with no core. Here, the sense of "I" has disappeared because the ego self has disintegrated. There is no "person" left, only random utterances and uncoordinated behavior. This is the inner world of the hospitalized schizophrenic or the hopelessly burnt-out alcoholic or drug addict. This is as close as we get to damnation while still alive. There is no further disintegration beyond it but death itself.

CHAPTER 12

THE 12 TRANSFORMATIONAL PRINCIPLES OF SPIRITUAL INTELLIGENCE

"Being new, nameless, hard to understand, we premature births of an as yet unproven future, we need for a new goal also a new means."

—Nietzsche, *Ecce Homo*

Articulating a new vision of the quantum organization and its quantum leader is my goal in this book, but it is a very lofty goal. It requires that we act from our higher, sometimes highest, motivations. It means nothing less than that we transform ourselves as human beings. To achieve this new goal, we need some new *means*. For that we must look to the principles of transformation available to spiritual intelligence.

A human being's IQ is pretty well steady throughout life, barring any brain illness or damage. But EQ, or emotional intelligence, can be learned, nurtured, and improved. As human beings are *essentially* creatures who seek and use meaning, all human beings are born with a potential for high SQ. Most children have a high potential for it. But our spiritually dumb culture and educational system, and our often spiritually deadening work patterns and pressures, reduce our capacity to practice our SQ. Like EQ, SQ must be nurtured. It can be relearned, and it can be improved. To do so, we must look for those qualities of a person's being and behavior that signify the presence of SQ at work. Finding and exploring these qualities also helps us better to understand the nature of quantum leadership itself.

We have seen that any chance of building quantum organizations requires a paradigm shift in our thinking about how businesses are structured and led. And we have also seen that paradigm shifts are most likely to happen at points of crisis. I have argued throughout this book that business today, and its whole capitalist system, is indeed at a point of crisis. We saw in Chapter Three when looking at three kinds of thinking that, when our habitual attitudes fail us, and something new and creative is needed, we need to bring our SQ to bear on the situation.

SQ is a recently discovered intelligence, and there has yet been little clinical research on the human qualities with which it can be associated. But as SQ functions as a complex adaptive system in the mind, the better researched and understood qualities of these systems seem an obvious first place to look for identifying qualities of SQ itself. Though in looking to these biological systems as models or forerunners of SQ qualities, we must bear in mind that SQ is a *conscious* complex adaptive system, and thus its qualities will have a uniquely conscious expression.

We saw in Chapter Ten, when introducing Quantum Systems Dynamics, that complex adaptive systems, "living quantum systems," are defined by ten distinctive characteristics: 1) they are self-organizing; 2) they are poised at the edge of chaos; 3) they are emergent, the whole larger than the sum of its parts; 4) they are holistic; 5) they are in creative dialogue with their environment; 6) they thrive through evolutionary mutations; 7) they are destroyed by outside control; 8) they are exploratory; 9) they recontextualize the environment; and 10) they bring order out of chaos.

In my earlier book, *Spiritual Capital*, I drew ten qualities of a conscious complex adaptive system (a human being!) from the above qualities of any complex adaptive system, bearing in mind the added factor of consciousness and the effect that a conscious expression would have on the quality. I called them the transformational principles of spiritual intelligence. And then I added two more drawn from the spiritual literature of all the world's great traditions.[1] Thus, though there are ten defining qualities of nonhuman complex adaptive systems, I suggested there are a total of *twelve* defining qualities of SQ.

Self-Awareness: To know what I believe in, value, and what deeply motivates me. Awareness of my deepest life's purposes.

Spontaneity: To live in and be responsive to the moment and all that it contains.

Being Vision and Value Led: Acting from principles, deep beliefs, and living life accordingly.

Holism (a sense of the system, or of connectivity): Ability to see larger patterns, relationships, connections. A strong sense of belonging.

Compassion: Quality of "feeling-with" and deep empathy. Groundwork for *universal sympathy*.

Celebration of Diversity: Valuing other people and unfamiliar situations *for* their differences, not *despite* them.

Field-Independence: To be able to stand against the crowd and maintain my own convictions.

Tendency to Ask Fundamental Why? Questions: Need to understand things, to get to the bottom of them. Basis for criticizing the given.

Ability to Reframe: Stand back from the problem/situation and look for the bigger picture, the wider context.

Positive Use of Adversity: Ability to own and learn from mistakes, to see problems as opportunities. Resilience.

Humility: Sense of being a player in a larger drama, sense of my true place in the world. Basis for self-criticism and critical judgment.

Sense of Vocation: Being "called" to serve something larger than myself. Gratitude toward those who have helped me, and a wish to give something back. Basis for the "servant leader."

Complex Adaptive Systems	Spiritual Intelligence
Self-organization	Self-awareness
Bounded instability	Spontaneity
Emergent	Vision and value led
Holistic	Holistic
In dialogue with environment	Compassion (feeling-with)
Evolutionary mutations	Celebration of diversity
Outside control destructive	Field-independent
Exploratory	Asking why?
Recontexualize environment	Reframe
Order out of chaos	Positive use of adversity
	Humility
	Sense of vocation

Table 7. Complex Adaptive Systems and Spiritual Intelligence

In this book, I want to introduce these twelve transformational principles of SQ as the active transformational principles of QSD. Thus, I think it is worthwhile at this point, taking another look at each of them in more depth.

SELF-AWARENESS

Chris Miller, CEO of Anglian Water in the UK, wrote, "If you really want to be a leader, the first thing you have to understand is yourself."[2] Two millennia earlier, Jesus promised his disciples, "If you know who you are, you will become as I am."[3] Yet knowing who we are is perhaps the last thing we know.

We live in a very self-obsessed culture, but we have very little self-awareness. In neither our personal lives nor in our organizations do we have many habits or structures for reflection. We take little or no time for catching up with ourselves, for looking inward. We don't even have any recent tradition for showing us what we might look inward *for*, or why. Our focus is outward, on events and problems in the world, with the consequence that we lose ourselves and all that is to be gained from self-knowledge.

In many parts of the East where Hinduism and Buddhism are widely practiced, people begin their day with the meditation or prayer,

Who is it that is acting?
Who is it that is willing?
Who is it that is thinking?
Who am I?

These questions take the questioner directly to the deepest and most spiritual level of self-awareness—an awareness that he or she has a "deep self" in the first place, a personal reality that lies beneath and acts through our daily actions and thoughts. This primary level of self-awareness enables us to escape the narrow restrictions imposed by our mere egos. They take us to the center of our awareness and freedom and empower us to act from our highest motives.

The awareness that I, or the organization of which I am a part, has a deep center in the first place, and my need to be in contact with it and to act through it confers meaning and authenticity on my projects and actions. It is to know that I have an inner compass and that I can be led by its sense of direction. This is one crucial meaning of integrity—to act in accord with my inner compass. To have self-awareness at this level is to know what I believe in, what I value, and what deeply motivates me. It is to know what I live for and, perhaps, even what I would die for. It is also having the courage to know when I am betraying these things.

Because deep self-awareness puts us (and our organizations) in touch with our deepest center; it allows us continuously to create or re-create ourselves. It puts us in touch with a fount of infinite potentiality. It also enables us to hear the "call" of the deep self, the voice of conscience and responsibility. It gives us a sense of focus, and often confers a deep sense of peace.

Daniel Goleman has argued that self-awareness is the keystone to emotional intelligence. If I don't know what or how I feel, emotions will control me and my reactions. "An inability to notice our true feelings," he warns, "leaves us at their mercy."[4] Knowing our deepest values and purposes is the keystone to our spiritual intelligence and allows us to raise and control our motivations.

SPONTANEITY

During one of the final rounds of the men's Wimbledon tennis tournament some years ago, there were some amazing acrobatics. One of the players—Andre Agassi, I believe—tripped during a volley and fell forward onto his chest. Nonetheless, he kept his head and right arm up and returned the ball just across the net. Then, standing up and with a second volley coming right toward him, Agassi lost his balance again and began to fall backward. This time he returned the volley in the midst of his backward fall and managed to win the point.

Agassi's winning shots were a combination of fierce inner discipline combined with the most radical spontaneity. Though off his balance both times, he was still instantly responsive to the position and momentum of the ball. He was in what sports psychologists call "the zone." This kind of being in the zone is our closest Western equivalent to the disciplined spontaneity practiced by the martial arts warrior. It is action or response that comes from beyond the ego, that issues from the "deep self." When in it, we are connected to our personal center, and hence to our inner power.

The word *spontaneity* comes from the same Latin root as the words *response* and *responsibility*. To be deeply spontaneous is to be deeply responsive to the moment, and then willing and able to take responsibility for it. It means greeting each moment, each person, each situation with the freshness of a child, without all the baggage of past conditioning, habit, prejudice, fear, not needing to seize control or being unnecessarily "polite." It means having the courage to put *oneself* in the moment. Deep spontaneity is, therefore, the necessary precondition for playfulness, improvisation, trial-and-error learning, and creativity. This is particularly true for mental spontaneity.

Mental spontaneity is the condition of being "in the zone" with our thinking. Too often we take refuge in what we already know, what we have already learned, in conditioned habits of thought. We get trapped in our minds' own personal paradigms—dogmas, prejudices, ideologies to which we subscribe, abstractions and "models," assumptions we hold, or simply thinking that feels comfortable and familiar. Mental spontaneity, like so many of the processes that distinguish SQ, often requires that we be willing to enter our discomfort zone. This can bring us face to face with fear.

Fear is usually the greatest barrier to achieving spontaneity. Fear of ridicule, fear of judgment or punishment, and fear of showing our own vulnerability. To be spontaneous, I must have the courage to suspend my defenses and to own both my vulnerability and my authenticity. These put me in touch with the spiritual dimension of spontaneity—a radical openness to life's possibilities and an existential readiness to become the person who I really am. Both are frequently accompanied by a sense of deep joy or even ecstasy. Both require a deep trust in life, a deep trust in myself, and a trust that I have a deep inner authority or inner compass that guides me.

VISION AND VALUE LED

In August 1963, I was among a crowd of some 100,000 people gathered before the Lincoln Memorial on the Mall in Washington, DC. We had prepared for this event all summer, and a great excitement filled the crowd. But none of us could have imagined or foreseen the electrifying wave of inspirational energy that swept through us as Martin Luther King almost sang out the ringing phrases of his now famous "I Have a Dream" speech. His words, their passion, and the vision they offered galvanized us, fired our motivations, and transformed the social and political landscape of our country. That is what real visions do.

Dr. King's words reached beyond the given realities of American race relations and painted the picture of a new, more just and loving society scarcely imagined by the American people at that time. He palpably ached in the whole of his being for the not yet born, and that ache carried in his voice as an inspirational longing. This, too, is a vital feature of great visions. They reach deeply into a well of human potentiality and present us with the not yet born. They make us dream. They make us long. They motivate us. It was with a similarly powerful vision that Mahatma Gandhi led India to independence and with which Nelson Mandela ended apartheid in South Africa. And that same visionary spirit is the key to quantum leadership.

Visions give rise to new realities through raising human motivations. But visions themselves are based on deep values. When Tex Gunning was CEO of Unilever Asia, he valued health and bringing health to people. He introduced the "5 rupee packet" that brought the advantage of Unilever products to India's poor.[5] Zhang Ruimin, CEO of China's Haier Group, values service, and he has made its practice of deep values the driving influence in the company transformation program he has undertaken. Martin Luther King valued equality and human dignity. Values are like quanta of energy. They make things happen. Our deepest values define us as the human beings that we are and lay the foundations for the kinds of organizations and societies that will bring out the best of human potential. If we want to shift human and corporate motivation beyond its currently low level on the scale, we can do so only through a healthy dose of the idealism that flows from serving fundamental values. The great German philosopher Immanuel Kant had a moral imperative that was the basis for his system of values: "Always act in such a way that it would be alright if *everyone* acted that way."[6] This may be a good criterion for all values, but it certainly applies to transpersonal values. It would be very creative if it could apply to corporate values.

HOLISM

At Blue Circle Cement there was a problem with profit margins. Delivery costs were running too high, and the company had pretty much decided to cut back on trips, and thus on drivers. The company had earlier adopted a policy of open dialogue and full consultation with employees, so a meeting was called to discuss the problem and to announce job cuts.[7] A tanker driver named Bill spoke up at this meeting.

"The problem isn't the number of trips and drivers," said Bill emphatically. "It's the size of the petrol tanks." A bemused CEO asked Bill to explain his thinking. Bill then pointed out that Blue Circle's petrol tanks were designed for long-distance journeys of 300-400 miles, whereas the average journey per delivery was only eighty miles. "All that weight could be used for carrying cement," he said, and then added, "You should also look at the weight of our metal hoses."[8] When technical experts followed through on these observations, they discovered that General Motors could supply trucks with smaller tanks at less cost, and that the heavy metal hoses could be replaced with light plastic ones. When these changes were made, productivity rose by 500 percent in the first six months without job cuts.

Blue Circle's action was holistic in the first place because it had in place a system of consultation that enabled a simple driver to speak up and be taken seriously by the bosses. And that driver's thinking was holistic because he looked at the productivity problem as a *full system* problem. He considered the interplay and connectedness of individual factors bearing on delivery costs, and thus brought a fresh perspective to the problem.

Holism in science is a defining quality of both quantum and complex adaptive self-organizing systems. It is an *internal* holism in that the relationship of the different parts of a system helps to define not just the system itself but even to give final form to the parts themselves. In physical holism, *it is the relationship between things that defines their reality*. We can't break a holistic system down into its separate parts without losing something vital of both those parts and of the system they comprise. We can't isolate the individual factors within the system. This is one of the qualities that made twentieth-century science revolutionary and paradigm-breaking.

Holism is also a defining quality of and process within using our SQ. It is an ability to see larger patterns and relationships, an ability to see the internally functioning connections between things, the overlaps and influences, an ability to think *systemically*. "The fish is in the water, and the water is in the fish."[9] It is an ability to look at a problem from every angle and to see that every question has at least two sides, and usually more. It is also a perception that a deeper, common reality underlies most differences. Seeing the holistic nature of a problem also taps us into the deeper potentiality within the situation from which it arises. (The possibility of using smaller petrol tanks and lighter hoses to address an under-lying weight problem in the case of Blue Circle.) At its most "spiritual" level, holism gives us the ability to see the infinite within the finite. And it gives us access to the deeper currents and patterns of a problem or situation. It taps us into *possibilities*.

Holistic people rely heavily on intuition, which is itself simply the initial and prelogical perception of patterns, relationships, and coherences. A holistic thinker is reflective, broadminded, and lives his or her life on a bigger stage. Such people are sensitive to the inner workings of groups or situations. They take responsibility for their part within the whole and are always aware how that whole affects them and others. Such people are needed to address, for example, the overwhelming problems issuing from human actions affecting the environment, and to appreciate that the environment human beings create impinges back upon our own well-being. The same is true of perceiving the complex interrelationships and patterns within a globalized economy, the social, political, and spiritual issues that bear on and create economic reality.

Traditionally, organizations have been described as machines, or collections of individuals (or at best, collections of teams), united by rules, practices, and a "culture." But this is bitty and piecey. The holistic aspect of SQ enables those parts or individuals to become a system and allows, literally, our organizations to become complex, self-organizing adaptive systems, with all the creativity that implies. It breathes life into a system from "below," from the deep well of potentiality latent within the system. Ensuring that one's organizational system is holistic, all parts meaningfully "entangled" is key to Quantum Systems Dynamics.

In my view, the real "glue" or holistic underpinning of a society or an organization (or even of an individual) is its vision and deep values, its sense of "being about something" meaningful. This is the driving force that binds together and motivates a human complex system and ensures its function. An organization that is aware, at least unconsciously, of this driving vision and values and is true to them, works. One that is not is bound to be dysfunctional. Preoccupation with the "bottom line" does not integrate or motivate at this level.

COMPASSION

A Dutch investment banker whom I shall call "Geert" wrote to me with a problem. Geert was at the top of his career, the senior investment analyst for one of Holland's big banks, but he wasn't happy. "I just spend all my time making money for myself and for my bank," he complained when we met. "There's a whole troubled world out there, and I feel I just have to do something about it."[10] What Geert wanted from me was just a little moral support for a decision he had already taken. A young man in his midthirties, he had decided to leave investment banking to set up a global ethical investment fund. Besides channeling his fund's money into ethical businesses, he intended to set aside 10 percent of all profits for the development of clean energy in the Third World.

In the Latin, *compassion* literally means, "feeling with." A quality of deep empathy, compassion is not just knowing the feelings of others, but *feeling* their feelings. It is knowing what it is like to walk in my neighbor's shoes, and perhaps wanting to help make my neighbor's journey less painful, less needy—*for his sake*. Hence it is an *active* feeling-with, a willingness—no, almost a compulsion—to get involved. Compassion requires that I feel the common humanity of my neighbor even if his or her views are alien to or opposite from my own, feeling-with him at a deep level even if I have to kill or destroy him because he is my "enemy" and threatens me. We are often able, through compassion, to draw out the potentiality for good from within even the very bad. This is the nurturing aspect of the quality.

All psychological evidence shows that we are more likely to be compassionate toward or cooperative with someone from our own family or group than toward members of other groups. This is no longer good enough given the global links that cause us to impinge upon one another even as strangers. A part of the paradigm shift enabled by using our SQ entails a paradigm shift about the so-called "otherness" of others. Can I call any person a "stranger"? Albert Einstein said that true compassion was compassion for the whole of existence, for every last speck of dust within it. Both quantum physics and the qualities of a universal field of meaning within which we all participate tell us that we are all pieces of each other, or at the very least all individual expressions of the same underlying reality. I am my brother's keeper because I *am* my brother.

True compassion requires the courage to be vulnerable and to own my vulnerability. My compassion for another is usually evoked by that other's vulnerability, but a healthy realization of "There but for the grace of God go I," prevents compassion from descending to mere pity. It acknowledges that today especially we all have a shared vulnerability. An honest awareness that now, "we are all in this together," can lead to a very pressing sense of feeling-with the plight of others.

The word *passion* is also hidden within *compassion*. If I feel-with someone or something, it can fill me with a passionate intensity within; it can stir me. Hence again, stirring me to become involved, active. That is why it is associated with one of the highest of our motivations, "Higher Service." Quantum leaders are driven by both passion and compassion.

CELEBRATE DIVERSITY

On a lecture tour of Finland I noticed and commented on the homogeneity of Finnish culture. "That is exactly our big problem," responded an executive from Nokia. "We are too alike. We all come from the same kind of schools, we went to the same few universities, and we all think alike. We lack the enrichment of diversity."[11] In our more diverse Western nations and economies, with their now common "diversity initiatives," diversity too often means an acceptable number of people from ethnic backgrounds on the payroll and a token woman on the board of directors.

A full appreciation of real diversity and its benefits is difficult for Western people and organizations to achieve. For over 2000 years, ever since Moses came down from Sinai with his Tablets of the Law, ours has been a culture of the one God, the one truth, the one way. This thinking runs through all our Western religions, appears again in Newtonian science (absolute space, absolute time, universal laws of nature), and is even built into our logic: either/or rather than both/and. This gives

Western people a negative view of conflict and difference. We see conflict as something to be "resolved," usually through the defeat of any opponents. At best we *tolerate* difference, allowing it to co-exist *despite* our disagreement or discomfort.

By contrast, complex adaptive systems in nature *thrive* on diversity. That bit of grit in the oyster becomes a pearl.

Genuine diversity means loving or at least highly valuing other people and conflicting opinions *for* their differences rather than *despite* those differences. It means seeing difference as opportunity. This requires, for Western people, making the quantum leap of recognizing that truth is multifaceted, perhaps infinite, and that there is no "one best way." (In Einstein's physics, there are as many valid points of view on space/time as there are observers; in quantum physics, the ground of all reality is a field of infinite potentiality—the quantum vacuum.) A celebration of diversity recognizes that my best approximation to understanding a problem or evolving a strategy is to capture as many points of view on it as possible. It means *cognitive* diversity. This requires a recognition that that which makes me uncomfortable or which challenges my assumptions is often my best teacher.

A full celebration of diversity means almost thanking God for the other's difference, because that difference enriches my own reality and opportunities. This allows me to respect a point of view (a religion, a belief, an argument) as valid and thus worth consideration, even though it is different from mine. And this of course requires that I be more humble about the importance of my own opinion. All these qualities require that I (or my organization) be deeply secure enough in myself to question myself and possibly all that I hold sacred. For this I must cultivate a deep trust that truth will emerge from conflict, or from a situation's self-organizing potential. I need to give up the need for total control.

There is a rich diversity underlying each one of us as individuals (and usually as organizations). Learning to appreciate it in others can help me learn to accept the rich chorus of my own many inner voices. This leaves me more open to intuition and hunches, more broadminded and more open to life's or a situation's different possibilities. It makes me more flexible, more self-questioning, thoughtful, open to learning, and willing to grow.

There is a rich lesson to be learned about diversity from its role in natural complex adaptive systems. In science, homogeneous systems are very stable, but hence slow to adapt. If an organization's dominate culture is *too* strong, it can share this flaw. By contrast, too much diversity or dissent in a system just tears it apart. Systems that are poised at the edge of chaos hold homogeneity and diversity in a critical balance. We might use the metaphor of "Her Majesty's Loyal Opposition" to illustrate the necessity of loyal dissent within a company culture.

FIELD INDEPENDENCE

Once during his long campaign for Indian independence, Mahatma Gandhi organized a national march from one side of India to the other. Tens of thousands walked with him in the dust and heat. Midway through, he suddenly stopped and announced, "No, no, this is a mistake! Turn back." Appalled, his followers questioned his judgment and consistency. Gandhi replied, "My commitment is to the truth as I see it each day, not to consistency."[12]

"Field independence" is a psychological term that means being able to stand against the crowd or, as in Gandhi's case, even against the previous dictates of my own mind. It is to have my own firm convictions that I live by, even if these isolate me or make me unpopular. It is to know my own mind and to be able to hold my own point of view, despite group pressure. More subtly, it is to see through and stand against the currents of my organization or culture that would influence my independent judgment. To be able to stand apart from immediate circumstances and see my way through.

More difficult still, field independence implies an ability to stand apart from the paradigms or habitual patterns of my own mind, to see when I am in error or thinking in boxes. Even more subtly, it means to be deeply independent from entanglement, from those tendencies in my own being that might imprison me—craving, hating, resenting, envying, a need for flattery or justification, the thrill of popularity. These are all things that influence my reactions and responses and that trap me lower down on the Scale of Motivations.

At its most spiritual, to be field independent is to stand on a high mountain in the clear air and have a wide, independent perspective. To have the strength to be lonely, to feel isolated, to feel that I am the only person on the planet who *sees* as I do—and yet carry on. It is to be steady, focused, steadfast, independent-minded, self-critical, dedicated, and committed. These are qualities necessary in the captain of a (corporate?) ship sailing a wild sea or the officer who must take command in the midst of battle. They are also the qualities of the scientist or the artist (or *any* innovator) who discovers a new way of seeing or doing something. Field independent people can seem stubborn; they can be genuinely subversive, but without them ideas and culture never move forward. The herd is always led by someone who can stand apart from the herd.

ASKING FUNDAMENTAL "WHY?" QUESTIONS

Several years ago there was a very serious accident at a Japanese nuclear power plant. The flow of coolant through the reactor was decreased and the control rods overheated. The reactor reached criticality, and there was an explosion. In the inquiry that followed it was discovered that engineers at the plant had taken a shortcut in an effort to boost the plant's efficiency. Not understanding the fundamental principles of a nuclear reactor, they caused an accident. The engineers forgot to ask, "Why?" Why did the rules for operating the plant ensure its safe operation? They didn't get to the bottom of the reactor's underlying *system*.

The natural curiosity of children makes them ask "Why?" incessantly, yet in both our schools and in our organizations we discourage questions. Questions are seen as bothersome, distracting, or even disloyal. Children attend school to be taught; employees (and even managers) are hired who will be told what to do. This is to discourage not just the child in us (the passion, freshness, and spontaneity), but also the creativity of the child's questions that has accompanied all great adult innovations and breakthroughs. Isaac Newton famously described himself as being like a young boy standing on a beach in awe of the great ocean of undiscovered truth that lay before him. Einstein, when asked about the secret of his great intelligence, answered that when he was a young boy in school he used to get into trouble for asking so many questions. Now a famous scientist, he could ask all the questions he liked, even "dumb" ones.

An active curiosity and a tendency to ask fundamental "Why?" questions are critical to the whole scientific spirit, which is a spirit of endless inquiry. In quantum science, Heisenberg's famous Uncertainty Principle established that asking questions (doing experiments) actually creates reality. Questions pluck possibilities from the infinite sea of potentiality (the quantum vacuum) and turn them into actualities. Yet we see that our corporate culture, drenched as it is in an atmosphere of fear, has little tolerance for questions. As such it represses both the higher motivations of exploration and creativity. As I wrote earlier, a quantum organization is a *questioning* organization. *Everyone* in the organization is encouraged to think and to question.

A need to ask fundamental "Why?" questions stems from our deeper motivation to understand things, to get to the bottom of them (exploration). It is accompanied by a tendency never to take anything for granted, but always to question the reasons, foundations, or inner workings, and to ask if it could be better or different. Asking "Why?" also takes us beyond the given, the present situation, and encourages us to explore the future. Why do we make this product rather than that one? Why do we use this distribution system or these raw materials instead of some others? Such questions are necessary to innovation and growth. And they allow us to thrive on uncertainty because we are not so frightened of moving on.

Their critics are right to fear questions. They are subversive. They usually question the *status quo.* They undermine smug assumptions and prejudices and rock the boat. The boat they rock may be my own. Thus the price of good questions is a willingness to question my own assumptions, values, and methods as well as those of others. This of course requires humility (reducing self-assertion). It also requires making that same quantum leap about the infinite nature of truth that is required by the celebration of diversity. I must see that truth is infinite to cultivate a tendency always to look for more behind any "answer," always to hold a preference for good questions over good answers. This can make me a player of the infinite game, one who plays *with* boundaries rather than *within* them. Can we imagine a corporate CEO who says to young executives on his board, "I want you to come in here tomorrow morning with ten good questions, ten things that you *don't* understand"?

THE ABILITY TO REFRAME

Peter Schwartz's *The Art of the Long View*, and the work on scenario planning at Royal/Dutch Shell that it describes, transformed strategic thinking. The essence of that transformation is an ability to rethink the past and to imagine the future—indeed, to imagine many *possible* futures, and to see how these might bear on present decision-making. Both rethinking the past and imagining the future are acts of reframing—literally, putting a different (larger, broader) frame around a situation or problem that we are thinking about and then seeing it from a larger or different perspective.

Reframing requires standing back from a situation, suggestion, strategy, problem, etc. and looking for the bigger picture, the wider context. Sometimes this wider context is "spatial," taking in a wider geographic perspective or a wider set of people/situations likely to be influenced by a decision. Sometimes it is temporal, noticing how different a strategy looks if viewed over a longer time frame. Some solutions to problems look brilliant in the short-term, but if looked at from a long-term perspective they seem quite dumb. Vandana Shiva has pointed out that the World Bank's policy of dumping industrial pollutants in Third World countries is such a dumb solution.[13] Over the long-term, the overall contamination of the earth's atmosphere is the same, and will affect us all, *wherever* on the globe we initially dump the pollutants. The same criticism can be made of those who choose to deny climate change because it is against their "national interests."

Perhaps the most critical block to reframing problems (or opportunities) is our own minds, the fact that most of us are always thinking inside some box, inside some set of assumptions. We have first to become conscious of this and of what these assumptions are, and then we have to blow up (or blow out) the walls of the box. This can take us into our discomfort zones. As Peter Schwartz described the process at Shell, "We evolved a discipline that allowed us to examine our mind-sets so that we could bring forth our prejudices and assumptions.... But what helped focus our attention on useful subjects was paying attention to those situations that made us uncomfortable or which we really did not understand."[14]

People (and organizations) that can reframe are more visionary, able to imagine (and perhaps bring about) futures that do not yet exist. Hence they are open to possibilities. They are creative (seeing the not yet seen) and broad in outlook. They are of necessity self-critical, and usually more adventurous. But because they can see beyond their own and others' paradigms, their insights can feel threatening or "mad" to those more comfortable with the given or with the narrow view. This has always been true in science and the arts as well as business.

Psychologists have found that we can predict which adolescents and adults will be better at reframing situations from their behavior as small children. In a famous experiment with marshmallows, a group of four-year-olds were offered two marshmallows, but told they could have two more later if they only ate one of these now. When retested at the age of fourteen, those children who had been able to delay their gratification at age four now showed wider and more sophisticated cognitive abilities, including an ability to reframe. An overall strength of character embeds many of these qualities of spiritual intelligence.

At the spiritual level, reframing can be seen as bringing something new into the world or something new into myself. In this sense, reframing my set of assumptions can be like undergoing an act of initiation or even rebirth.

THE POSITIVE USE OF ADVERSITY

Charles Handy described an "alchemist" as somebody who can make things happen, someone who can create something out of nothing. Such people are the innovators in business, the arts, and the sciences. A common feature of alchemists is their "doggedness," their ability to stick with a project or an idea and see it through no matter how tough or disaster-ridden it gets. "Alchemists have the extraordinary ability," says Handy, "to turn disaster into new life."[15]

One of Handy's alchemists is Virgin's Richard Branson, a man who even did a brief stint in jail for one of his early business mistakes. Says Branson, "My businesses grow out of my experiences, usually my bad experiences. I see something done badly which I know that we could do better—like the airline."[16] Like all English schoolboys, Branson would have grown up with Rudyard Kipling's character-forming poem, "If": "If you can meet with triumph and disaster and treat those two imposters just the same . . . you'll be a man, my son."[17]

The positive use of adversity is an important quality of spiritual intelligence because it enables us to learn from and use our mistakes. It teaches us to recognize our limits, not just to live within them but often to surpass them. We grow and learn from suffering or failure and make gains from our setbacks. "Pick oneself up, dust oneself off, and start all over again." Yet such wisdom goes against the grain of an existing corporate culture that takes no prisoners: "Here is your budget," say most senior managers. "It is tight, so don't make any mistakes." I know of no corporation that gives an award for the most creative mistake of the week. Rather the ethos is: screw up, and you pay for it. This is one of the chief reasons an atmosphere of fear permeates corporate culture.

The positive use of adversity requires great strength of character, but it is also the only thing that really builds character. Think of Nietzsche's now common phrase, "That which does not kill me makes me stronger." Using adversity requires the courage to look at my own weaknesses, faults, and past mistakes, to own them, learn from them, and grow beyond them. It requires that I be brave enough to face the pain that accompanies shame, and thus have the resilience to grow beyond the causes of that shame. As American sociologist Richard Sennett pointed out, this in turn requires that I have an underlying and abiding sense of self, a sense of self that transcends the short-term working experiences, flexible institutions, and constant risk-taking that characterize corporate culture.[18] Such a sense of self can arise only from living true to my deepest values. Sennett calls this "fidelity to oneself."[19]

More subtly, the positive use of adversity requires a tragic recognition that not all problems have solutions, not all differences can be resolved—and yet the ability to carry on just the same. To be able to bear the sadness that lies at the heart of all creativity. Such recognition confers a deep wisdom and maturity, a sense of having made my peace with life, or at least of having given life "a good run for its money." To fly in the face of tragedy or setback in turn helps to build a basic trust in life, and thus a greater ability to live with uncertainty.

HUMILITY

The director of executive education at a major international business school criticized my list of the twelve transformational principles of SQ for including "humility." She said that businesspeople aren't interested in being very humble. Yet humility was described in the *Harvard Business Review* as one of two essential defining qualities of a "Level 5 Leader." These are leaders who can "transform a good company into a great one . . . catalysts who elevate companies from mediocrity to sustained excellence."[20] The other defining quality of a Level 5 Leader is possession of a fierce resolve.

A sense of humility, or modesty, is the first SQ transformational principle process that raises our scale and responses into the positive zone of higher motivations. It gets us beyond the isolation of and preoccupation with our own egos and assumed self-importance. It opens us to the possibility of learning from others and from experience. If I think that I am God's gift to the world and know more than anyone else, I have little motive to listen or learn.

Healthy humility gives me a sense that I am but one player in a larger drama and makes me more aware of the good qualities and achievements of others. It makes me aware how much my own achievements are grounded on those of others and on the gifts and good fortune that life has thrown my way. This, in turn, makes me more sensitive to the needs of others, and more likely to be a leader who creates space where others can realize their own best talents. It makes me ask questions and seek advice, and gives me a readiness to admit that I could be wrong and others could be right. This promotes a healthy self-criticism and makes me both aware of and ready to admit my own limits. It also prevents me from taking myself too seriously.

At a more spiritual level, a sense of humility puts us in touch with a sense that our true self-importance comes from something deeper than, or from something beyond, our mere ego selves. Beyond a purely secular sense of "knowing my place" in the natural and social worlds, it helps my self-awareness evolve into seeing myself as a part of humanity, a part of the universe, as a child of God, or as an excitation in the common field of vacuum energy shared by all. It provides a wider context and deeper meaning for my life. This makes humility a companion of gratitude, of deeper self-awareness, and of a wish to serve. Very great leaders like Abraham Lincoln, Mahatma Gandhi, and Nelson Mandela have all combined deep personal humility with great political vision and fierce resolve.

A SENSE OF VOCATION

A British fashion designer told me she thought there were three reasons that someone might start a business. The first reason, she said, was just that there is an exploitable hole in the market. "You see that something is wanted or needed, and you decide to provide it." The second reason is personal opportunity. I may have inherited a business from my family, or I may have a special skill or talent to provide a certain kind of thing, like fashion design or sound systems. "But the third reason is different," she said. "The third reason for starting a business is just a sense of *I have to*; it just *has to be*."[21] This third reason is more visionary, a felt need to bring something into the world.

A sense of vocation is the active accompaniment to having a vision. It is a desire and the will to make that vision come true. Literally from the Latin word *vocare*, "to be called," a vocation originally meant a call to take up holy orders, to be called by God. As an SQ quality, I mean it as any calling to higher service, a sense of being called upon to make something good or beautiful happen in this world. It is a call to pursue a certain course in life, a sense of deep personal (transpersonal!) purpose, a need to act from and act upon my deepest ideals and values. Teaching and medicine have traditionally been viewed as vocations; the law used to be. The ideal posed by the paradigm of quantum leadership is that being a business leader should also become a vocation.

A sense of vocation is far deeper than merely having an ambition or a goal. There is no vocation in saying, "I want to be a millionaire by the time I am thirty." Rather, having a sense of vocation is being driven by a wish to make my life useful, by a strong need to make a difference. It often comes from following an inspiration. It need not be a grand vocation like saving the world. A person can be called to become an honest leader, a good parent, or an active citizen. The essential quality is that *it has to be*.

A sense of vocation usually follows from a deep sense of gratitude, a sense that I have been given very much and now I want to give something back. That something I wish to give is not used or intended to manipulate those whom I will serve. It is a gift. Beyond mere gratitude, this quality may arise from a sense of reverence, reverence for the existence of some quality or example, or even for the gift of life itself. The Trappist monastic order has as its motto, *Laborare est orare*, "To work is to pray." Their reverence for God's works led them to work in the world. What if such a sense of reverence were to inspire our business leaders to do something good for the world with the companies they lead. That *would* be a paradigm shift!

Business leaders I work with often ask me, "What can I *do* to become a quantum leader?" I think that practicing the twelve principles of spiritual intelligence, embedding them in one's company culture, and articulating them in one's company vision is a pretty good way to start. That is why their practice is a key element of Quantum Systems Dynamics.

CHAPTER 13

THE DIALOGUE GROUP: A WAY TO TRANSFORM COMPANY CULTURE

In a recent conversation, the head of global leadership development at a major pharmaceutical company, expressed a frustration she has felt about shifting the thinking, motivation, and behavior of individuals going through the company's leadership development programs. She used the metaphor of fish swimming in the dirty water of a fish tank.

"We've been concentrating on taking the fish out of the tank and cleaning them. But then we just throw them back in the dirty water, and all our efforts are wasted. We realize now we've got to clean the water, the company culture."[1] One method she has been experimenting with to achieve this is the introduction of dialogue groups. This pharmaceutical company is one among many big companies turning to dialogue as a transformation tool.

Much of this book has been about thinking, and about using new thinking to rewire the corporate brain. But using thinking implies doing. It requires actions and tools for transformative action. If a corporation wants to think and operate at the edge, it needs some methodology or infrastructure for doing so. Dialogue is such a method. Properly understood and practiced, the dialogue process and the dialogue group are a practical tool with which companies can make the transition from old thinking and less effective business practices to new being and doing. Even the decision to undertake the dialogue process can change the way a company operates and the way its employees are empowered. The medium is the message.

Remember the example of Bill, the Blue Circle Cement driver, described in Chapter Twelve. The fact that a simple driver was able to present his thinking to the CEO at a company meeting was enabled by the company's earlier decision to introduce mixed dialogue groups where employees drawn from all levels of the company structure could express themselves freely.

The word *dialogue* is familiar to most of us. Too familiar, because it is used in so many ways to mean so many different things. Most people think they engage in dialogue whenever they engage in conversation, or at least whenever they have a good discussion or a good debate. But I mean something more specific by the word. I want to describe dialogue as a very particular process of *thinking together* and a powerful group exercise by which members can grow new neural connections. I think it is a quantum process, a means for doing collective quantum thinking. Used in a corporate context, the dialogue group can be a crucial infrastructure for any thinking or learning organization, an infrastructure through which the corporate brain can rewire itself continuously.

The history of dialogue is important. Its origins go back to ancient Athens. It was the main teaching method used by Socrates, the method immortalized in Plato's famous dialogues. The word *dialogue* itself is Greek, coming from *dia* and *logos*. *Dia* means "through," or "by way of." *Logos* has traditionally been translated as "word," so *dia-logos* would mean "through words," "through talking." But there is an earlier and more original Greek meaning of *logos*. This is translated as "relationship." *Dia-logos* is "through relationship." This gives the word a radically different and far more powerful meaning, particularly when we remember the creative importance of relationship in quantum science. Imagine *logos* translated in the Bible as "relationship." "In the beginning was relationship." A whole new metaphysics and theological perspective would be suggested.

In ancient Athens, dialogue was the special relationship between Socrates and his students. It was a form of ongoing conversation in which Socrates would teach people by asking them a seemingly endless series of questions. Each question was intended to undercut some assumption or prejudice or false belief in the student's last answer. Socrates believed that all human beings are born knowing everything, but that life is a process of forgetting. Truth, then, for him was "unforgetting" or "recalling" what we have always known, coming into possession of our original wisdom. The most famous instance of this Socratic dialogue technique used for unforgetting is in Plato's dialogue *The Meno*. Here, Socrates gets an ignorant slave boy wholly without education and, through a series of questions, elicits from him all the principles of higher mathematics. "See," comments Socrates, "he really knew all along."[2]

Dialogue was also a special relationship among the citizens of Athens, enabling them to resolve their differences. Whenever there was an important issue to be considered, the citizens would meet in the *agora*, the marketplace, and hold a dialogue about it—for hours, for days if necessary, until they had seen some way through. This allowed the emergence of collective insight, collective wisdom, and a nonconfrontational way of solving problems. But, as the years passed, the citizens of Athens became too numerous and too busy to engage in dialogue. So they hired paid advocates to put their positions, and they voted on the advocates' arguments. Dialogue was replaced with debate, and representative democracy as we know it today was born. A democracy of equal citizens exploring ideas and problems together became a focus on voting between set positions instead of a relationship allowing many positions and new insights to emerge.

Ever since the appearance of those paid advocates in ancient Athens, confrontational debate has been our familiar Western form of solving disagreements or arriving at decisions. We teach the art of debate in our schools and look for it in our politicians. It has become the dominant model for most conversation between individuals and within groups in Western societies. I think debate is a particularly Newtonian, mechanistic form of conversation. It is about the conflict of ideas and the confrontation between their advocates, like the clash of two billiard balls in Newton's model of the atomistic universe. We even use the expression, "Let's bounce some ideas off each other." Public debates are formal, constrained by rules and boundaries, and accepted speaking techniques.

DEBATE VS. DIALOGUE

We can look at some contrasting features of debate and dialogue to see what radically different approaches they are to conversation and relationship. The difference is important to corporate thinking and the transformation of corporate cultures. It certainly has wider societal and education implications.

Knowing vs. Finding Out

In a debate, I know which position I am advocating or defending. I know the many points of my argument and—if well prepared—know the most clever way to present them. I know my position is right. Debate is clever; it is cerebral. I do it with my head.

Dialogue is about finding out, about exploring and discussing something openly until I break through to some new knowledge or insight. I might go to a dialogue believing what I think is the case, but I am willing to suspend my conviction and listen to the discussion with an open mind. And with an open heart. Dialogue involves my emotions and my deeper sensitivities, as well as my best intellectual-thinking faculties. I engage in dialogue with my whole being.

Answers vs. Questions

In a debate, because I already know, I have all the answers. You have nothing to teach me. I am here to teach you, or to convince you, or to defeat you. I talk *at* you.

Dialogue is about questions, about the things I don't know or things I would like to find out. It's about exploration—of myself, of the others, of the matter at hand. Why do your words make me feel angry or anxious? Why have you said that? Where are you coming from? What is your point of view, and why do you hold it? Is there possibly another way to look at things? What assumptions have I been making? Where has my own point of view been coming from? What has been the larger framework of my thinking?

Winning or Losing vs. Sharing

In a debate, somebody knows, somebody has the answers, and the other person is wrong. So one of us will win, and the other will lose. One point of view will be judged better than the other, one line of argument best. There is one best way from A to B, and we'll vote on that.

Dialogue is about sharing. We share our points of view; we share our assumptions, our doubts, and uncertainties, our questions, our fears, our suggestions and wild ideas. We propose many paths from A to B, and we jointly imagine and consider them. We *feel* them together.

Unequal vs. Equal

Debate is unequal because one of us is right and one of us is wrong. One of us will win, and the other must lose. One of us has the answers; the other is in error. One point of view will be judged better than the other. We will choose, or our listeners will choose. One of us has been more clever, more eloquent, more entertaining.

Dialogue is equal because we all have something to contribute. Unless a person is insane, he or she has some valid reason for holding a particular point of view or for harboring a feeling. There is something valid about any point of view or any feeling that any of us might entertain. There are no "wrong" points of view, no invalid ways to feel. I am here to learn your reasons and your feelings and to understand their origins. And to understand my own response to them.

Power vs. Respect or Reverence

Debate is about power. My power to defeat you or to win you over or make you compromise. It is about my power to persuade you or to make you look like a fool.

Dialogue is about respect. My respect for your point of view and how you have arrived at it, my respect for your feelings, for your contribution. It may even be about reverence. My gratitude to you for seeing things differently than I do, my reverence for your different personality, your different history and experience, and your ability to enrich me with them. Each of us can only express one of life's (reality's) many possibilities. I revere you for showing me there are others and sharing them with me.

Proving a Point vs. Listening

Debate is about proving a point or defending a position. I attack you, and I build defenses against you, against your point of view. I close myself to you and your words and your feelings. I don't want to know.

Dialogue is about exploring new possibilities together. It is about listening. I create a space inside myself where I can hear myself, where I can listen to and feel my own reactions to what you say—thus *questioning* myself and becoming aware of underlying unconscious assumptions. Most of us are not very good at listening, to ourselves or to others. Our experience and our education have prepared us always to be ready with a thought or a reaction or a good argument. This overpreparedness blocks out what we might learn or hear. It makes us deaf. And insensitive—insensitive to others and to ourselves.

DIALOGUE ITSELF

Like good quantum thinking, dialogue makes us surface and challenge our assumptions. It leads to us changing our existing mental models, to reframing. It is a structure that dissolves previous structures.

Dialogue is not necessarily about reaching consensus. Our Western culture teaches us there is one best way, one best point of view, one God, one truth. Ideally, we should all be able to agree on this. The convergence of all differences toward one cozy agreement is our cultural ideal, the end and goal of Western history. We feel ill at ease with difference or ambiguity. We resist the possibility that two people might disagree and yet both might be right. We can't handle that, can't handle "both/and."

There is a famous Sufi story about the Mullah Nasruddin. Nasruddin was a wise man or a fool, depending on your point of view. In this particular story, two men have come to the mullah with an argument. The first man puts his case, and Nasruddin says, "I perceive that you are right." Then the second man puts his own, contradictory case, and once again Nasruddin says, "I perceive that *you* are right." A third man looking on objects. How can Nasruddin say that both men are right when they entirely disagree? To him Nasruddin says, "I perceive that you also are right." A Chinese citizen would find this entirely natural, but to the Western mind it is a brainteaser.

The Mullah Nasruddin, like Socrates, was a practitioner of dialogue. In my own experience, some of the best dialogue groups I have ever facilitated have ended with nobody agreeing with anybody else. Yet everyone has emerged enriched. Dialogue is about that enrichment. It is about what we can learn from difference, and the wisdom of knowing that truth isn't always simple. It's about knowing that human nature and human situations and human problems are not simple and that if there are any solutions, these, too, are not simple.

The concept of dialogue lay dormant in Western culture for centuries. It was revived by the group psychology movement in the 1940s as psychologists working with traumatized soldiers returning from the war discovered it was an effective means of fostering group discussion and conflict resolution. In the 1970s, quantum physicist David Bohm took up the cause of dialogue. Bohm saw that it was a particularly quantum approach to conversation, where ambiguity, the celebration and exploration of many points of view ("potentialities"), the *holding* of many points of view in one nonconfrontational conversation gained real power. He felt it could be used to change society. Through Bohm's work,[3] "Bohmian dialogue" began to spread. It was taken up by the MIT Learning Center and featured strongly in Peter Senge's best-selling *The Fifth Discipline*. Bill Isaacs, a young protégé of Bohm's, began the MIT Dialogue Project and took the practice into big companies. Today it is practiced widely, and the practice is spreading. Isaacs has said, "We can think of companies as networks of power or hierarchy or we can think of them as networks of conversation. Dialogue can change companies."[4]

THE DIALOGUE GROUP

In group psychology and in the corporate world, dialogue is practiced in what are called dialogue groups. There are also dialogue groups being run in schools, prisons, and regions of political or religious conflict. I personally have run them with companies, schools, and local politicians.

In the dialogue group, people sit in a circle to emphasize the absence of hierarchy. In a corporate group, it is always most effective to have participants who represent all levels of the organization, from janitors and tea ladies to members of very senior management. The ideal group size ranges from seven to twenty, so that everyone can participate fully. There should be no observers in a dialogue group, no fence-sitters. But one or two members of the group act as facilitators. They participate fully; they are members of the group, but they also have the job of holding the group's energy, of maintaining a spirit of inquiry in the conversation, and if there is a theme, of gently assuring that the conversation sticks to it more or less.

The only real rules in dialogue are that each group member should express openly and honestly what he/she thinks or feels and that no one should be confrontational or abusive. The facilitators ensure that one person does not interrupt another who is speaking, and that no one person monopolizes the conversation. If the dialogue becomes too cerebral, if there is abuse, or if the conversation collapses back into debate, the facilitators gently bring it back on track.

There is an assumption that the dialogue group is a sacred space. If people are to be honest and open, they have to feel safe. Comments should not go beyond the group. There should be no comeback for expressing unpopular ideas or for surfacing criticism. No one should fear sounding the fool. The facilitator has to build what Bill Isaacs calls "the container"[5]—the safe space where dialogue can happen freely.

The dialogue group enables group feeling and a group intelligence to emerge. As in quantum physics, the whole (the group) is larger than the sum of its parts (its individual members, their thoughts and feelings). This is why it can be a powerful tool for organizational learning. It gives the corporation access to the corporate brain. During the dialogue itself, the corporate brain is almost tangibly present in the center of the group. Bill Isaacs describes this tangible presence as "a field," the field of inquiry, the field of shared intelligence.[6] It is very much like the quantum field, the vacuum, out of which all things emerge. Dialogue is always full of surprises.

Dialogue group practitioners differ (as they should!) about the nature of the dialogue conversation. Some, following the tradition of Chris Argyris and "Action Science," think the conversation should be goal-directed, aimed at solving some particular problem or dispute. Critics, like David Bohm himself, feel this goal-directedness is too mechanistic. Others prefer a completely open and nondirected conversation, letting whatever comes to mind spontaneously emerge. Personally, I usually use a both/and approach, setting some vague theme but letting the conversation run widely.

Nondirected conversation is alien to companies, and many corporate people feel uncomfortable with nondirected dialogue. "What's it for? How does it justify the time it takes up in the working day?" Some companies have got around this by having a group within the group. The larger dialogue group meets weekly or biweekly for at least six months, allowing itself a wide range of free-flowing inquiry. A small subgroup with the dialogue group then meets separately to discuss how insights that emerge in the dialogue might be implemented for practical use.

THE DIALOGIC ATTITUDE

Dialogue groups are powerful vehicles for organizational learning and transformation. They are a way of evoking and embedding quantum thinking, and thus form a useful "quantum infrastructure." But I think that dialogue is more than just a special kind of conversation.

To me, dialogue is essentially an *attitude*. It is a radically different attitude toward oneself, toward others, toward knowledge and problems and relationships. It is part of the new quantum worldview, quantum thinking in practice. If, deep inside ourselves and in our approach to others, we replaced knowing with finding out, answers with questions, inequality with equality, power with respect and reverence, and proving points with exploring possibilities and listening, then I think we really could change ourselves and our world. There would certainly be a different approach to work, innovation, challenge, and relationship in corporate cultures. It is because we believe in this transformative power of the dialogue process that I see it as a fundamental tool of both Quantum Systems and Quantum Strategy Dynamics.

Dialogue can be within a group, but it can also be internal. Each of us has so many simultaneous conversations going on in our heads, simultaneous and conflicting impulses and desires. Usually we repress most and follow one. "This is my true voice and the real me." But they are all voices of me. The quantum self is a whole chorus of conversations and personalities. Inner dialogue can allow me to listen to myself in a new way. At the same time, it can teach me to listen to intimate associates and work colleagues in a new way. It can teach me to hear the possibilities inside myself, inside others, and inside situations. In the next chapter, we will explore this inner dialogue process as we look at meditation and reflective practice.

CHAPTER 14

MEDITATION AND REFLECTIVE PRACTICE

It might not be too strong to say that a Mindfulness meditation movement is sweeping corporate America. Such well-known companies as Google, General Mills, Goldman Sachs, and Black Rock have introduced programs to teach employees meditation on the job. At the Aetna Insurance Company based in Hartford, Connecticut, CEO Mark Bertolini made meditation instruction available to all his 50,000 employees. More than a quarter took him up on it, and the results have been good for business. Increased on-the-job focus has boosted productivity, with an estimate added value to the company of $3,000 per employee. Reduction in pain, improved sleep capacity, and reduction in stress levels among these employees has saved the company an estimated $9 million in healthcare costs in just one year.[1] Aetna has now launched instruction packages for Mindfulness as a very lucrative product to its customers.

Spiritual Intelligence, SQ, is our ultimate working intelligence. Meditating and reflecting upon its twelve transformational principles is, in itself, a path to its improvement. And it is primarily through the strengthening of our SQ that we can bring all of our intelligences to their fullest development, and get them to work in synchrony. But more than simple reflection is required for bringing SQ to its fullest efficacy. We also need a daily practice that can develop and initiate change. We need a practice that allows us to stand back from, and become fully aware of, the way that our consciousness itself works.

We have seen that the mind can get itself locked into patterns of thought. It can develop mental and emotional habits that turn our experiences of ourselves and our world into mere objects that we then manipulate. Our minds are also filled with noise, with the jumble of reactive thinking and feeling required to deal with the many demands of everyday life. By the end of a busy day, we are left feeling exhausted and confused by the welter of mental activity needed to cope with that day's demands. Many of us feel almost brain-dead by the end of the day, and resort to alcohol or mindless television viewing just to relax. We have no means to digest the day and to begin a new one with a cleansed and fresh mind. We certainly have little enhanced awareness of ourselves or of the underlying thought patterns that dictated our actions, decisions, and feelings of the day. Our bodies carry the tension of all the day's stress, dulling our perceptions and leaving us physically as well as mentally exhausted.

Self-awareness is the most primary of the twelve transformational principles of SQ. It, on its own, takes us beyond mere ego awareness and all the distortions and traps that entails. It enables us to work with all the other principles more creatively. So if we are looking for a daily practice to improve SQ, we need a practice that frees us from the ego and brings us insights about how our minds block or distort our conscious experience. As Mark Bertolini described his own experience, "It's made me question what I do and how I look at the world. It's made me consider my influence and how I treat people."[2] One consequence of this was that he raised all his lowest-paid employees' salaries by 33 percent!

In these past fifty years, we in the West have become much more aware of and open to many of the meditation practices used for thousands of years in the East. Millions of us practice some form of meditation often, if not daily. Some of us do this just as a relaxation technique, others for health reasons, to improve concentration or alertness, or to clear our minds of noise. Some do it to gain insights into how our minds work and to alter destructive or distorting patterns of thought. For many, meditation is a serious spiritual practice.

Transcendental Meditation (TM) was the first such practice to gain a popular following, and millions still use it today. Many other meditation techniques, also usually derived from the Hindu tradition, are popular, and all have some beneficial effect. But most are just that, techniques, rather mechanical processes for achieving a desired end without altering deeply the mental habits that had blocked achieving that end in the first place. They do still the noise in our heads, and usually relax our bodies, but they don't take us into that deep, inner, silent place where real self-understanding occurs and from which truly transforming insights arise. These techniques are like recipes from a cookbook, a set of stages we go through to produce a promised product at the end. Most of us rely on recipe books when we first learn to cook, but a really good cook has a more intuitive felt sense of the dish he/she wants to prepare, a sense of ingredient combinations, cooking processes, flavors, smells, textures, and final appearance. A really deep meditation practice needs to have this same felt sense about it.

MINDFULNESS MEDITATION

The meditation practice now being taken up in great numbers by corporations and schools, mental health and counseling services in America and Europe is known as Mindfulness. Originating in thousands of years of Buddhist tradition and previously known as *Vipassana*, or Insight meditation, it was re-represented to the world in its present form a few decades ago by Harvard professor Jon Kabat-Zinn. Mindfulness is a practice that does take us deeply into a felt understanding of the role our egos play in distorting experience. It frees us from those distorting processes and the noise that attends them, and takes us into a deep, silent region of the self where our own deepest self and the center of the universe itself are at one. This is a place from which insights emerge that can guide us for leading more meaningful and more purposeful lives. They certainly leave us more self-aware.

Such insights are the "end result" of this meditation practice, but we must not "go for" these results. The silence from which the insights flow may produce "highs" and "otherworldly" experiences, but we must not aim for these, nor cling to them. If practiced in the wrong spirit, these resulting insights and highs can actually generate a sense of self-importance—the very thing that Mindfulness is meant to dissolve. Reaching a place from which we can observe desires, such as a desire for guaranteed results, is one of the points of doing the practice. It generates its effects just by being practiced, without force or willfulness or desire. Left to their own process, these results come "as surely as night follows day."

The very fact that we sit down quietly for some time each day and observe the things that flow through our minds in itself opens a distance between this ego-centered brain activity and our unconscious deeper self. Creating this gap is, in itself, one of the desired effects of Mindfulness. It allows us to disengage from our thoughts and feelings, and even from subconscious material, and to realize how much these have restricted and dominated our experience.

Freed from these, our whole being can begin to breathe, and we get a sense of spaciousness all around. We realize that this new state of being is different from our ordinary, everyday awareness, and we begin to identify with something larger than our ego selves. We come into contact with what I call "the Witness," a state of awareness, or a self outside the ego self, that can observe "the monkey mind" from a detached perspective. Becoming one with this Witness self is the second desired effect of Mindfulness. It invites us to see the Witness as wholly different from our ordinary ego selves, and puts us in touch with a direct, lived, immediate intelligence.

As we now have our experience through this lived intelligence, a whole stream of insights issues from our deep unconscious to guide us on many matters. Five of these are particularly important:

- We come to understand the underlying dynamics and forces that shape our experience of everyday reality.
- We come to understand, in an immediate, lived way, the actions and attitudes that can free us from the ego self.
- We come to understand how to use the ego in a more effective way once we have disengaged from it. The ego becomes our servant rather than our master. Conscious mind becomes sharper and more focused.
- We gain insight into having new goals for our lives, and the ful-

fillment and sense of satisfaction that pursuing these goals would bring.

- We gain insight into the attitudes, motivations, and actions that might have made it impossible to achieve these goals.

The practice of Mindfulness gives us a living sense of wholeness, of the deeply interconnected nature of reality and the interconnectedness of events in our daily experience. It puts us in touch with the foundation or root of things, with the roots of our being and, ultimately, in touch with the very ground of reality itself. Thousands of research studies done on the effects of Mindfulness have established that this sense of wholeness comes about because, during meditation, the brain really *is* whole—Mindfulness practice unites the activity of the brain's right and left hemispheres, while at the same time integrating conscious and unconscious mind. The 40 Hz oscillatory field that sweeps across the brain to integrate the experiences of the mind is at its most coherent during meditation.[3] This is why I consider Mindfulness an important "tool" for nourishing quantum thinking.

From this much deeper perspective, we are in a good place to reflect upon and to practice the transformational principles of our spiritual intelligence. We have the Witness with us as a constant companion throughout our everyday experiencing of our world, thus raising both our critical thinking and our reflective intelligence. We become, all around, more alert and more effective.

PRACTICING MINDFULNESS

As with most meditation practices, we begin by sitting comfortably, in a quiet and restful place, either in a half-lotus position on the floor, or in a chair, with our feet flat down, in touch with "the earth." The spine must be kept straight, and the hands are rested, palms upward, on our knees. We close our eyes.

Many Mindfulness teachers advise that we begin by relaxing our bodies, ridding ourselves of some of our physical stress. This bodily relaxation is a preliminary to practicing Insight meditation, *not an integral part of that meditation itself.* We do this relaxation by focusing first on our feet and, breathing deeply, experiencing silently in ourselves, "Feel the feet breathing." Slowly, we repeat this as we move up the body—"Feel the calves breathing," "Feel the thighs breathing," "Feel the pelvis breathing," and so on, until we experience, "Feel the brain breathing." We finish by feeling the whole organism breathing. This part of the exercise, on its own, is a good meditation to perform in bed at night to relax the body, making it ready for sleep.

Now, starting the Mindfulness practice itself, we begin to focus on our breathing, as it enters and exits the nose. No force, no huge concentration, just a gentle, focused awareness. We continue to follow the flow of our breathing for as long as we can. Then, just naturally, we will enter a state of *samadhi*, a still, deep, inner silence wholly devoid of content. Just a pure awareness. We won't even, any longer, be aware of our breathing.

Allowing the state of samadhi observation to continue for as long as it wishes, we begin again to observe our breathing, moving its focus to the lower abdomen. Gently, without force or effort, just noting the flow of breath in and out. As we do this, thoughts and feelings, memories of events, will begin to pass through our field of consciousness. We notice them, but we don't fix on or engage with them. We don't feel that we have to do anything about them. We just let them be, and pass by.

But as we view them thus, from the perspective of the Witness, we slide into total stillness, and may begin to have insights. We achieve an immediate, lived intelligence about them, or things we associate with them. This lived intelligence is not mediated by concepts, and we should not force it into concepts. Just let it be, with disengaged awareness. We may get excited by some of these insights and be tempted to stop, to write them down. But we should not do this. Insights that come to us in this way, even if apparently forgotten, will reappear later in life when and if we need them.

To become really effective, this meditation should be practiced for at least twenty minutes daily. It should become a natural part of each day's structure, and its effects will build as time goes by. There is no need for harsh asceticism to get the benefits of Mindfulness. We don't have to become vegetarians, give up spices, sex, or alcohol. But it is best to do the practice on an empty stomach, preferably early in the morning, before supper, or before bed: making it a daily practice will strengthen our spiritual intelligence, thus improving our physical, emotional, and rational intelligences, and pave the way to achieving "total intelligence," whole-brain intelligence.

What I have described here is only a written guide to Mindfulness practice. But no written text can be used as a blueprint for practicing this, or any other, meditation—even if written by a great guru, or the Buddha himself. It is always best to seek out a personal teacher, who can guide us through the subtle stages and distinctions that occur throughout the practice.

REFLECTIVE PRACTICE

We saw in Chapter Three that reflection is one of the key skills of quantum thinking. When we reflect on an incident during the day, a problem, or even our own thoughts, we stand back from them—i.e., we step outside whatever box or fishbowl the brain's normal thinking has put them in. Reflection also integrates the activities of the whole brain, the fast thinking of the unconscious mind and the slow thinking of conscious mind as well as the thought processes of both the brain's left and right hemispheres. Reflecting on things also acts to digest them, and to dissolve any stress associated with keeping them locked away. It both stills and clears the mind and relaxes the body.

A kind of automatic reflective process is one of the benefits of regularly practicing Mindfulness meditation. But there is another practice I have invented for myself that greatly helps me to digest and gain beneficial perspective on both myself and on the day's events, and I want to share this with readers. I call this "reflective practice."

Reflective practice is best done at the very end of the day. It must be done in a quiet place where one can be comfortable and free from distractions. Personally, I go into my sitting room and sit by fire and candlelight.

After just sitting for a few minutes to place myself in the room, I bring my attention to my body. Where is my body tense or uncomfortable? Is there a "lump" in my stomach? Is my breathing fast or shallow? Is my chest tight? Do I have a headache or a stiff neck? Am I clenching my fists or fidgeting? In my own case, I usually combine this bodily awareness by thinking, "What kind of music does my body want to feel tonight?" Music can, for many people, act like a tuning fork that resonates with the body's own rhythms and soothes them. Others may prefer silence.

After we've become aware of where the flow of the body's energies might be blocked, we begin to ask Why? Or What? What happened today that might have upset me? Was it an incident at work? An exchange with someone at home? Am I stuck on a problem? Do I just feel too much has come at me today? Did something not happen that I had hoped? Did someone or something disappoint or frustrate me? Does the answer to any of these questions increase the tension in my body? If so, then that issue needs further inquiry. So I begin to ask Why?

Why did that exchange I had today upset me? Why did I get upset by something like that? What is it about me that I was vulnerable in that situation? Was the situation caused by something I said or did? Why did I say or do it? Could I have handled it differently? Could I have avoided it? Why didn't I? Do I get into exchanges or situations like that because of some habit or leaning in my personality? Why am I like this? Could I change? Why? Why? Why? Each act of reflection gets me deeper into the situation and deeper into the way that I think or act about things. It surfaces assumptions and attitudes and habits of which I had previously been unaware. It also gives me a broader and deeper perspective on others who are part of my life.

The reflective process of plunging deeper into some disturbing incident of the day is not endless. Inevitably, the act of repeatedly asking Why? will generate an insight that causes the body to let out a deep sigh of relief, and the tension it had been holding dissolves. Like Mindfulness meditation itself, this will have positive consequences for blood pressure, quality of sleep, and clarity of thought. It can be thought of as a daily house cleaning of the psyche.

This same kind of reflective practice can also be used to work with and nurture the twelve transformational principles of SQ. Without question, the very act of reflecting like this increases self-awareness. But one could also choose any one of the twelve principles and reflect on the extent to which one does or does not live by it. Why was I not as compassionate as I might have been today? Why was I a bit arrogant in that situation? Why do I have difficulty working with people who think differently than I do? Why do I always zero in on the first answer that comes to mind? What stops me from being more spontaneous? In each such chain of inquiries there will be bodily clues to guide us as we probe more deeply.

I've said many times throughout this book that, in essence, we human beings are the species that asks questions, especially questions of meaning. When I outlined the quantum worldview in Chapter One, it was clear that asking such questions could be seen as the reason for our existence—Heisenberg's Uncertainty Principle! The questions I ask give me the answers that I get. The questions that I ask tease out the potentialities latent in underlying quantum reality. The questions I ask create the world I live in. And, most definitely, the questions I ask create the person that I am.

CONCLUSION

THE QUANTUM LEADER AS SERVANT LEADER

Oh, this is the animal that never was.
They did not know it and, for all of that,
they loved his neck and posture, and his gait,
clean to the great eyes with their tranquil gaze.
Really it was not. Of their love they made it,
till in this clear uncluttered place lightly
he raised his head and scarcely needed to be.
They did not feed him any corn,
only the possibility he might exist,
which gave the beast such strength,
he bore a horn upon the forehead.
Just one horn. Unto a virgin he appeared,
all white, and was in the silver mirror and in her.

—Rainer Maria Rilke,
Sonnets to Orpheus, "The Unicorn"

Rainer Maria Rilke is generally considered the most influential German poet of the twentieth century. His work has caught and reflected some of the century's major concerns. This poem about the unicorn is one of the central readings in the concept cafe that my colleague and I run for business leaders. I think that it adds important new dimensions to discussions of the servant leader concept. More than that, I think these are particularly quantum dimensions, and that the servant leader concept is vital to understanding quantum leadership.

As I understand the term, servant leadership involves practicing the essence of quantum thinking. Servant leaders lead from that level of deep, revolutionary vision that is accessed only by the third of our three kinds of thinking. They change the system, invent the new paradigm, clear a space where something new can be. They accomplish this not just from "doing" but, more fundamentally, from "being." All this makes servant leadership the essence of what this book is about. Such leaders are essential to deep corporate transformation. For this reason, I have chosen servant leadership as the book's final and summary theme.

The unicorn has always been a special symbol in our culture. He is that most impossible creature of the human imagination, a beast conjured up by longing and the human capacity to dream. In Rilke's poem he is conjured up by love, and given a space to be by those who dare to believe in the possibility that he might exist. In quantum science, the whole of existence is a set of possibilities plucked out of the quantum vacuum's infinite sea of potentiality. Some of these possibilities are plucked out by observers, by human beings living our lives. An awareness of our role as cocreators of existence can increase our capacity to fulfill that role. Each of us is a servant of the vacuum, a servant of the manifold potentiality at the heart of existence.

Business leaders who become aware of servanthood in this sense know that they serve more than company or colleagues, more than markets or products, more even than vision and values as these are normally understood. They serve that longing that conjures up unicorns, and through this service they build or contribute to a successful, profitable business that adds some new dimension both to business and to human well-being.

I mentioned earlier that an independent company founder with whom I spoke told me she could see three reasons why people might start up a business. The first reason is opportunity. The would-be entrepreneur looks at the market and sees that there is an opening for some service or product, and says, "Someone needs to provide this. I will." The second reason is talent or unmet need. The would-be entrepreneur looks inward at personal resources and skills or outward at the local environment and says, "I can provide this." The third reason is more spiritual. The future entrepreneur doesn't begin by thinking about business or a career, but about a feeling of inner necessity. "This has to exist. This has to happen. I have to do it." I think this is the beginning of the servant leader's business career.

There seems to me an interesting and useful interplay between these three motives for going into business, the three kinds of thinking our brains can do, and the three models of self and organization that we have looked at. The opportunity motive is very logical. I analyze the market, see what is missing, and decide to provide it. This is the way my rule-bound, goal-oriented serial thinking operates. It's compatible with seeing myself as a Newtonian billiard ball in human form, as able to place myself in the scheme of things through manipulating and controlling the forces and bodies around me. It is management by objectives.

The skill motive is very associative. I am this sort of person with these sorts of resources, so I can see that I fit in here. This is the way the brain's parallel, networked thinking operates. Those things are most natural (those neural connections strongest) that conform to past experience, to habit, to the relationships around me. This is compatible with seeing myself in terms of my relationships to others, to what I can offer them. I find my place in some existing network. I go into the family craft or the family business. I deal locally, with familiar things and familiar people.

The inner necessity, "I have to" motive, is quantum. The existing provisions, products, services, and so on are not adequate. Something new is needed here, and I have to provide it. This is the way the brain's creative, rule-breaking, rule-making kind of thinking operates. Experience throws up things and events for which there are no previous neural connections, therefore no concepts or categories. So the brain creates new ones. It rewires itself. This is compatible with the quantum model of self where I see myself as a cocreator, as an active agent in this universe who makes things happen. If I want the world to change, *I* have to change it. If this product or service should exist, *I* have to provide it.

We've seen that in both the brain and in life's experiences, one reason why quantum thinking kicks in is that there is a crisis. We have little motive to change our neural wiring or our paradigm if the existing one is doing its job. Such crisis is common in the shift from normal or conservative science to revolutionary science. It often plays a role in the making of servant leaders. In their case this is often a spiritual crisis, some threat to their usual self-esteem, to their usual framework of meaning and value, some longing for something more.

REAL SERVANT LEADERS AT WORK

I have had the good fortune to know four such leaders personally and to know a bit about their stories. I want to share brief episodes from each because they throw light on those deeper dimensions of servant leadership that I think are associated with the vision of the new science.

Juliette's Story

This is a true story, but the names have been changed at the request of its subject. The leader I will call Juliette Johnson owns a small but growing business, Juliette's Fashion Studios. The founding studio is located in southeast England. She is in her early forties, a French immigrant to the United Kingdom who is married to an Englishman. It was Juliette who outlined the three reasons I have described why someone might start up a business.

In France, Juliette was an opera star. She is a large woman with the broad chest and wide neck that are usually associated with a successful opera singing career, and she was successful. She had her success, a husband, two teenaged children, and a wide circle of friends. She dabbled in spiritual quest, but not seriously. Then, within the space of a year, her husband left her, her children decided to join their father, and her friends became critical and distant. "I was devastated," she says. "I didn't know what had happened. I didn't know where to turn."[1]

On the advice of associates in England, Juliette signed up for a six-month extensive study course at a spiritual community in Scotland. She studied the writings of an eleventh-century Sufi mystic, Ibn al-'Arabi, and those of ancient Eastern and more modern Western mystics, all of whom used their work to celebrate the unity of existence. Life at the community was quiet, disciplined, and reflective. Juliette was thrown back on herself and on a quest to discover what really mattered to her. During the course she met her future second husband, an Englishman, and they moved on to the south of England.

Living in a small flat above a shop and supported through state welfare funds, Juliette had no clear sense of career direction. Then a friend asked her to help with a handmade dress. She had done sewing ever since she was in her early teens, and the dress she now made for her friend awakened something. She made a few others and felt that in her original designs she saw an expression of the passion she had felt during her study course in Scotland, a passion to celebrate the unity of existence and the true reality that lies behind the human form. She felt that she had to make more dresses, whether or not anyone wanted to buy them. But people did buy them. Her designs were fresh; they brought out some special, deeply feminine quality in any woman who wore them. She consciously designed in a way that made bodily shape and size unimportant. "All bodies are beautiful," she says. "Every woman should be able to feel good about her body. She should feel happy about herself."[2]

In fact, Juliette's clothes flatter something beyond the body, something even beyond the feminine. She smiles and says, "Yes, of course. It's a celebration of that Source from which all form arises." The passion and the vision it inspired led to more designs, to the opening of a large shop, to the growth of a promising business. "It had to be a business," she says. "I had to show that I could serve something sacred and that I could do this inside a business. I wanted my business to be an act of service." Nonetheless, she is loath to describe herself as a servant leader. It seems too grand, too lacking in humility. Quoting the mystic who inspired her, she says, "Just say what you know. Don't say how you got there."[3]

Andrew Stone's Story

We've met Andrew Stone and his quantum leadership practices throughout this book. But there is a story behind Stone's career, a crisis that inspired his life and his work.

Andrew Stone is extremely well-read, but he has little formal education. As he put it, he left school "in disgrace" at age fifteen with only five "0" level exams, one of which was in woodwork. He began to live by his wits, as they say in England, and by the age of seventeen he was a spiv in the street markets of Cardiff in Wales. A spiv is a seller of "dubious" goods. He had his own market stall where he could offer these wares, and he made a good living from it. "I had a car, a flat, and some good mates who, admittedly, were in the criminal world. I could pull any bird I wanted. I thought I was a very big deal."[4]

Stone is from a Jewish family, though that had meant little to him. Still, in 1967, when the Six Days War broke out and friends chided him that if he was really such a big deal, he would go to Israel and fight, he went. As so many of us of that generation found, the war was over by the time he got there, but he decided to stay on for a while. But Israeli life didn't live up to his expectations. Or at least he felt his own life didn't live up to Israeli standards.

"I was used to pulling birds with a flashy car and fast line and a big wad of pound notes," he says. "Israeli girls could not have cared less. They wanted philosophical conversations about Jewish destiny and the meaning of life. They were attracted to war heroes and guys who wanted to dedicate themselves to something. I felt like shit. I felt I was a total nothing, a germ that ought to be eradicated." He spent a year in Israel feeling this way until he suddenly felt that he had to be of service. He couldn't justify living otherwise. "Even when I was a spiv," he says, "I wanted to make my customers happy. I always wanted to get them a good deal. Now I felt I had to play that out on a wider stage."[5]

Stone wrote to his father, also a Jewish street trader back in Wales, about his new feelings, saying he wasn't sure how to act on them, what to do next. "My father reminded me of my skills at retailing and told me about the principles of Marks & Spencer, an idealist Jewish firm with a vision of serving the community. He said it was rare to combine in one person an intense belief in caring principles and knowledge of how to buy and sell profitably. There are do-gooders who can write and talk. There are traders who can turn a profit. But a great challenge would be to work for Marks & Spencer and try to carry on to the next generation this combination of great retailing done in a socially responsible way. I was inspired by this."[6]

Stone went back to England and applied for a job at Marks & Spencer (M&S). He took the standard recruitment test and failed on every point. The recruitment officer at that time was David Sieff, son of the then chairman, and later director of community affairs at M&S. Sieff told Stone that by any of the normal criteria, he was unemployable. But at the same time, M&S then was aware of the growing dangers of its size and a tendency to become bureaucratic and institutionalized. They wanted to retain the skills of the entrepreneur that had built the company. "I have an instinct about you," Sieff told Stone. "I'll try you out for a year."[7] The rest has become part of company history.

Chen Feng's Story—A Confucian Gentleman

Chen Feng is the forty-one-year-old CEO of Tian Jian Water, a water treatment company based in the Chinese province of Zhejiang. To understand the power, inspiration, and relevance of his story, we need to look at the state of Chinese society today.

China is one of the world's oldest and richest traditional cultures, over 5,000 years old. But in the 1950s, Mao Tse-tung's infamous Cultural Revolution set out to destroy the nation's past, to eradicate its history and "start fresh." Mao wanted to build an entirely new society free of all past traditions, attitudes, and values. Great books were burned, beautiful buildings that had stood for hundreds of years and art treasures dating back thousands of years were destroyed, and values such as respect for elders and care for the community were literally spat upon. Intellectuals and "elites" were either murdered, imprisoned, or sent to the countryside to become rural laborers. In one generation, China as the world had known her, and as she had known herself, was no more. "The Chinese you find today are not the Chinese of before the Revolution," I have been told by countless modern-day Chinese—as a warning!

Many Chinese today feel the country has a crisis of values. One person commented to me, "Everyone is out for themselves. They just want to make money, and they don't care how they do it. The people are very materialistic, and they have no respect."[8] My friends speak of a "moral vacuum" at the heart of Chinese society, and even President Xi Jinping has spoken of a spiritual crisis in today's China.[9] The situation became worse in the 1960s when Chairman Deng Xiaoping introduced his policy of "one state, two systems"—the introduction of capitalism. The guiding mantra of the Communist Party became, "It is glorious to be rich." The people were instructed that the best way to serve self, community, and country was to make a lot of money. Everywhere in China's cities today one sees very wealthy people wearing the latest designer clothes, shopping for Western luxury goods in expensive department stores, and driving big Western cars—Mercedes are the most popular. But the business community's reputation as "a pack of cheats and liars" now poses great problems for China's ambitions in the wider world as China seeks to become a global economic power. And there is widespread unease and unhappiness among China's more thoughtful and reflective people.

When he assumed the presidency in 2014, Xi Jinping made his own intentions clear by introducing a huge national anti-corruption campaign. Many senior Communist Party officials and senior generals have been sent to prison as examples of bad behavior that will no longer be tolerated. At the same time, Xi has encouraged the Chinese people to return to the wisdom and values of the Chinese classics, the *I Ching*, the *Tao Te Ching*, and the teachings of Confucius. More people are returning to the ancient Chinese Taoist and Buddhist traditions—again, with the encouragement of Xi Jinping. My friends in China tell me it will take two or three generations for the country to recover from the damage done by the Cultural Revolution, but my own experience makes me more optimistic.

I have been invited to China three times in the past year, and have several more invitations pending for the near future because everywhere I go in the country people love the "quantum message." I have not experienced anything like the same enthusiasm for myself and my work anywhere else in the world. People tell me it is because "quantum" resonates with the ancient Chinese teachings they wish to rediscover, that it gives them a "modern" way to express old beliefs and values they are trying to recapture. I was recently appointed professor of quantum philosophy at the Center for Confucian Entrepreneurs and East Asian Civilizations of Zhejiang University and asked to teach a course on quantum philosophy and Chinese thought. My young students are eager to learn, they show deep concern for the state of their nation's soul, and they are filled with ambition to become better people. Many say they want to become "quantum leaders" and act to change Chinese society. I believe them, and I believe in them. And then there is Chen Feng, whose story I want to tell here.

Chen Feng was born in Stone Creek Village, a rural farming community in Zhejiang Province, just as Deng Xiaoping was assuming power and transforming China's economic model. He was a bright student and, at age fourteen, won a place at an elite boarding school to gain his high school education. But, away from the discipline of home, he "fell by the wayside," neglected his studies, and spent three years immersing himself in volumes of the Swordmen martial arts stories so popular with Chinese boys. These books of honorable and magical heroes with positive energy who helped ladies and had a strong gentleman's code of honor were to shape his character, but they nearly destroyed his education. He failed the entrance exam for the final year of high school and was sent home to receive a harsh beating from his father. Told that he now faced a life of hard farm labor, he cried and begged to be given another chance to complete his studies. Back at school, he made up in one year the three years he had lost reading Swordmen books and was the most successful student in his class. He graduated, won a place at a university, and then entered the business world. That was when he began to feel like "a total outsider" in Chinese society.[10] The values of the Swordmen warriors, Chen Feng's values, were not the values of the business community.

"I began to feel a total failure at business," he remembers. "In one job I worked for two years in sales and I didn't win a single customer." In 2003 he founded his company, Tian Jian Water, but had trouble competing with other water treatment companies that were cheating and selling dirty water. "After two years, I was experiencing the worst crisis of my life," he told me. "I was sincere, I was honest, I liked serving people, but modern Chinese society didn't want these qualities. I wondered, should I just be a cheat like everyone else in business?"[11]

At that point, perhaps partly because he was worn down with personal doubt, Chen Feng suffered a very serious illness. He was in the hospital for two weeks with a high fever, and the doctors thought he had contracted the SARS virus. Eventually, they sent him home to die. His mother wrapped his head and his body in packets of ice, but the fever would not break.

"Then, one night, in my feverish state, I had a vision of an old lady like my grandmother. She came walking towards my bed and said to me, 'It is right to behave like a good man.'" He thought the old lady was Quan Yin, the Buddhist goddess of compassion and the feminine face of the Buddha. The next morning his fever broke, and he slowly regained his health. And his commitment to his own business vision. "I wanted to build a good company staffed by good people." He decided to hire only honest and trustworthy people who would never betray their friends or customers. "We are looking for people with inner drive," says Chen Feng, "not those who work because of outside pressure. I want people with positive energy."[12]

All new Tian Jian employees are put through a three-day training/induction program to familiarize them with company culture and to know what is expected of them. The program includes some teachings from the *I Ching*, such as "The highest excellence is like that of water," and other messages from the Chinese classics about the importance of learning and service. The company's name, *Tian Jian*, is taken from the first two characters in the *I Ching*, meaning "heaven/sky" and "energetically." The third character meaning "living/operating" is implied. There is an Isle of Learning, a very long corridor lined with recommended books, at company headquarters. New employees are told that interdepartmental and intradepartmental cliques and conspiracies, and lies and cover-ups with bosses and customers will not be tolerated. All are very common in China's large state industries. Each employee is taught that the whole (the company, the team) is greater than the sum of its parts, and that each individual is responsible for the whole. They are also taught that at Tian

Jian, the customer is the true employer and that, "The ultimate goal of management is to manage myself." And they are inducted into the company's culture of constant and open questioning. "To ask questions is the most important ability," says Chen Feng. "It is important to ask questions of those with whom you disagree, not just those with whom you agree."[13]

Tian Jian is still a small but rapidly growing company. Chen Feng started the company in 2003 with RMB 2000. With 30 percent annual growth ever since, turnover is currently RMB one billion. The company has now expanded beyond Zhejiang Province into three other provinces, and it is predicted that within ten years it will be the largest water treatment company in China. Yet it remains a happy, friendly company where human relationships are treasured. Chen Feng himself is much loved for his habit of visiting sick employees in the hospital and personally greeting visiting parents from rural districts at the station. "He is our father and our brother," one employee told me.[14] One of his senior vice presidents added, "I feel safe here. Whatever difficulties I face I feel safe, because the company is always backing me."[15] At a lunch with his senior leadership team (average age twenty-nine years), people spent time telling me why they are happy with their work.

Walking with me one evening by the West Lake near his company headquarters in Hangzhou, Chen Feng asked me, "What do you think is my product?"

"Water, of course," I replied.

"No," he said, "my product is people. I want to build the 'Tian Jian person,' and I want the Tian Jian person to be a model for all of China's business community." He calls the company culture he is building "the Gentleman culture."[16] The idea comes from the Confucian ideal of the gentleman who stands as a bridge between heaven and earth. He hopes the Tian Jian person will be a bridge between the old China and the new.

THE CONCEPT OF SERVANT LEADERSHIP

Western businesspeople who have been discussing the servant leader concept do mean by this a leader who has a sense of deep values and a leadership style that involves conscious service to these values. But we don't always mean the same thing when we speak about values. The usual Western corporate values, at their best, speak of things like excellence, fulfilling one's potential and allowing space for others to do so, achievement, quality of products and services, and commitment to never-ending growth. In the East, traditionally, deep values have centered around things like compassion, humility, gratitude, service to one's family and community, service to the ancestors or to the ground of Being itself. Traditionally, the East has emphasized cooperation and trust, the West, competition and control. A "good man" in the East has a quality of being. In the West, a "good man" is usually measured by his quality of doing. Robert Greenleaf, who wrote the original paper on servant leadership, had something more Eastern in mind. Indeed, he used the example of a Nepalese Buddhist monk. And in his book, *Synchronicity*, Joe Jaworski emphasizes the importance of being before doing in corporate leadership.[17] He uses dialogue practice extensively as a way of helping leaders access the level of being within themselves. Jaworski's own life was turned around during an interview with David Bohm about the thinking in quantum science. I deeply believe the conceptual structure and spiritual implications of this new science can give us a more solid underpinning for understanding the true meaning of the servant leader. And a deeper understanding of what that leader serves.

As someone trained in physics at MIT, I know well from my own educational background the role that science and the wider spirit of Newtonian mechanism have played in widening the gulf between values associated with doing and those associated with being. Newtonian science is preoccupied with objects, obsessed with analysis and measurement. It draws a sharp divide between spirit and matter, between man and nature. And it gives us a concern with the here and now, a view of truth as black or white, a preoccupation with achievement and progress as measured by doing and acquiring. These are not the values that have inspired the three leaders whose stories I have cited.

We have seen that the new science that emerged during the twentieth century has a very different philosophical and conceptual basis. Quantum science tells us that the world is all of a piece, holistic. We human beings are in and of nature. We help to make reality happen. We are free agents with a responsibility for co-creation. More than that, quantum science shows us that we are, in our essential physical and spiritual makeup, extensions, "excitations," of the underlying ground state of Being. As I put it earlier, a quantum view of the self shows us that we are "thoughts in the mind of God."

To qualify as servant leaders in the deepest sense, I think that leaders must have four essential qualities. They must have a deep sense of the interconnectedness of life and all its enterprises. They must have a sense of engagement and responsibility, a sense of "I have to." They must be aware that all human endeavor, including business, is a part of the larger and richer fabric of the whole universe. And perhaps most important of all, servant leaders must know what they ultimately serve. They must, with a sense of humility and gratitude, have a sense of the Source from which all values emerge.

Describing the unicorn, Rilke said, "Really it was not. Of their love they made it."[18] The servant leader serves from a base of love. The three whose examples I quoted do so—not from some gooey, sentimental love of all humanity and wish to do good works, but out of a deep, abiding passion for and commitment to service. And that service itself is to something beyond the given. A wish to make women feel good about themselves inspired by the underlying nature of existence. A wish to make people happy inspired by the Jewish love of community. A wish to serve his nation by the cultivation and nurturing of good people, honest people.

To these servant leaders and others like them, the business of business no longer restricts itself to manipulating things and nature and people for profit. Rather, business becomes a spiritual vocation in the largest sense of that word. The brain's "spirit" (quantum thinking) integrates the abilities of the brain's "intellect" (serial thinking) and the brain's "heart" (parallel thinking). As such, it initiates and perpetuates the brain's necessary rewiring. I believe that it is only from such a basis of spiritual servant leadership that really deep transformation can come about in the corporate world. And thus I close this book with "The Oath of the Quantum Leader," the leader who is a servant leader *par excellence*:

OATH OF THE QUANTUM LEADER

I believe that global business has the money and the power to make a significant difference in today's troubled world, and that by making that difference it can help itself as well as others. I envision business raising its sights above "the bottom line." I envisage business becoming a vocation, like the higher professions. To make this possible I believe that business must add a moral dimension, becoming more service- and value-oriented and largely eliminating the assumed natural distinction between private enterprise and public service institutions. I envisage business taking responsibility for the world in which it operates and from which it creates its wealth. And I envisage myself becoming one of those business leaders who are "servant leaders"—leaders who serve not just stockholders, colleagues, employees, products, and customers, but leaders who also serve the community, the planet, humanity, the future, and life itself.

NOTES

INTRODUCTION: WHY BUSINESS NEEDS A REVOLUTION

    1. Danah Zohar and Ian Marshall, *Spiritual Capital: Wealth We Can Live By* (San Francisco: Berrett-Koehler Publishers, 2004), p. 9.

    2. James Carse, *Finite and Infinite Games* (New York: Ballantine Books, 1986).

    3. Nikhil Swaminathan, "How the 'Plastic' Brain Rewires Itself," *Scientific American*, February 28, 2007, http://www.scientificamerican.com/article/brain-plasticity-juvenile-adult/ (accessed May 11, 2016).

    4. Zohar and Marshall, *Spiritual Capital*, pp. 38–39.

    5. David Bohm, *On Dialogue* (London: Routledge, 1995).

CHAPTER 1: ENTERING THE QUANTUM AGE

    1. Li Yang and Xie Chuanjiao, "A Chinese Business Model For the Internet Age," *China Daily*, December 3, 2014, http://www.chinadaily.com.cn/opinion/2014-12/03/content_19014331_2.htm.

    2. Haier Group, China, in letter to the author, November 2014.

    3. Eric Hobsbawm, *The Age of Extremes* (London: Michael Joseph, 1994).

    4. Arthur Fine, *The Shaky Game: Einstein, Realism and the Quantum Theory* (Chicago and London: University of Chicago Press, 1986), dust jacket.

    5. Vlatko Vedral, "Living in a Quantum World," *Scientific American* (June 2011).

    6. Business leader, from a national broadcast following the tsunami in Japan in 2011.

    7. Max Lederhausen in a letter to the author, 1992.

    8. Andrew Stone (former managing director of Marks & Spencer), in discussion with the author, 1990.

    9. Christopher Giercke (CEO of Altai Himalaya), in discussion with the author, July 2014.

10. David Bohm, *Unfolding Meaning* (London and New York: ARK Paperbacks, 1985).

11. Eckhart Tolle, *The Power of Now: A Guide to Spiritual Enlightenment* (New York: New World Library, 1999).

12. David Bohm, "A New Theory of the Relationship of Mind and Matter," *Philosophical Psychology* 3, no. 2 (1990): 271–86.

13. Eknath Eswaran, trans., *The Bhagavad Gita* (Canada: Blue Mountain Center of Meditation and Nilgiri Press, 2007).

14. Howard Lutnick, interview with Piers Morgan, *Piers Morgan Tonight*, CNN, September 9, 2011.

15. Ibid.

16. Ibid.

17. Eswaran, *Bhagavad Gita*.

18. James Joyce, *Portrait of the Artist as a Young Man* (New York: Viking, 1956).

19. Carlos Castaneda, *The Teachings of Don Juan: A Yaqui Way of Knowledge* (New York: Washington Square, 1996).

20. Archibald MacLeish, *Act Five and Other Poems* (London: Bodley Head, 1950), p. 114.

21. Ibid.

CHAPTER 2: THREE LEVELS OF REAL TRANSFORMATION

1. Rene Descartes, *Meditations* (New York: Bobbs-Merrill, 1960).

2. Abraham Maslow, *Motivation and Personality* (New York: Harper, 1970).

3. Danah Zohar and Ian Marshall, *Spiritual Capital: Wealth We Can Live By* (San Francisco: Berrett-Koehler Publishers, 2004), p. 17.

4. Viktor Frankl, *Man's Search for Meaning* (New York: Pocket Books, 1985).

5. Roger Penrose, *The Emperor's New Mind* (Oxford: Oxford University Press, 1989).

6. Nikhil Swaminathan, "How the 'Plastic' Brain Rewires Itself," *Scientific American*, February 28, 2007, http://www.scientificamerican.com/article/brain-plasticity-juvenile-adult/ (accessed May 11, 2016).

7. Thomas S. Kuhn, *The Structure of Scientific Revolutions: 50th Anniversary Edition* (Chicago: University of Chicago Press, 2012), p. xxxvi.

8. Quoted in David Mielach, "5 Business Tips from Albert Einstein,"

BusinessNewsDaily, April 18, 2012, http://www.businessnewsdaily.com/2381
-albert-einstein-business-tips.html (accessed May 11, 2016).

    9. Kuhn, *Structure of Scientific Revolutions*, p. 151.

CHAPTER 3: THREE KINDS OF THINKING:
HOW THE BRAIN REWIRES ITSELF

    1. Quoted from a personal address to a leadership conference author
attended in mid-1990s.

    2. Daniel Kahneman, *Thinking, Fast and Slow* (New York: Allen Lane,
2011), p. 13.

    3. James Carse, *Finite & Infinite Games* (New York: Ballantine Books,
1986).

    4. Kahneman, *Thinking, Fast and Slow*, p. 20.

    5. Iain McGilchrist, *The Master and His Emissary: The Divided Brain
and the Making of the Western World* (New Haven and London: Yale University
Press, 2012).

    6. John Seely Brown and Estee Solomon Gray, "The People are the
Company: How to Build Your Company Around Your People," *Fast Company*,
October 31, 1995, http://www.fastcompany.com/26238/people-are-company
(accessed May 5, 2016).

    7. Ibid.

    8. Ibid.

    9. Wolf Singer, "Striving for Coherence," *Nature* 397(February 4, 1999):
391–93.

    10. Richard Tanner Pascale, *The Art of Japanese Management: Applications
for American Executives* (New York: Warner Books, 1982).

    11. Michio Kaku, *Hyperspace: A Scientific Odyssey Through Parallel Uni-
verses, Time Warps, and the Tenth Dimension* (Oxford University Press, 1994),
pp. 4–5.

    12. David Mielach, "5 Business Tips from Albert Einstein," *Business
NewsDaily*, April 18, 2012, http://www.businessnewsdaily.com/2381-albert
-einstein-business-tips.html (accessed May 11, 2016).

CHAPTER 4: EIGHT PRINCIPLES OF QUANTUM THINKING APPLIED TO LEADERSHIP

1. Abraham Pais, *Niels Bohr's Times: In Physics, Philosophy, and Polity* (New York: Oxford University Press, 1994).

2. Ibid.

3. Ibid.

4. Albert Einstein in a letter to Harry Lipkin on July 5, 1952, quoted in Arthur Fine, *The Shaky Game: Einstein, Realism and the Quantum Theory* (Chicago and London: University of Chicago Press, 1986), p. 1.

5. Margaret Thatcher, interviewed by Douglas Keay, *Woman's Own*, October 31, 1987, pp. 8–10, quoted in "Margaret Thatcher: A Life in Quotes," *The Guardian*, April 8, 2013, http://www.theguardian.com/politics/2013/apr/08/margaret-thatcher-quotes (accessed May 23, 2016).

6. Sigmund Freud, *Civilization and Its Discontents* (New York: Norton, 1962).

7. David Bohm, "A New Theory of the Relationship of Mind and Matter," *Philosophical Psychology* 3, no. 2 (1990): 271–86.

8. David Bohm, *Wholeness and the Implicate Order* (London: Routledge, 1980).

9. Andrew Stone (former managing director of Marks & Spencer), in discussion with the author, 1990.

10. Ibid.

11. Reported to author at a dinner party in Guizhou, 2000s.

12. Quoted in "The Life and Times of Arthur Miller," *BBC Media Centre*, http://www.bbc.co.uk/mediacentre/proginfo/2015/41/the-life-and-times-of-arthur-miller (accessed May 17, 2016).

13. Freud, *Civilization and Its Discontents*.

14. Benny Shanon and Henri Atlan, "Von Foerster's Theorem on Connectedness and Organization: Semantic Applications," *New Ideas in Psychology* 8, no. 1 (1990): pp. 81–90.

15. Marks & Spencer meeting in which the author attended, 1997.

16. Art Kleiner, "The Man Who Saw the Future," *Strategy + Business*, February 12, 2003, http://www.strategy-business.com/article/8220?gko=0d07f (accessed May 23, 2016).

17. Marks & Spencer meeting.

18. Ibid.

19. Lord William Thomson Kelvin, quoted in *Scienceworld*, http://scienceworld.wolfram.com/biography/Kelvin.html (accessed May 24, 2016).

20. Discussion with a senior consultant, 1990s.

21. Ibid.

22. Conversation with a manager at a European consultancy firm meeting, late 1990s.

23. Ibid.

24. James Carse, *Finite & Infinite Games* (New York: Ballantine Books, 1986).

25. Ibid.

26. Taken from business events author attended in 1990s.

27. Discussion with a Shell Oil senior manager, 2000s.

28. Discussion with senior consultant.

29. Fons Trompenaars, *Riding the Waves of Culture* (London: Nicolas Brealey, 1993), p. 19.

30. Discussion with secretary, late 1990s.

31. A conversation with a member of Shell Oil's Leadership Council, late 1990s.

32. Stone, in discussion with author.

33. Rabindranath Tagore, *Essays* (New Delhi: Atlantic, 2007), p. 379.

34. Richard T. Pascale and Anthony G. Athos, *The Art of Japanese Management: Applications for American Business* (New York: Simon and Schuster, 1981).

35. Carse, *Finite & Infinite Games*.

CHAPTER 5: LEADING AT THE EDGE

1. Anna Nilsson-Ehle (vice president for corporate transformation) in a conversation with the author, mid-1990s.

2. Andrew Stone (former managing director of Marks & Spencer) from a meeting the author attended in 1997.

3. Walter J. Freeman and Walter Schneider, "Changes in Spatial Patterns of Rabbit Olfactory EEG with Conditioning to Odors," *Psychophysiology* 19, no. 1 (1982): 44–56.

4. John Micklethwait and Adrian Wooldridge, *The Witch Doctors: Making Sense of the Management Gurus* (New York: Times Books, 1996), p. 172.

5. "Soros: 'I've Lost My Touch,'" *CNNMoney*, June 16, 2000, http://money.cnn.com/2000/06/16/worldbiz/soros/ (accessed May 14, 2016).

6. George Soros, "The Capitalist Threat," *Atlantic*, February 1997, http://www.theatlantic.com/magazine/archive/1997/02/the-capitalist-threat/376773/.

7. Ibid.

8. Eric Hobsbawm, *The Age of Extremes* (London: Michael Joseph, 1994).

9. Soros, "Capitalist Threat."

10. Ibid.

11. Friedrich Nietzsche, *Thus Spoke Zarathustra* (New York and London: Penguin, 1961).

12. Ibid.

13. Arthur William Edgar O'Shaughnessy, "Ode," *The Oxford Book of Victorian Verse* (Oxford: Clarendon, 1925).

14. Plant manager statement from a business event author attended in late 1990s.

15. From a Marks & Spencer meeting the author attended in 1997.

16. From a conversation with a Volvo manager, mid-1990s.

17. Stone in an interview with author, 1997.

18. From a company visit at Marks & Spencer the author took in 1997.

PART II: THREE MODELS OF ORGANIZATIONAL STRUCTURE AND LEADERSHIP

1. Hamish McRae, *The World in 2020: Power, Culture and Prosperity* (Boston: Harvard Business School, 1995), p. 12.

2. Xiaotong Fei, *From the Soil: The Foundations of Chinese Society* (Berkley: University of California Press, 1992), p. 41.

3. Ibid., p. 65.

CHAPTER 6: THE WESTERN MODEL: THE NEWTONIAN SELF AND THE NEWTONIAN ORGANIZATION

1. Nicholas Tredell, *C. P. Snow: The Dynamics of Hope* (UK: Palgrave MacMillan, 2012), p. 146.

2. Conversation with a senior manager, 2005.

3. Ibid.

4. Conversation with CEO, 2007.

5. Conversation with employee at Delhi workshop the author conducted in 2007.

CHAPTER 7: THE EASTERN MODEL: THE NETWORKED SELF AND THE NETWORKED ORGANIZATION

1. Xiaotong Fei, *From the Soil: The Foundations of Chinese Society* (Berkley: University of California Press, 1992), p. 62.

2. Ibid., p. 67.

3. Ibid., p. 69.

4. Hsu Dau-lin, "The Myth of the 'Five Human Relations' of Confucius," quoted in Fei, *From the Soil*, p. 28 (63).

5. Fei, *From the Soil*, p. 32.

CHAPTER 8: THE QUANTUM MODEL: BRIDGING EAST AND WEST

1. Danah Zohar and I. N. Marshall, *The Quantum Self: Human Nature and Consciousness Defined by the New Physics* (New York: Quill, 1990).

2. Wolf Singer, "Striving for Coherence," *Nature* 397 (February 4, 1999): 391–93.

3. Nick Mathiason, "Three Weeks That Changed the World," *The Guardian*, December 27, 2008, https://www.theguardian.com/business/2008/dec/28/markets-credit-crunch-banking-2008 (accessed May 11, 2016).

4. Learned during author visit to Volvo in mid-1990s.

5. Personal conversation with a Volvo manager, mid-1990s.

6. Linus Pauling in a letter to David Harker quoted in *The Pauling Blog*, October 28, 2008, https://paulingblog.wordpress.com/2008/10/28/clarifying-three-widespread-quotes/ (accessed May 20, 2016).

7. Anna Nilsson-Ehle (vice president for corporate transformation) in a conversation with the author, mid-1990s.

8. Personal conversations with Volvo executives, mid-1990s.

9. Ibid.

10. M. Mitchell Waldrop, "The Trillion-Dollar Vision of Dee Hock," *Fast Company*, October 31, 1996, http://www.fastcompany.com/27333/trillion-dollar-vision-dee-hock.

CHAPTER 9: QUANTUM CASE STUDY: HAIER GROUP, CHINA

1. Zhang Ruimin (Haier Group CEO) in an interview with the author, June 2015.

2. Conversation with Haier strategy department staff, June 2015.

3. Ibid.

4. Ibid.

5. Interview with Haier Group business unit leader, June 2015.

6. Quotes and information from interviews at Haier Group, June 2015.

7. Daniela Wei and Dave McCombs, "Haier Electronics Annual Profit Growth Slows as Sales Drop," *Bloomberg*, March 22, 2016 (updated), http://www.bloomberg.com/news/articles/2016-03-21/haier-electronics-annual-profit-growth-slows-as-sales-slump (accessed May 12, 2016).

8. John Seely Brown and Estee Solomon Gray, "The People are the Company: How to Build Your Company Around Your People," *Fast Company*, October 31, 1995, http://www.fastcompany.com/26238/people-are-company.

9. Interview with Haier platform manager, June 2015.

10. Interview with a Haier vice president, June 2015.

CHAPTER 10: QUANTUM SYSTEMS DYNAMICS

1. Danah Zohar and Ian Marshall, *Spiritual Capital: Wealth We Can Live By* (San Francisco: Berrett-Koehler, 2004), p. 79.

CHAPTER 11: THE MOTIVATIONS THAT DRIVE US

1. Abraham Maslow, *Motivation and Personality* (New York: Harper, 1970).

2. Ibid.

3. Raymond B. Cattell, *Personality and Motivation Structure and Measurement* (New York: World Book Company, 1957).

4. Hazel Guest and Ian Marshall, "The Scale of Response: Emotions and Mood in Context," *International Journal of Psychotherapy* 2, no. 2 (1997): 149–69.

5. Ludwig Wittgenstein, *Philosophical Investigations*, trans. G. E. M. Anscombe (New York: Macmillan, 1953).

6. Daniel Goleman, *Emotional Intelligence* (New York: Bantam Books, 1996).

7. Conversation with a senior manager, March 2000.

8. Goleman, *Emotional Intelligence*.

9. David Hawkins, *Power vs. Force* (Sydney: Hay House, 1995).

10. Steve Boggan, "'We Blew It': Nike Admits to Mistakes Over Child Labor," *CommonDreams*, October 20, 2001, http://www.commondreams.org/headlines01/1020-01.htm (accessed May 24, 2016).

11. Aaron Bernstein, "Online Extra: Nike's New Game Plan for Sweatshops," *Bloomberg*, September 20, 2004, http://www.bloomberg.com/news/articles/2004-09-19/online-extra-nikes-new-game-plan-for-sweatshops (May 24, 2016).

12. Reported to author in personal conversation with a professor at Wits University Business School, 2004.

13. Ibid., p. 76.

14. Cattell, *Personality and Motivation*.

15. Ibid., p. 46.

16. Ibid., p.82.

17. Michael Harrison, "How Branson Won the 'Dirty Tricks' Air War: Virgin's Libel Battle with BA Is Likely to be Settled Today. Michael Harrison Plots the Background," *Independent*, January 10, 1993, http://www.independent.co.uk/news/business/how-branson-won-the-dirty-tricks-air-war-virgins-libel-battle-with-ba-is-likely-to-be-settled-today-1477920.html.

18. Hawkins, *Power vs. Force*.

19. Ibid.

20. Malcom W. Browne, "The Benzene Ring: Dream Analysis," *New York Times*, August 16, 1988, http://www.nytimes.com/1988/08/16/science/the-benzene-ring-dream-analysis.html.

21. Rainer Marie Rilke, *Rilke on Love and Other Difficulties*, trans. J. J. L. Mood (New York: Norton, 1975).

22. Alison Feeney-Hart, "Richard Branson's Top 10 Tips For Success," *BBC News*, March 15, 2014, http://www.bbc.com/news/entertainment-arts-26575792 (accessed May 19, 2016).

23. Mohit Chakrabarti, *Swami Vivekananda: Excellence in Education* (Delhi: Kalpaz, 2008), p. 63.

24. Stanley Appelbaum et al., ed., *Macbeth* (Mineola, NY: Dover, 1993), 5.5.17–28. References are to act, scene, and lines.

25. Gia-Fu Feng and Jane English, trans., *Tao Te Ching* (New York: Vintage Books, 1989).

26. St. John of the Cross, "The Dark Night of the Soul," quoted in *The Mystical Element in the Metaphysical Poets of the Seventeenth Century* p. 231.

27. Ibid.

28. Galatians 2:20.

29. T. S. Eliot, *Four Quartets* (New York: Mariner Books, 1968), p. 3.

CHAPTER 12: THE 12 TRANSFORMATIONAL PRINCIPLES OF SPIRITUAL INTELLIGENCE

1. Danah Zohar and Ian Marshall, *Spiritual Capital: Wealth We Can Live By* (San Francisco: Berrett-Koehler Publishers, 2004).

2. Chris Miller (CEO of Anglian Water) in a letter to the author in 1990s.

3. Galatians 4:12.

4. Daniel Goleman, *Emotional Intelligence: Why It Can Matter More Than IQ* (New York: Bantam Books, 1997), p. 43.

5. Tax Gunning (former CEO of Unilever) in a conversation with the author, 2000s.

6. Immanuel Kant, *Groundwork for the Metaphysics of Morals*, trans. H. J. Paton (New York: Harper, 1948).

7. William Isaacs (CEO of *Dialogos*), in conversation with the author, 1995.

8. Workshop run by William Isaacs (CEO of *Dialogos*) author attended, 1995.

9. Quoted in "The Life and Times of Arthur Miller," *BBC Media Centre*, http://www.bbc.co.uk/mediacentre/proginfo/2015/41/the-life-and-times-of-arthur-miller (accessed May 17, 2016).

10. Personal conversation with a senior investment analyst, 2000s.

11. Personal conversation with a Nokia executive, 2000s.

12. Ram Dass, *Journey of Awakening: A Meditator's Guidebook*, ed. Daniel Goleman et al. (New York: Bantam Books, 1990), p. 201.

13. Vandana Shiva, *India Today* conference author attended in Delhi, 2000s.

14. Peter Swartz, *The Art of the Long View: Planning for the Future in an Uncertain World* (New York: Doubleday, 1996), p. 45.

15. Charles Handy, *The Alchemists* (London: Hutchinson, 1994).

16. Charles Handy and Elizabeth Handy, *The New Alchemists* (London: Hutchinson, 2004), p. 84.

17. Rudyard Kipling, "If," *Poetry Foundation*, http://www.poetryfoundation.org/poems-and-poets/poems/detail/46473 (accessed May 23, 2016).

18. Richard Sennett, *The Corrosion of Character* (New York: Norton, 1998), p. 133.

19. Ibid., p. 145.

20. James C. Collins, "Level 5 Leadership," *Harvard Business Review* (January 2001).

21. Personal conversation with a fashion designer, 2000s.

CHAPTER 13: THE DIALOGUE GROUP: A WAY TO TRANSFORM COMPANY CULTURE

1. Personal conversation with head of global leadership development, 2014.

2. Plato, *The Meno* (Newburyport, MA: Focus, 1998).

3. David Bohm, *On Dialogue* (London: Routledge, 1995).

4. William Isaacs, *Dialogue* (London, New York, etc.: Currency, 1999).

5. Ibid.

6. Ibid.

CHAPTER 14: MEDITATION AND REFLECTIVE PRACTICE

1. David Gelles, "At Aetna, a CEO's Management by Mantra," *New York Times*, February 27, 2015, http://www.nytimes.com/2015/03/01/business/at-aetna-a-ceos-management-by-mantra.html?_r=0.

2. Ibid.

3. Wolf Singer, "Striving for Coherence," *Nature* 397(February 4, 1999): 391–93.

CONCLUSION: THE QUANTUM LEADER AS SERVANT LEADER

1. "Juliette" (fashion designer) in an interview with the author, 1997.

2. Ibid.

3. Ibid.

4. Andrew Stone (former managing director of Marks & Spencer), in discussion with the author, 1990.

5. Ibid.

6. Ibid.

7. Ibid.

8. Conversation with a Chinese citizen, July 2015.

9. Benjamin Kang Lim and Ben Blanchard, "Xi Jinping Hopes Traditional Faiths Can Fill Moral Void in China: Sources," *Reuters*, September 29, 2013, http://www.reuters.com/article/us-china-politics-vacuum-idUSBRE98 S0GS20130929 (accessed May 19, 2016).

10. Chen Feng (CEO of Tian Jian Water) in an interview with the author, October 2015.

11. Ibid.

12. Ibid.

13. Ibid.

14. Personal discussion with Tian Jian employee, 2015.

15. Personal discussion with a senior vice president of Tian Jian, 2015.

16. Feng interview.

17. Joseph Jaworski, *Synchronicity: The Inner Path of Leadership* (San Francisco: Berrett-Koehler, 2011).

18. Rainer Maria Rilke, *Sonnets to Orpheus*, trans. C. F. MacIntyre (Berkeley: University of California Press, 1967), p. 63.

BIBLIOGRAPHY

Aerts, D. et al. "A Case for Applying an Abstracted Quantum Formalism to Cognition." *Mind in Interaction*. Edited by R. Campbell and John Benjamins.

Bohm, David. "A New Theory of the Relationship of Mind and Matter." *Philosophical Psychology* 3, no. 2 (1990): 271–86.

———. *On Dialogue*. London: Routledge, 1995.

———. *Unfolding Meaning*. London and New York: ARK Paperbacks, 1985.

Carse, James. *Finite & Infinite Games*. New York: Ballantine Books, 1986.

Cattell, Raymond B. *Personality and Motivation Structure and Measurement*. New York: World Book Company, 1957.

Chakrabarti, Mohit. *Swami Vivekananda: Excellence in Education*. Delhi: Kalpaz, 2008.

Collins, James C. "Level 5 Leadership." *Harvard Business Review* (January 2001).

Descartes, Rene. *Meditations*. New York: Bobbs-Merrill, 1960.

Eswaran, Eknath, trans. *The Bhagavad Gita*. Canada: Nilgiri, Blue Mountain Center of Meditation.

Fei, Xiaotong. *From the Soil*. Berkeley: University of California Press, 1992.

Feng, Gia-Fu and Jane English, trans. *Tao Te Ching*. New York: Vintage Books, 1989.

Fine, Arthur. *The Shaky Game: Einstein, Realism and the Quantum Theory*. Chicago and London: University of Chicago Press, 1986.

Frankl, Viktor. *Man's Search for Meaning*. New York: Washington Square, 1959.

Freud, Sigmund. *Civilization and Its Discontents*. New York: Norton, 1962.

Goleman, Daniel. *Emotional Intelligence*. New York: Bantam Books, 1996.

Hawkins, David. *Power vs. Force*. Sydney: Hay House, 1995.

Hobsbawm, Eric. *The Age of Extremes*. London: Michael Joseph, 1994.

Isaacs, William. *Dialogue*. New York: Currency/Doubleday, 1999.

Joyce, James. *Portrait of the Artist as a Young Man*. New York: Viking, 1956.

Kahneman, Daniel. *Thinking, Fast and Slow*. New York: Allen Lane, 2011.

Kaku, Michio. *Hyperspace: A Scientific Odyssey Through Parallel Universes, Time Warps, and the 10th Dimension*. Oxford: Oxford University Press, 1994.

Kant, Immanuel. *Groundwork for the Metaphysics of Morals.* Translated by H. J. Paton. New York: Harper, 1948.

Kuhn, Thomas S. *The Structure of Scientific Revolutions.* Chicago: University of Chicago Press, 1970.

MacLeish, Archibald. *Act Five.* London: The Bodley Head, 1950.

McGilchrist, Iain. *The Master and His Emissary.* New Haven and London: Yale University Press, 2009.

Maslow, Abraham. *Motivation and Personality.* New York: Harper, 1970.

Micklethwait, John, and Adrian Wooldridge. *The Witch Doctors.* London: Heinemann, 1996.

Nietzsche, Friedrich. *Thus Spoke Zarathustra.* New York and London: Penguin, 1961.

O'Shaughnessy, Arthur William Edgar. "Ode" in *The Oxford Book of Victorian Verse.* Oxford: Clarendon press, 1925.

Pais, Abraham. *Niels Bohr's Times: In Physics, Philosophy, and Polity.* New York: Oxford University Press, 1994.

Pascale, Richard Tanner and Anthony G. Athos. *The Art of Japanese Management.* New York: Penguin Books, 1982.

Penrose, Roger. *The Emperor's New Mind.* Oxford: Oxford University Press, 1989.

Rilke, Rainer Marie. *Rilke on Love and Other Difficulties.* Translated by J. J. L. Mood. New York: Norton, 1975.

Soros, George. "The Capitalist Threat." *Atlantic* (February 1997).

Tolle, Eckhart. *The Power of Now.* New York: New World Library, 1999.

Trompenaars, Fons. *Riding the Waves of Culture.* London: Nicolas Brealey, 1993.

Vedral, Vlatko. "Living in a Quantum World." *Scientific American* (June 2011).

INDEX

40 Hz oscillatory field, 66

actuality versus potentiality, 98–99
adaptive systems, complex, 15, 17
adversity, positive use of, 217, 233
Aetna Insurance Company, 247
Agassi, Andre, 220
Age of Extremes, The (book), 116
aging and neural connections, 55
agrarian societies, 143
Aikido, 206
alchemists, 233
Altai Himalaya, 28
ambiguity, 82
analysis, 83
Anger (-2 on Scale of Motivation), 203
Anglian Water, 218
Anguish (-5 on Scale of Motivation), 208–209
answers vs. questions, 240
Apathy (-6 on Scale of Motivation), 210
Argyris, Chris, 245
artificial intelligence (AI), 80
Art of Japanese Management, The (book), 106
Art of the Long View, The (book), 231
Art of War, The (book), 170
Asian societies, difference between, 142–43, 150

assets, intangible, 98–99
associative thinking, 61–64
Athos, Anthony, 106
Atlantic Monthly (magazine), 114
atomism, 39, 73–74, 76, 131
atomistic souls, 131
attractors, 183–84, 191, 200

balance, symbiotic, 78
Bank of America, 166–68
basic needs, 42–45
behavior, organizational, 101
Bertolini, Mark, 247–48
Bhagavad Gita, The (book), 33–34
big bang, the, 28, 32
Black Rock, 247
Bohm, David, 12–13, 17, 29, 33, 76, 243, 245, 268
Bohmian dialogue techniques, 19, 243
Bohr, Niels, 71–72
brain
    adult, 115
    capacity to change, 54
    cognitive processes of, 128
    constant rewiring of, 53–56
    corpus callosum, 124
    energy use of, 115
    and the firing of neurons, 26
    "gamma wave" activity of, 66, 151